# AWAKENING
# TO ZEN

# AWAKENING
# TO ZEN

## THE TEACHINGS OF
## ROSHI PHILIP KAPLEAU

EDITED BY POLLY YOUNG-EISENDRATH
AND RAFE MARTIN

SHAMBHALA
*Boston · 2001*

Shambhala Publications, Inc.
Horticultural Hall
300 Massachusetts Avenue
Boston, Massachusetts 02115
*www.shambhala.com*

9  8  7  6  5  4  3  2  1

First Shambhala Edition
Printed in the United States of America
⊗ This edition is printed on acid-free paper that meets the
American National Standards Institute Z39.48 Standard.
Distributed in the United States by Random House, Inc.,
and in Canada by Random House of Canada Ltd

"What Will God Do When I Die" by Rainier Maria Rilke, translated by Babette
Deutch, from *Poems from the Book of Hours*. Copyright © 1941 by New Directions
Publishing Corp. Reprinted by permission of New Directions Publishing Corp.

Many of these essays originally appeared in *Zen Bow*, the private publication
of the Rochester Zen Center. "What Is Zen?" was originally published in *Texas
Quarterly*. It appears courtesy of the University of Texas. "Waking Up with Zen"
has been adapted from Roshi Kapleau's introduction to *Zen Keys* by Thich Nhat
Hahn, Doubleday, 1974. It appears courtesy of Doubleday. "Of the Same Root:
Animals and Our Relationship with Them" was originally published in the May
1983 issue of *Parabola*. It appears courtesy of *Parabola*. "Diet and Zen Practice" was
originally published in the *San Francisco Oracle*. "Mind-Altering Drugs" originally
appeared in *The Review*, from the *McGill Daily Supplement* (Montreal),
January 16, 1970. "An Age of Destruction and Spiritual Resurgence"
was originally published in *Quality Profiles* magazine.

Library of Congress Cataloging-in-Publication Data
Kapleau, Philip, 1912–
Awakening to Zen: the teachings of Roshi Philip Kapleau / edited by
Polly Young-Eisendrath and Rafe Martin.
p. cm.
Originally published: New York: Scribner, c1997.
Includes bibliographical references and index.
ISBN 1-57062-806-8
I. Young-Eisendrath, Polly, 1947-II. Martin, Rafe, 1946-III. Title.
BQ9286'.K36   2001
294.3'927—dc21

# Contents

## PART III: ZEN TRAINING/ZEN TEACHING

## PART IV: ON ILLNESS, DYING, AND DEATH

## PART V: SUFFERING AND MEANING

There are no mundane things outside of Buddhism, and there is no Buddhism outside of mundane things.

—Yuan-Wu

Ummon, a great Zen master of the T'ang period in China, said to his assembly of monks, "The world is vast and wide. Why do you put on your seven-piece robe at the sound of the bell?" Ummon is urging us: Experience for yourself this limitless universe—touch it, taste it, feel it, be it. Thoroughly savor it. Don't speculate about life and the world. Live it! That is true freedom—religious freedom, spiritual freedom. Yes, even political freedom.

Ummon is saying, if you are a monk, put on your robes when the bell rings announcing the morning service. If you are an office worker, go to the office at eight-thirty. If you are a husband, kiss your wife and children and drive to work. If you are a student, go to school. If you are a school teacher, open the door and ring the bell. Don't drag your feet and complain, "Why should I?" Awakening brings the experiential awareness that the world is illimitable, an unfathomable void. Yet every single thing embraces this immense cosmos. At breakfast, Mother says, "Here's your oatmeal, Johnny." It's on the table before you. Now what do you do? Why, yum, eat it up!

—Philip Kapleau, 1985

# Author's Preface

As I look over this book, I am struck by the fact that it covers thirty years of my Zen teaching—the first thirty years of Zen in America. There's much I had thought to say in my author's preface, but looking over the editors' note, I find that most of what I intended is already succinctly covered there. So, let me here simply acknowledge the real debt I owe my three friends who put this book together—Jim Robicsek, Polly Young-Eisendrath, and Rafe Martin. Following Jim's initial impetus to create a meaningful volume from a vast body of unpublished work, Polly and Rafe dove in and did the necessary organizing, editing, and rewriting that allowed these disparate pieces to stand together as a book. How grateful I am to have had such help from such friends.

Scott Moyers, my editor at Scribner, has also done a careful, intelligent job of keeping this manuscript on track. His support and enthusiasm have been a great encouragement.

I also want to acknowledge the debt I owe all the many students I've worked with over these thirty years. A teacher really learns from students. It was my students, some of them teachers in their own right now, who taught me the meaning of Sangha's wisdom and warmth. They helped me, too, in countless ways to further mature my understanding of Zen Buddhism in the intricacies of daily living. As the great English visionary, artist, and poet William Blake said, "The bird a nest, the spider a web, man friendship." Zen is a path of discovering one's true, innate friendship with the universe. But it is also a Path walked hand in hand with many Dharma friends. To each I am grateful.

Lastly, I am especially grateful to the three outstanding Zen masters who trained me in Zen and long ago guided my own faltering steps toward Truth—Nakagawa Soen Roshi, Harada Sogaru Roshi, and Yasutani Hakuun Roshi. Nakagawa Roshi took me

9

under his wing. Together we traveled to visit his many Zen friends from all walks of life. This grounding in Zen's reality in ordinary people's lives made it possible for me to stay in Japan and commit myself to the practice and training. Without such first-hand knowledge of Zen's warm, living heart, I might have turned tail and run. Later, through Nakagawa Roshi's guidance, I came to Harada Roshi, who accepted me for training at Hosshin-ji Monastery, famed for its bleak climatic conditions and powerhouse sesshins. From him I learned something of the strength, courage, and determination—the rigorous dedication—that Truth-seeking requires. I learned, too, to have a deep respect for the ancient, monastic heritage of Zen. Finally, Yasutani Roshi shared with me his open manner of accomplished lay practice and the alert wisdom of one who walks the Path in the midst of life. With a tender heart he opened to me the inner door of Zen. To all of these revered teachers I owe the deepest possible debt of gratitude. I place my hands palm to palm and bow before them now in thanks.

Today Zen in the West is becoming psychologically astute. Much of this has been needed. And, indeed, Zen's innately creative religious genius complements our Western interest in the workings of the psyche and the life of the individual. Still, I have concerns that the constant psychologizing can lessen Zen's real depth—which is, after all, the spiritual, the religious life. At its deepest levels Zen offers true liberation, not just stress reduction. I fervently hope, too, that Zen's deep, Bodhisattvic aspiration will not be lost amidst tangles of self-interest as Zen unfolds in the West. In other areas, such as that of lay practice in general and the integration of family life into Zen and Zen into family life, I look forward with both expectation and great interest to all further explorations. These are clearly going to remain sources of deep, ongoing vitality for Western Zen. Yet I hope that our Western Sangha will someday also include monastics, men and women with a full-time dedication to the Buddha's Way.

These are some of my concerns and hopes for the future. As for now, I am content that the foundation is securely in place. The Path is open to all in the West who wish to walk it.

—ROSHI PHILIP KAPLEAU, 1996

# Editors' Note

This volume is a collection of writings, talks, lectures, and interviews by Roshi Philip Kapleau, spanning a thirty-two-year period from 1964 to 1996. Some of these pieces have been published before in specialized publications, such as small magazines, but others have had no previous broad public exposure, having been published only in pamphlets or the newsletter of the Rochester Zen Center. The rest are lectures, presentations, and Zen training talks that have been edited for publication for the first time here.

From a wide selection of previously unpublished talks, lectures, and pamphlets, with the help of Roshi Kapleau and Jim Robicsek, Polly Young-Eisendrath chose those that struck the most resonant chords for general accessibility, immediate engagement, and relevance to everyday life. Many of these are also representative of the form and substance of Roshi Kapleau's teachings over the past thirty years.

Rafe Martin then looked over each piece carefully, consulting as needed with Roshi Kapleau, Sensei Bodhin Kjolhede, abbot of the Zen Center and Roshi Kapleau's Dharma Heir, and with Sensei Sunya Kjolhede, also an ordained Zen teacher and the sister of Sensei Bodhin. The editing at this point consisted of maintaining Roshi's "voice" while bringing informal elements from the original talks into the completion that written text demands. Teachings that may have been partial were rounded out with teachings presented at other times, in other talks, or gleaned in private conversation.

Whatever your depth of acquaintance with Buddhism, you will find these papers relevant to everyday life and your own spiritual quest. Because Roshi Kapleau is already a prodigious author, well-known for his broad knowledge of Buddhism and

Zen, we have had the freedom and privilege of introducing him here in the kind of personal, down-to-earth style that character-izes his live teaching. Our aim was to give readers a feeling for what it's like to actually train with him and to clarify what is unique about his contribution to American Zen through his sin-gular insights, humor, compassion, and dedication.

Though there is a wide range of topics and styles in these papers, they are arranged so as to give any reader a path to fol-low. At the beginning are pieces about Zen and everyday life, followed by commentaries on practice, discipline, and training, and then by a set of interviews that Roshi conducted with health-care professionals—doctors and nurses—on the subject of dying and death. Finally, we have closed with three very dif-ferent pieces: a brief interview with Vondell Perry about the destruction and spiritual resurgence of our time, a recent essay that asks penetrating questions about the meaning of suffering and injustice, and an epilogue—an interview with Ken Kraft—that provides an overview of these past thirty years of Zen prac-tice and teaching with Roshi Kapleau.

This book is about living a life based on zazen, or Zen medita-tion. Roshi Kapleau has defined *zazen* in this way:

> Literally, "sitting Zen," to be distinguished from meditation [that] involves a visualization or putting into the mind of a con-cept, idea, or other thought form. During true zazen the mind is one-pointed, stabilized, and emptied of random, extraneous thoughts. Zazen is not limited to sitting but continues through-out every activity.

Zazen is now the daily practice of many thousands of Westerners in all walks of life. Some are seeking greater peace and peaceful-ness amidst the stresses of contemporary life. Some are seeking full realization of the Buddha's liberating call to Awakening.

Roshi Kapleau has written in great depth about how to do zazen in his classic *The Three Pillars of Zen*. Another of his books, *Zen: Merging of East and West*, is about integrating zazen into one's life and carrying on this 2,500-year-old spiri-tual practice in today's complex world.

Many Zen centers now exist outside Asia, in North and South America, Europe, New Zealand, and Australia, to help in the ongoing practice of a life of zazen. These groups offer instruction, inspiration, and support. Most people today practice zazen at home, coming to a Zen center for periodic sittings, instruction, talks by a teacher, and longer retreats. Most of the talks in this collection were presented at the Rochester Zen Center in such contexts.

Although nothing can replace actual Zen practice—daily zazen, periodic interviews with a teacher (dokusan), Zen talks (teisho), and retreats (sesshin)—some spiritual questions can be asked and answered through reading. It has been a great privilege to collect and edit these pieces because of the teachings they offer and the warmth they express.

—RAFE MARTIN AND POLLY YOUNG-EISENDRATH, 1996

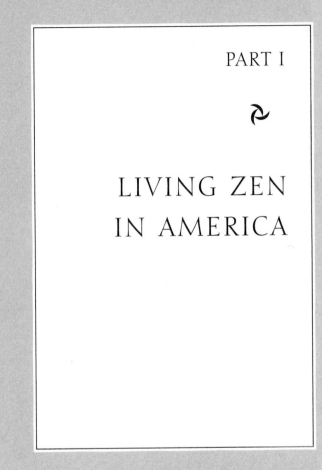

PART I

LIVING ZEN
IN AMERICA

# What Is Zen?

## (1973)

Rather than give you a detailed explanation of Zen doctrine and history, which could mislead and even bore, and in any case would be contrary to the spirit of Zen, let me put before you three typical Zen koans, or spiritual problems. These koans are Zen's method of demonstrating truth directly and concretely without recourse to logic or reason. Were you to reflect on them deeply and awaken to their innermost meaning, you would come to understand Zen.

Here is the first koan. A monk came to the Master Ummon (Yun Men in Chinese) and said, "Suppose you meet up with someone deaf, dumb, and blind. Since he couldn't see your gestures, couldn't hear your preaching, or, for that matter, ask you questions, you would be helpless. Unable to save him, you'd prove yourself a worthless master, wouldn't you?"

"Bow, please," said the master. The monk, though taken by surprise, obeyed the master's command, then straightened up in expectation of having his query answered. But instead of an answer he got a staff thrust at him and leaped back.

"Well," said Ummon, "you're not blind. Now approach closer." The monk did as he was bidden. "Good," said Ummon, "you're not deaf either. Well, understand?"

"Understand what, sir?"

"Ah, you're not dumb either."

On hearing these words the monk awoke as from a deep sleep.

Before going on to the next koan, let us reflect a moment on this one. Some people can never get away from theoretical, abstract questions, perhaps with the sense that the way to learn is to ask questions—the more the better. Questions frequently asked me are "What does the Zen person think of the Vietnam War?" or "What does Zen think of sex?" or "What does Zen have to say about morality?" The "Zen person" is an abstraction; he or she doesn't exist; only a specific person with Zen training does. One person's enlightenment may be deeper and training more thorough. One person may be wiser, more compassionate, and steadfast. This is all you can say. So the questions are really meaningless. More often than not, such questions are a dodge, a subterfuge to avoid facing up to one's own life problems. When a Zen teacher hears such questions, he must quickly determine the state of mind of the person asking them and treat them accordingly.

Observe how masterfully Ummon handles this student. He wastes no words probing or analyzing his motives, engaging him in a Socratic dialogue, or challenging his sincerity. In a direct, concrete, existential manner that would be the envy of any contemporary pedagogue (and remember, this incident took place in ninth-century China), he makes the student realize that he has the power of sight, speech, and hearing: everything, in fact, he needs to save himself. Why, then, doesn't he do so and stop engaging in speculations? Moreover, this koan points out a fundamental doctrine of Zen, namely, that in our essential nature each one of us lacks nothing, but is like a circle to which nothing can be added and nothing subtracted. We are each of us whole, complete, perfect, and so is everything else. Even a blind man, as a blind man, lacks nothing.

Why then do we suffer? Why is there so much greed, folly, and violence in the world? The Zen answer is that because our bifurcating intellect and our five senses deceive us into postulating the dualism of self and other, we are led to think and act as though each of us were a separate entity confronted by a world external to us. Thus in our unconscious the idea of "I," or selfhood, becomes fixed, and from this arises such patterns as "I hate this," "I love that," "This is mine," "That's yours." Nourished by this fodder, ego—and this is not the psychological ego whose healthy functioning is necessary, but the delusive sense of oneself standing apart from others, from the whole universe—comes to dominate the personality, attacking whatever threatens its domination and grasping at anything that will enlarge its power. Antagonism, greed, and alienation—in a word, suffering—are the inevitable consequence of this circular process. To see through this mirage and grasp the ungraspable is to realize that "heaven and earth and I" are of the same root, to use a Zen phrase.

The Buddha, the master physician for the ills of the spirit and the heart, deeply understood this question syndrome. Replying to a monk who threatened to quit religious life unless his questions about whether the enlightened man exists after death were answered, he said, "It is as if a man had been wounded by an arrow thickly smeared with poison, and his friends and companions, his relatives and kinfolk, were to procure for him a physician or surgeon, and the sick man were to say, 'I will not have this arrow taken out until I have learnt whether the man who wounded me was tall, short, or of middle height, was from this or that village, town, or city, whether it was an ordinary arrow or claw-headed arrow.' That man would die without ever having learned this." At another time the Buddha stated, "The religious life does not depend on the dogma that the world is eternal or not eternal, infinite or finite, that the soul and the body are identical or different, or that the enlightened man exists or does not exist after death. It profits not, nor has it to do with the fundamentals of religion, nor does it tend to the absence of passion, to supreme wisdom, and *nirvana*."

Now for the second koan. One day a master was taking a walk in the woods with his disciple. Suddenly a pure white rabbit darted in front of him. The master, taking advantage of the moment, said to the disciple, "What would you say as to that?" The disciple gushed, "It was just like a god!" The master, looking at him in disgust, said, "You're a grown man but you talk like a child." "All right," said the student, slightly miffed no doubt, "What would *you* say about it?" "It's a *rabbit!*" replied the master.

A rabbit is a rabbit is a rabbit. How many truly see when they

19

look, truly hear when they listen? Not many. The average person is perpetually weaving ideas and embroidering notions *about* what he sees or hears. An art student studying a painting probably analyzes the formal structures; another may try to recall what he had read or heard about the painting; to another the painting may turn the mind to the circumstances of the painter's life. A flash of lightning may set a person's mind to thinking, "What a dazzling sight!" If philosophically inclined, he might reflect, "Man's life is as brief as that lightning." If fear was his dominant emotion and he was looking out the window when the lightning struck, he could think, "I'd better pull my head in before I lose it!" The haiku poet Basho has a verse that goes, "How fortunate the man who sees a flash of lightning and does not think, 'How brief life is!' "

With each mental judgment or coloration the viewer or hearer is being taken farther and farther away from the object itself, the experience itself, so his knowledge becomes correspondingly weaker and more distant and limited. Truly to look at a painting, one has to see it with one's own eyes and ears, one's whole body.

Concert pianist Vladimir Horowitz tells about the time he played a dissonant contemporary composition at a private gathering. When he had finished, someone asked, "I just don't understand what that composition means, Mr. Horowitz. Could you please explain?" Without a word, Horowitz played the composition again, turned to his questioner, and announced, *"That's* what it means!"

The mind of the ordinary person is a checkerboard of crisscrossing reflections, opinions, prejudices, fears, and anxieties, so that his life, far from being centered in reality, is grounded instead in his *notions* of reality. The rabbit koan is urging us to empty our minds of all false values and notions and directly experience things in their wholeness and purity. To one who enters into every action with no separation, empty-minded, so to speak, yet filled with attention and awareness, a rabbit is the whole universe. Or if you like, it is everything and it is nothing. This koan celebrates a life of truth, a life of Zen, a life of full, undiluted participation at every moment and in every circumstance. It proclaims that to experience the core of a person or a thing we must ourselves be fully, wholeheartedly, *present* without reservation.

The responsible life is the responsive life. As long as we stand apart weighing, analyzing, and judging, people and things confront, even menace, us. So we feel, as the poet A. E. Housman wrote, like "a stranger and afraid in a world I never made." But embrace the whole world, take it and all things into your hara, your belly, and you have the Buddha's "Throughout heaven and earth I am the most honored one." With this realization birds fly in the sea, a cow gives birth to a calf on a flagpole, the Rocky Mountains stride over the Mississippi River. Is this not true, limitless creativity?

Now for the third and best-known koan, one that illustrates the Zen principle that from unity flow freedom and creativity, while from separateness come pain and confusion. A Zen master said, "Zen is like a man up in a high tree hanging from a branch with his mouth. His hands can't grasp a bough, his feet won't reach one. Under the tree is another man who asks him, 'What is the innermost truth of the Buddha's teachings?' If he doesn't answer, he evades his duty. What should he do?" Zen, we must remember, is not a philosophical game or a literary embellishment, but life itself, absolute life. The problem posed by this koan is central to every life, namely, when to speak and when to remain silent.

It's a vital problem between a teacher and pupil, a husband and wife, a parent and child, between friends and lovers. So much of our lives, personal and professional, is about communication, isn't it? What could be more vital to understand truly? In Zen, of course, there are dead words and there are live words. Words that merely analyze and explain are dead, while words that issue from the heart and gut, that stir our depths and fire the imagination, are alive. We *feel* their power. Every explanation, including this one, no matter how subtle, is but looking from a single side at something that has infinite dimensions. Overly long interpretations and elucidations often tire the brain and leave us feeling torpid. One live word—"Goddamnit!" for instance or even a real "Yes!" or a real "No!"—uttered from the gut reveals more than a dozen words of explanation. The gut word is the true word, the word that cuts away all stratagems and makes us One.

Silence, while said to be golden, can also be yellow. Discretion may be the better part of valor, yet not to speak when our words may help another is craven. There are other situations involving words and silence. What do we do when we are unjustly accused or abused? Do we maintain a monumental silence, or do we stimulate further argument and abuse by fighting back? Or is there a middle way? The most creative silence is beyond speech and stillness, and it is really to this Silence that our koan points.

Please understand that I have merely talked *about* koans here, not given answers to them. To resolve a koan, one must be able to *demonstrate* one's understanding and not merely talk about it. Each of us, whether endowed with subtle intellect or little intelligence, whether male or female, whether physically or mentally handicapped, possesses as a birthright the primal source of all creativity, namely, Buddha-nature, or Mind. Now, what is Zen? Zen is another name for Mind, and Mind is the foundation of Zen. Zen therefore never provides creeds or dogmas. Zen is not something to be philosophically thought of or intellectually understood. It has to be a concrete fact personally attained by one's own realization experience. Until one has this experience, Zen is merely an idea, a concept, an image. The real life and spirit of Zen is in the spiritual experience attained by each individual. Zen is the doctrine of the true, living self. Conventional wisdom says, "Where there is smoke, there is fire." Zen wisdom says, "Where there is smoke, there is smoke."

From the ground of Mind each of us is creator even as we are the created. Each one embraces every world and every being. At every millionth of a second this unique being, arbitrarily defined as "John Jones" or "Jill Smith," is dying and being re-created. With the lifting of my finger I re-create heaven and earth. All existence is the creation of my own mind—it therefore belongs to me as I belong to it. The energy of the cosmos is my energy; its sounds, my speech; its movements, my movements. The Rocky Mountains are not the Rocky Mountains. The Rio Grande is not the Rio Grande. The strength and grandeur of that incalculable conglomeration of protons, neutrons, and electrons we arbitrarily call the Rocky Mountains are my strength and my grandeur. The flow of the Rio Grande is myself streaming and gushing on. Were I to die, the Rio Grande would stop flowing, the Rocky Mountains crumble. Zen Master Eisai says, "Because I am, heaven overhangs and earth is upheld. Because I am, the sun and the moon go round; the four seasons come in succession, all things are created, because I am—that is, because of mind." Shelley, the poet, says, "I am the eye with which the universe beholds itself and knows that it is divine."

To create, the painter needs paint, brushes, and canvas; the sculptor, wood, stone, or metal, and tools; the poet, words and a pen and paper—or computer; the composer, sounds, notes, paper. But for one awakened to the nature of Mind, the entire universe is the canvas; hands, feet, emotions, and intellect the implements. Each moment is joy unbounded, ripe, and creative, when we are liberated from the enslaving notions of "This is *my* head, this is *my* body, this is *my* mind." Here, at the core of each of us, is creativity, here is the art of living. If the mission of the artist is "to make the invisible visible," in the words of Leonardo da Vinci, the purpose of Zen is to bring into consciousness the substrata of both the unconscious and the conscious.

The aim of Zen training is awakening, and the living of a life that is creative, harmonious, and *alive*. These "goal-less goals," for there really are no goals to attain, no place to *get* to, are brought into being through a process of concentration and absorption. In the sense of purging and freeing the mind from enslavement to fugitive, useless ideas, ideas that bog us down and limit us, Zen meditation, or zazen, might be called "brainwashing." Perhaps this statement will be clearer if I tell you briefly the experiences with zazen of two Americans in Japan. The first, after he had been practicing Zen a short while, said, "Zen discipline, I know, involves ridding the mind of all tightly held beliefs and values so that it becomes a clean slate. But look, I spent four years getting a good education at Harvard. This knowledge cost me a considerable effort and my parents much money. If you think I'm going to throw it all away for a pig in a poke called 'enlightenment,' you're crazy. To tell the truth, I'd rather read about Zen than practice it; that way I don't lose, I gain."

The second fellow, after longer training, said, "Some people ask me what I have gained from Zen practice. I must answer truthfully that I've lost, and that whatever gains I have made are the result of this loss. I have lost much that was not really myself, and as a result the burden of the false self which I was carrying around has become lighter. Unhappily I do not yet know who I really am, but I know better who I am not, and this means I can move about and flow more easily through life."

Our ordinary mind is an Augean stable of stale impressions, of theories, opinions, assumptions, standards, dogmas, prejudices, and facts in which our lives become mired. This is the stuff of mind we endlessly argue about and even fight for, bringing upon ourselves and others much pain and suffering, not to mention confusion. We sacrifice our inborn freedom to these abstract notions. When they are swept from the mind through zazen—the concentrated sitting meditation particular to Zen—our true Mind rises to consciousness in all its beauty and effulgence. Furthermore, through zazen, energies that were formerly squandered in compulsive drives and purposeless actions are preserved and channeled into a unity, and to the degree that the mind attains one-pointedness, it no longer disperses its force in the uncontrolled proliferation of idle thoughts. The entire nervous system is relaxed and soothed, inner tensions eliminated, and the tone of all organs strengthened.

In other words, by realigning the physical, mental, and psychic energies through proper breathing, concentration, and sitting, zazen establishes a new body-mind equilibrium. With the body and mind consolidated, focused, and energized, our emotions respond with increased sensitivity and purity, and our will exerts itself with clearer strength of purpose. No longer are we dominated by intellect or driven by unchecked emotions. Eventually daily zazen transforms our personality and character; dryness, rigidity, and self-centeredness give way to warmth,

24

resiliency, and compassion. Self-indulgence and fear are, in time, transmuted into self-mastery and courage.

Let me close with some words on Zen by Bernard Philips, an old friend who trained with me for a time in Japan:

> Zen is three things. First, externally and objectively considered, it is a sect of Buddhism. As such, it has its own history and institutionalized forms.
>
> Second, from a deeper point of view, it is the heart and essence of Buddhism, having no doctrine or scriptures of its own but pointing to the ultimate source of all Buddhist teaching, namely, the enlightenment experience of the Buddha. On this level, it is a discipline oriented towards that illumination of mind, pacification of the heart, and freedom of action, in the context of a disciple's life, that the historical Buddha achieved through his enlightenment.
>
> Third, and still more profoundly considered, Zen transcends the particulars of Buddhism as such and is not one religion so much as it is religion itself in its most universal intention. In other words, it is the life of truth, of authentic being, wherein the self has overcome its alienation from itself and from all other things. When Zen in this sense is fully concretized, there is no longer anything to be called Zen, and the uniqueness of Zen is that when it is realized, it bows out of being. Life in its unconditioned integrity calls for Zen no more than water calls for wetness or fire for heat.

# Toward a Meaning of Buddhism for Americans

## (1964)

Zen Buddhism springs from the great awakening, or enlightenment, of the Buddha. What in the West we term Buddhism has its origin, historically speaking, in the person and life of Siddhartha Gautama, later to be known as the Buddha Shakyamuni. Among Buddhists he is revered not as a deity or a savior who takes upon himself the sins of others, but as a fully awakened, fully perfected human being who attained liberation of body and mind through his own efforts and not by the grace of a supernatural being. People often asked him, "Are you a god?"

"No," he would answer.

"An angel?"

"No."

"A saint?"

"No."

"Then what are you?"

"I am awake," he would reply, and this indeed is the meaning of the term *Buddha:* one awakened or enlightened to his own Self-nature and all existence.

Upon his enlightenment, the Buddha is recorded as having said, "Wonder of wonders! Intrinsically all living beings are complete and whole, endowed with virtue and wisdom, but because of their delusive thoughts, they fail to perceive this." How truly marvelous that all human beings, whether clever or stupid, male or female, ugly or beautiful, are whole and complete just as they are. That is to say, the nature of every being is inherently without a flaw, perfect, no different in fact from that of the Buddha himself. Yet most people are restless and anxious, living half-crazed lives because the mind, heavily encrusted with delusive thoughts, is turned upside down. We need therefore to return to our original perfection, to see through the false image of ourselves as incomplete and sinful, and to wake up to our inherent purity and wholeness.

In Zen the fundamental problem is not God but man. Not what is God, but what am I? How can I realize my original perfection? The religious question in Zen is, Why was I born, why must I die? What is my link with my fellow human and other beings? This is the primary concern in Zen. Dostoyevsky, in a letter to his brother, wrote, "How terrible to watch a man who has the Incomprehensible within his grasp, does not know what to do with it, and sits playing with a toy called God." Toys are for the amusement of children; they are not for adults. Zen demands maturity and responsibility of its adherents. It admonishes them to stand on their own two feet, not God's or anyone else's, and to respond wholly to what is most true in themselves and others. Our inborn freedom and spontaneity must not be fettered by attachment to God or Buddha.

So in Zen there is nothing to search for. Search implies some goal or object outside oneself and a subject "I" that does the searching, a dualistic notion that fractures our inherent Wholeness. But since our True-nature is like, as I have said, a circle to which nothing can be added and from which nothing can be subtracted, what is there to seek? Many people, proudly calling themselves seekers, become attached to the idea of searching, and so they never find.

# Waking Up with Zen

## (1974)

*An earlier form of this essay appeared as the introduction to Thich Nhat Hanh's* Zen Keys *in the mid-seventies. The essay has been rethought and revised, and I'm grateful for the opportunity to have given it new life here. I found it especially important to clarify the discussion of ego. The last twenty years have brought much greater sophistication to our thinking on this subject. Most importantly, we need to distinguish the psychological concept of ego from the spiritual one.*

### WORK

We live in a society where the object for so many is to do as little work as possible, where the workplace, whether office or home, is looked upon as a place of drudgery and boredom, where work, rather than being a creative and fulfilling aspect of one's life, is seen as oppressive and unsatisfying.

How different is Zen! In Zen everything one does becomes a potential vehicle for self-realization. Every act, every movement, done wholeheartedly, with nothing left over, is an "expression of Buddha," and the greater the pure-mindedness and unself-consciousness of the doing, the closer we are to this realization. For what else is there but the pure act itself—the lifting of the hammer, the washing of the dish, the movement of the hands on the typewriter, the pulling of the weed? Everything else, such as thoughts of the past, fantasies about the future, judgments and evaluations concerning the work itself, what are these but shadows and ghosts flickering about in our minds? Right before us is life itself.

28

To enter into the awareness of Zen, to "wake up," means to free the mind of its habitual disease of uncontrolled thought and to return it to its original purity and clarity. In Zen it is said that much more power is generated by the ability to practice awareness in the midst of the world than by just sitting alone and shunning activity. Thus one's daily work becomes one's meditation room, the task at hand one's practice. This is called "working for oneself."

An opera singer is reputed to have responded to Descartes's famous phrase "I think, therefore I am" by saying, "I *work*, therefore I am." In Zen all labor is viewed with the eye of equality. Only a dualistically ensnared mind discriminates between agreeable and disagreeable jobs, between "creative" and "uncreative" work. It is, in part, to root out such weighing and judging that Zen novices are set to work pulling weeds by hand, licking envelopes, or doing other seemingly unimportant, "noncreative" work at the start of their training, and why the abbot himself often cleans the toilets. For true creativity is possible only when the mind is empty and totally absorbed in the task at hand. Only at the point where one is freed of the weight of self-consciousness is there transcendence and the joy of genuine fulfillment. In this natural creativity our intuitive wisdom and joy are released and brought into play.

All this does not mean, of course, that attempts at bettering working conditions and making work more meaningful are worthless. But for someone to constantly resent the work itself or his or her superiors, to become sloppy and slothful in working habits, and embittered toward life, these attitudes cause unnecessary harm and do little to change working conditions. When it's time to work, one works, nothing held back. When it's time to make changes, one makes changes; when it's time to revolt, one even revolts. In Zen everything is in the doing, a doing arising from Awareness, not in the contemplating.

There is one more area in which the untrained, ego-dominated mind plays thief to us, and this is in terms of energy. The fatigue that grips many at the end of the workday is not simply natural tiredness, but the product of a day filled with wasted thought, with feelings of anxiety and worry, not to speak of anger and resentment, whether openly expressed or inwardly held. These negative mental states probably do more to sap energy than anything else. In contrast, the trained Zen person can move through the day aware and alert. The task at hand receives its due share of energy, but little is wasted in unnecessary anxiety, fantasy, or smoldering resentment. Such a person is present, and so, even at the end of a full day's work, his or her store of energy, having not been destructively depleted, remains unexhausted.

## AWARENESS

Awareness—and this is more than mere attentiveness—is everything. A lack of awareness is responsible for so much of the violence and suffering in the world today. For it is the mind that feels itself separated from life and nature, the mind dominated by an omnipresent "I," which lashes out to destroy and kill in order to satisfy its desire for more and more—at whatever cost. This unaware mind breeds insensitivity to people and things, for it doesn't see or appreciate the value of things as they truly are, only seeing them as objects to be used in satiating its own desires. The deeply aware person sees the indivisibility of existence, the rich complexity and interrelatedness of all life. Out of this awareness grows a deep respect for the absolute value of all things, each thing. From this respect for the worth of every single object, animate as well as inanimate, comes the desire to see things used properly, and not to be heedless, wasteful, or destructive.

To truly practice Zen therefore means not leaving lights burning when they are not needed, not allowing water to run unnecessarily from the faucet, not loading up your plate and leaving food uneaten. These unmindful acts reveal an indifference to the value of the object so wasted or destroyed as well as to the efforts of those who made these things possible for us: in the case of food, the farmer, the trucker, the storekeeper, the cook, the server. This indifference is the product of a mind that sees itself as separated from a world of seemingly random change and purposeless chaos. This indifference robs us of our birthright of harmony and joy.

## IMPERMANENCE

From a Buddhist point of view, the teachings of impermanence and non-self hold the key to resolving the anxiety of a mind that sees itself as separated from a world of random change. Anyone alive to the realities of life cannot but acknowledge, for example, that impermanence is not a creation of mystical philosophers but simply a concretization of what "is." In the last hundred years this process of constant and explosive change on the social and institutional level has accelerated to a degree unknown to people of earlier ages. Almost daily the newspapers report new and dizzying crises in the world: famines and natural disasters, wars and revolutions; crises in the environment, in energy, and in the political arena; crises in the world of finance and economics; crises in the piling up of divorces and nervous breakdowns, not to speak of crises in personal health.

The average person looking out on this ever-changing world sees anything but natural karmic laws at work; nor does he perceive the unity and harmony underlying this constant and inevitable change. If anything, he is filled with fear and anxiety, with a feeling of hopelessness, and with a sense that life has no meaning. And because he has no concrete insight into the true character of the world or intuitive understanding of it, what else can he do but surrender to a life of material comfort and sensual pleasure?

And yet in the midst of all this seemingly meaningless chaos can calmly stand the Zen Buddhist. Her equanimity is proof that she knows there is more to life than what the senses tell her—that in the midst of change there is something always permanent, in the midst of imperfection there is perfection, in chaos there is peace, in noise there is quiet, and finally, in death there is life. So without holding on or pushing away, without accepting or rejecting, she just moves along with her daily work, doing

31

what needs to be done, helping wherever she can, or as the sutras say, "In all things one is neither overjoyed nor cast down."

## NON-SELF

Like the law of impermanence, the teaching of non-self is no mere philosophical speculation, but the expression of the deepest religious experience. It affirms that, contrary to what we *think*, we are not merely a body or a mind. If not either or both, what are we? The Buddha's answer, stemming from his experience of Great Enlightenment, is ego-shattering: "In truth I say to you that within this fathom-high body, with its thoughts and perceptions, lies the world and the rising of the world and the ceasing of the world and the Way that leads to the extinction of rising and ceasing."

What could be grander or more reassuring? Here is confirmation from the highest source that we are more than this puny body-mind, more than a speck thrown into the vast universe by a capricious fate—that we are no less than the sun and the moon and the stars and the great earth. Why, if we already possess the world, do we try to enlarge ourselves through possessions and power? Why are we afraid, at times self-pitying and mean, at other times arrogant and aggressive?

It is because our image of ourselves and our relation to the world is a false one. We are deceived by our limited five senses and discriminating intellect (the sixth sense in Buddhism), which convey to us a picture of a dualistic world of self-and-other, of things separated and isolated, of pain and struggle, birth and extinction, killing and being killed. This picture is untrue because it barely scratches the surface. It is like looking at the one-eighth of an iceberg above the water and being unaware of the seven-eighths underneath. For if we could see beyond the ever-changing forms into the underlying reality, we would realize that in essence there is nothing but harmony and unity and stability, and that this perfection is no different from the phenomenal world of incessant change and transformation.

But without spiritual training, our vision is limited and our intuitions weak.

## EGO

Nor is this the whole of it. Sitting astride the senses is a shadowy, phantomlike figure with insatiable desires and a lust for dominance. Its name? Ego, ego the magician, and the deadly tricks it carries up its sleeve are delusive thinking, greed, and anger. Where it came from no one knows, but it has surely been around as long as the human mind. This wily and slippery conjurer deludes us into believing that we can only enjoy the delights of the senses without pain by delivering ourselves into its hands. Now, let me clarify something else here. In saying this, I am speaking of the Buddhist meaning of *ego*, a spiritually technical term for the delusive sense that oneself and the Universe are fundamentally separate. This delusion is the source of our suffering. However *ego* can also refer to the *psychological* ego, which is not a negative thing, not a spiritual enemy. Indeed one needs healthy ego functioning to live and work, to create and love, as well as to carry on and deepen spiritual practice.

## LANGUAGE

Of the many devices employed by the delusive ego to keep us in its power, none is more effective than language. The English language is so structured that it demands the repeated use of the personal pronoun *I* for grammatical nicety and presumed clarity. Actually this *I* is no more than a figure of speech, a convenient convention, but we talk and act as though it were real and true. Listen to any conversation and see how the stress invariably falls on the *I*—"*I* said . . . ," "*I* did . . . ," "*I* like . . . ," "*I* hate. . . ." All this plays into the hands of ego, strengthening our servitude and enlarging our sufferings, for the more we postulate this "I" the more we are exposed to ego's never-ending demands.

We cannot evade responsibility for this state of affairs by claiming ignorance, for the machinations of ego, as well as the way to be free of them, have been pointed out time and again by the wisest of people. After all, language is our creation. It reflects our values, ideals, and goals and the way we see and relate to the world. There are languages that do not insist on the constant repetition of the vertical pronoun for clarity or grammatical completeness. In Japanese, for example, it is possible to make sentences without the *I* or other personal pronouns in all but a few cases. The Japanese ideal of personal behavior, which the language reflects, is modesty and self-effacement, in theory at least if not always in practice. The strong assertion of the *I* in contemporary American speech, as well as the decline of the passive voice in favor of the active, may reveal that we no longer value humility and self-effacement, if we ever did.

The dualism of "I" and "not-I," aided by language, deceives us in other ways. It constantly tempts us into distinctions and judgments that take us further and further from the concrete and the real into the realm of the speculative and the abstract. Take the case of an individual walking alone who suddenly hears the sound of a bell. Immediately that person's discriminating mind evaluates it as beautiful or weird, or distinguishes it as a church bell or some other kind. Ideas associated with a similar sound heard in the past may also intrude upon the mind, and these are analyzed and compared. With each such judgment the experience of pure hearing becomes fainter and fainter until one no longer hears the sound but hears only *thoughts* about it.

Or again, we tacitly agree among ourselves to call a certain object a "tree." We then forget that "tree" is an arbitrary concept that in no way reveals the true identify of this object. What, then, is a tree? A philosopher might call it ultimate truth; a botanist, a living organism; a physicist, a mass of atoms; an artist, a unique shape with distinctive coloring; a carpenter, a potential table. To a dog, however, it is merely a urinal. All descriptions, explanations, or analyses are but a looking from one side at that which has infinite dimensions. The true nature of the tree is more than anything that can be said about it.

Similarly we tinker with time by dividing it into past, present, and future and into years, months, days, etc. This is convenient, but we need to remember that this "slicing" is artificial and arbitrary, the product of a discriminating mind, which discerns only the surface of things. Timelessness is unaccounted for. Thus we conceive a world that is conceptual, limited, and far removed from actuality.

The moment one says, "This rose is red," it has already changed into something else. Besides, to someone else the rose may appear pink. For Zen, however, a rose is not merely red, pink, yellow, but it is all colors and at the same time it is no color. Does not "a rose is a Rose is a ROSE" more nearly convey the cosmic grandeur and infinite beauty of a rose than "This rose is—or appears—red"? But why say anything? Enter the heart of the rose—smell it, touch it, taste it—and what is there to say except perhaps "Ah, wonderful!" or better yet, simply "Ah" or best of all, just smile—a smile that flowers.

The Zen masters have always been alert to the snare of language, which "fits over experience like a glove," and have used it in such a way so as to liberate their disciples from its bind. What are these methods? The Sixth Patriarch used to teach: "If someone asks you about the meaning of existence, answer him in terms of nonexistence. If he asks about the worldly, speak of the saintly. If he asks of the saintly, speak of the worldly. In this way, the interdependence and mutual involvement of the two extremes will bring to light the significance of the Mean. Suppose someone asks you, 'What is darkness?' Answer him thus: 'Light is the primary cause of darkness and darkness is the secondary cause of light. It is the disappearance of light that causes darkness. Light and darkness exhibit each other, and their interdependence points inevitably to the significance of the Mean.'"

Another famous master, Joshu (Chao-chou, in Chinese), when asked, "Is it true that even a dog has the Buddha-nature?"—the implication of the question being that if such an exalted being as man has the pure, all-embracing Buddha-nature, how can such a lowly creature as a dog also have it—sometimes answered, "No, it hasn't" (*mu* in Japanese, *wu* in

35

Chinese), and at other times, "Yes, it has." The questioners may
have been genuinely puzzled by the statement in the Buddhist
scriptures that all beings possess the Buddha-nature, or they
may have been feigning ignorance to see how the master would
respond. Since Buddha-nature is common to all existence, logically neither answer makes sense. But more than logic is
involved here. So what is the master up to? Is he flouting the
logic of language to show the monks that absolute truth lies
beyond affirmation and negation, or is he, by the manner in
which he utters yes or no, actually thrusting this Buddha-
nature at his questioners?

An episode involving Nansen (Nan-chuan, in Chinese), Joshu's
own master, became a vital koan for generations of Zen students. One day Nansen returned to his monastery to find some of
his monks quarreling about a cat sitting in front of them. Presumably they were arguing whether a cat, like a dog, has the
Buddha-nature. Sizing up the situation at once and taking advantage of the occasion to bring home to them the truth they were
obscuring, the master suddenly seized the cat, held it aloft, and
demanded, "One of you monks, give me a word of Zen! If you can,
I will spare the life of the cat, otherwise I will cut it in two!" No
one knew what to say, so he boldly cut the cat in two. (Most Zen
teachers would say he mimed this. No Zen teacher would literally
kill a cat.) That evening when Joshu, who had also been away,
returned, the master told him of the incident. Without a word
Joshu took off his slippers, placed them on his head, and slowly
walked out of the room. "Ah," said the master admiringly, "had
you been there, you would have saved the cat."

A ZEN WORD

Now what does it mean to say that a word is "of" Zen? In Zen
there are live words and dead words. The admired live word is
the gut word, concrete and vibrant with feeling; the dead word
is the explanatory word, dry and lifeless, issuing from the head.
The first unifies, the second separates and divides. Neither the

monks nor Joshu spoke a word, yet the master rejected the monks' silence and praised Joshu's "eloquence." Why? What was the significance of Joshu's putting his slippers on his head and walking out? What did the master demonstrate by his act of "cutting" the cat in two? The master's gesture restores that unity of life split apart by the monks' arguments. Commenting on this incident, another master said, "He didn't cut the cat in two, he cut it in one."

Such episodes or teaching methods were collected by later generations of masters and given to their students to solve as part of their training. They came to be called koan (kung-an in Chinese; literally, "a public record"), that is, cases that could be relied upon as pointing to and embodying ultimate truth. Koans, then, are religious problems, not linguistic ones, for despite their perplexing formulations, all point to man's true Self, his Face before his parents were born.

## ZEN EAST AND WEST

In the East, Zen is declining due to many cultural influences, including the heavy inroads made by materialism and technology—in short, "Westernization." In the West, paradoxically, it is precisely the spiritual emptiness of the "good" life produced by materialism and technology, and the failure of traditional religions to fill this void, that is driving so many into Zen. For together with the realization that technology makes "major contributions to minor needs of man" is the awareness that we have become cogs in a wheel that is spinning out of control, living by a value system that does not see the person as a human being but merely as a consumer of things.

## POLLUTION, INFLATION, AND THE ENERGY SHORTAGE

The contamination of our own and the world's environment and our squandering of dwindling natural resources through overconsumption, waste, and mismanagement speak eloquently of our greed and irresponsibility. How long will the rest of the world stand by while we in North America, with only 6 percent of the world's population, consume 40 percent of its resources?

However much our self-indulgent living habits have contributed to the world energy shortage and to pollution and inflation, these ailments are but outward manifestations of our inner malaise. The energy crisis is really an internal one: how to mobilize the unlimited energy locked within us—how to split the atom of the mind—and use it wisely for ourselves and mankind. Behind economic inflation is the inflated national ego. As for pollution, the most fundamental pollution of all is that of the mind by the mind.

We need to recover our basic humanity. The choice before us is clear: a disciplined life of simplicity and naturalness or a contrived and artificial one; a life in harmony with the natural order of things or one in constant conflict with it. It is a choice of freedom or bondage, growth or decay. But even having chosen the way of regeneration, to walk this path requires spiritual training and discipline. Only through purifying the heart and mind of each of us can we hope to purify the world and restore a measure of peace and stability in our global community.

# Why Buddhism?

## (1968)

*This essay is based on a talk given to several hundred parents of Zen Center members. The parents had come to a Rochester Zen Center "Parents Weekend" to find out why their children were now practicing Zen. It was the late sixties, and so many young people had come to Zen that it seemed important for parents to understand what their offspring (mostly eighteen- to twenty-five-year-olds) were up to—and why. Without such clear communication, much misunderstanding and pain for families already stressed by the Vietnam War, psychedelics, and "the generation gap" would clearly lie ahead.*

Buddhism teaches that the primary cause of our being born is the desire for rebirth, and that the secondary, or contributing, cause is a mother and a father. It also teaches that we pick our parents, which means that we are born through a set of parents with whom we have a karmic affinity. So the parent-child relationship is, spiritually speaking, the most profound. Brother and sister are biologically closer, but the bond of spirit that unites parents and child is of a deeper order. The child who estranges himself from his parents, and the parents who renounce their children, are inviting pain at the root level of their being. The practice of Zen Buddhism leads, within the family, to increased love, affection, and respect. We hope parents will want to do zazen themselves and transform their own lives. The door is open to everyone. I hope you will want to begin, not so much for your children's sake as for your own.

Why the appeal of Buddhism? At least five reasons can be stated, as detailed in the following, of which two are most pronounced: peace, inner and outer, and personal experience as a replacement for abstract conjecture about fundamental questions.

## PEACE

How strong is the yearning for peace in the minds of our people, especially among the draft-age young, who have to fight this immensely unpopular war and who therefore feel its terrible suffering so personally?

This yearning for peace has grown up with the young—a consciousness nurtured into growth by awareness of concentration camps and atomic bombs. It is intrinsic to their pain and aspiration. It is the persistent voice of their spiritual quest.

Buddhism, I think it is fair to say, is preeminently a religion of peace. Throughout its long history, which began more than five hundred years before Christ, it has never fought or urged a religious war. The Buddha emphasized that peace in and among nations is the consequence of a peaceful, loving heart. This in turn springs from right understanding and selfless activity. Where there is no inner harmony and understanding, there can be no outer peace. Wherever you go in Asia, the figure of the Buddha symbolizes our own potential for harmony and compassion. The appeal of Zen Buddhism is that it offers a tested way, a proven method, to realize for oneself this inner peace.

## PERSONAL EXPERIENCE

In Zen, there is abhorrence of the abstract, of the nonconcrete. And so Zen is usually described as a religion beyond words and letters. It also abhors an intoxication with words for their own sake, empty verbalization. We've all heard the high-flown phrases of politicians and heads of governments: "All we seek is a just peace," et cetera, et cetera, but their actions belie these fine words. To counteract this, Zen emphasizes deep intuition, feeling and acting rather than just thought and talk. Please understand this: Zen does not condemn thought. It encourages thought grounded in something deeper than mere verbalization.

Parents know how much young people insist upon the need to experience for themselves. This goes back to the best tradition of our pragmatic philosophers, Dewey and James. It seems to be an existential theme of our culture. Zen's appeal is to personal experience and not philosophic speculation as a means of verifying ultimate truth. Another's experience of Truth is never your own. And no one can do zazen for you. You must discover the truth of yourself and others by yourself. A picture of food won't fill an empty stomach.

You can't seriously practice Zen and remain phony, not for long. There's no way to play the usual games. Nothing less than purity and genuine sincerity will open the gates of Truth, Compassion, and Wisdom. When true inner freedom comes—the freedom to be the master and not the slave of your life—it comes not from the teacher, not from the Buddha, and certainly not from any supernatural being. It comes from one's own unfaltering exertions.

## SIMPLICITY AND NATURALNESS

This appeal of Zen is often overlooked. Precisely because modern life is so complex, with the machines and technology as manipulators and us as the puppets, life has become dry and fractured. We yearn deeply, spontaneously, for a natural life. The turns toward healthy unrefined food, unpretentious clothes, and simple living conditions are some visible manifestations of this yearning.

There's another, deeper aspect: Buddhism teaches that we are all rooted in the same fundamental reality. What is common to all, both animate and inanimate, is the ungraspable Buddha-nature. The absolute value of *every* thing makes it a great transgression against our own fundamental nature to willfully destroy or waste *any* thing. Americans are so used to wasting

41

and squandering, particularly things that seem so common—water, paper, electricity. But waste makes for insensitivity. It implies an indifference to the ultimate value of the wasted thing. Insensitivity breeds greater separation, greater ego, and ego breeds pain. So we find ourselves removed from life through dull indifference.

When one accepts, practices, and realizes the Buddhist teaching that human beings do not stand apart from nature, then there can be no abuse, exploitation, or pollution of the material world, for to do so is to abuse, exploit, and pollute ourselves.

ENLIGHTENMENT

This is really an abstract term. What is preferred in Zen is the phrase "to open the Mind's eye." And this means to answer the most essential of all questions—namely, "Who am I?" or more properly, "What am I? What is my True Nature? Why was I born? Why must I die? What is my relation to my fellow man?" To be human means to ask these questions, and to be truly human means we must get an answer. Until these questions arise to consciousness, we can lard our lives over with all kinds of activities, worldly involvements that leave us no chance to reflect on ourselves. But sooner or later these questions arise, and then there is no escaping them. They burn within us, and intellectual answers give us no peace. We pick up books dealing with the human condition, the meaning of life, and get all these beautifully set-out phrases, these flowing metaphors, but they do not answer the question. Only the gut experience of self-awakening satisfies the gut questioning. Personal experience is the final testimony of Truth.

This is the flavor of Zen discipline. Self-deceiving games won't work. You must be utterly sincere. Enlightenment never comes until we have achieved this kind of selfless purity. And you must work hard to become pure-minded in Zen, to clear away the clouds of irrelevant ideas, prejudices, notions, and hard-set opinions that constantly pass through and pollute our

minds. This is the primary pollution, the defilemen
mind. In one sense, zazen is a discipline to cleanse the
that our inherent purity, wholeness, and radiance, wnicn are
obscured by all this mental grime, can emerge. Then our inborn
love and compassion will shine. In another sense, zazen is itself
the expression of the truth that from the very beginning we and
all beings have been whole and complete; that our true nature is
a circle to which nothing can be added and from which nothing
can be taken away. That is what Enlightenment is about.

## CONTINUITY AND UNITY OF ALL EXISTENCE

This may strike some of you as a rather dubious reason why
people would want to come to the Center to train in Zen. But
actually it is valid. We are not strung up in sequence like tele-
graph poles. Life is interrelated. We can look at all existence
from two points of view: the relative and the absolute. When we
say relative, we mean from the point of view of things changing.
From this standpoint we can speak of the summer changing to
fall, of cause and effect, time, space, Buddhas and Bodhisattvas.
*Bodhisattva* translates from Sanskrit as "wisdom being." It
refers to one in whom compassion and wisdom are functioning
for the welfare of all living beings. At the same time we must
experience life in its absolute aspect, as One Mind without distinctions of any kind. The most remote star, the most distant
supernova, is nothing but One Mind in which we all equally
participate.

In our culture many people, particularly the young, sense
this in a vibrant, alive way. They feel it intuitively and naturally,
even before formal practice. Overall, though, our culture has
become increasingly empty of rituals and ceremonies that might
point to this Truth, and people feel this absence deeply. So the rituals and ceremonies that we have at the Zen Center are much
more than a foreign import; they clarify the nature of Mind and
give our experiences of it a poetic grandeur that enriches and
sustains us. Above all they acknowledge the unity of life.

Karma, a Sanskrit word that means "action," is a principal Buddhist teaching that reveals how we ourselves create the effects that surround us, how our own actions and intentions carry over into consequences in our daily lives. This principle of karma teaches us that we must take responsibility for our actions, that we are the architects of our fate. Karma also emphasizes the continuity of existence. If we are dissatisfied with our life today, which is the product of the way we have thought, felt, and acted in previous times, that is sour Karma, then we certainly can change it. Zen further says, "You can't change anyone or anything unless *you* change first, unless you purge yourself of your false thinking and wrong acting." When this happens, you find those around you changing, and pretty soon an arc of influence develops. More than any teaching I know of, Zen provides a method and a discipline that have stood the test of twenty-five hundred years, and it has behind it the experience of so many people who have looked into their own minds and awakened to the Truth.

# Of the Same Root: Animals and Our Relationship with Them

### (1982)

I want to focus on the origin and significance of the deep relationship between human beings and animals and to show how that relation, an outcome of the fundamental laws of karma and rebirth, is demonstrated in Buddhist scripture, art, and ceremonies.

The deeply rooted belief that Buddhahood is latent in all creatures is vividly portrayed in the Buddhist art of ancient China and Japan. Of such works perhaps none is more sublime than the class of paintings depicting the Buddha's Great Demise, or Parinirvana—that is, his attainment of perfect emancipation beyond all conditioned existence. Interestingly, animals figure prominently in these works of art.

Before me as I write is the original of one such painting. It is a long scroll, six feet long and four feet wide; like most religious art of the past, it bears no signature. The artist, obviously imbued with deep religious feeling, has succeeded in conveying the grandeur and solemnity of the occasion. The Buddha, stretched out, lying on his right side, is painted in golden tones and is as brilliant and commanding as the sun. Like a magnet, the figure of the Buddha draws the upper and lower halves of the picture into the person of himself, into the Buddha-nature underlying all forms of life.

Surrounding the World-Honored-One are beings from the six realms of existence: demigods (devas), humans, fighting demons (ashuras), animals, hungry ghosts (pretas), and hell-dwellers. All have come to pay their last respects. Among the humans one sees monks, nuns, royal personages, and ordinary men and women. Sorrow and pain are etched on the faces of the assembled multitude. Many are openly weeping.

Occupying the bottom half of the scroll is a massed group of animals: an elephant, horse, ox, dog, goat, monkey, camel, badger, fox, mongoose, deer, hare, snake, crane, tiger, leopard, duck, squirrel, chipmunk, rat, quail, eagle, dove, peacock, goose, egret, heron, crow, hawk, raven, mandarin duck, cock, tortoise, crab, butterfly, and dragonfly. Also present are the legendary dragon (representing absolute Mind) and the phoenix (symbolizing rebirth and regeneration).

Why should animals be represented in a religious painting? They are there because in Buddhism they are as integral to the life cycle as humans themselves. And the cycle includes other non-human beings as well. In the upper right-hand portion of the painting, a host of demigods (devas) are descending from the heavens. Below them is the natural world of oceans, trees, and plains, with a full moon shining in the upper left-hand corner of the picture. No sun is shown because the Buddha himself embodies the Light that spreads throughout the universe and resides within all things.

The Buddha radiates sublime peace—peace within himself and with the whole world of animate and inanimate existence. The painting portrays the multiform Buddha-nature that unifies all elements of creation, and the nobility of every creature gracing heaven and earth.

The high status accorded animals in Buddhism is attested to as well in the Jataka stories, parables about the Buddha's previous animal and human existences. It is significant that the Buddha himself, narrator of these tales, regarded his own animal incarnations as no less meaningful than his human ones. Implicit in all these stories are the Buddhist teachings of karma and rebirth—the teachings that an unbroken chain of cause and effect binds all existences, and that every creature has passed through many kinds of life and will pass through many more.

Writer and storyteller Rafe Martin, who has enacted these stories many times and who has written at length about them, writes:

The Jataka tales are dramatic presentations of one of the most fundamental aspects of the Buddhist vision. They express the essential unity of all life. After entering the world of the Jatakas, one notices animals more. They live their own lives, have their own tests and purposes. And as often brief and painful as their lives can be, they are also touched with purity and clarity. The Buddha-nature, equally common to all things, can often be seen flowing transparently in them. In the Jatakas one sees their inner life revealed and finds it to be the very same as one's own.

What strikes us most directly about the Jatakas is the focus on compassion, the self-sacrifice that flows from compassion, and identification of oneself with all living and suffering beings. In the Jatakas, animals freely sacrifice themselves for humans, and humans sacrifice themselves for "lower" animals. Imagine, humans sacrificing themselves for animals! It is almost unimaginable in our culture today. Yet, we do have the example of Greenpeace, whose leaders have put their own bodies between the harpooners' cannons and the whales.

The first of the two Jataka tales that I'd like to share, taken from Rafe Martin's book *The Hungry Tigress*, tells about such caring. It presents the future Buddha in a former life in which he sacrificed his body so that a starving tigress and her cubs might live. Again, to many this may seem unbelievable. But is it? Animals often sacrifice themselves for humans—think of dogs who have gone to the aid of their masters in danger, even when to do so cost them their lives. Are the beasts nobler than we? To sacrifice oneself for another, even for a "lower" four-legged creature, is the purest form of compassion, the noblest attribute of man or animal. For those in whom pity and compassion flow abundantly, the response to suffering, whether in man or beast, is unpremeditated and complete. Perhaps because animals are so much less caught up in the intellect than we, they may be more, not less sensitive. Indeed, their sufferings may be greater than our own.

A complete Jataka usually entailed four sections: (1) a story set in the present that gives the circumstances that led the Buddha to reveal his former birth, (2) the story of the former birth, (3) the original verses on which the stories are commentaries, and (4) the Buddha's statement revealing who the characters are in their present lives. Only the second of these four is included here.

## THE HUNGRY TIGRESS

Once, long, long ago, the Buddha came to life as a noble prince named Mahasattva in a land where the country of Nepal exists today. One day when he was grown, he went walking in a wild forest with his two older brothers. The land was dry and the leaves brittle. The sky seemed alight with flames.

Suddenly they saw a tigress. The brothers turned to flee, but the tigress stumbled and fell. She was starving and desperate and her two cubs were starving, too. She eyed her cubs miserably, and in that dark glance the prince sensed long months of hunger and pain. He saw, too, that unless she had food soon, she might even be driven to devour her own cubs. He was moved by compassion for the hardness of their life. "What after all is this life for?" he thought.

Stepping forward he removed his outer garments and lay down beside her. Tearing his skin with a stone he let the starving tigress smell the blood. Mahasattva's brothers fled.

Hungrily the tigress devoured the prince's body and chewed the bones. She and her cubs lived on, and for many years the forest was filled with golden light.

Centuries later a mighty king raised a pillar of carved stone on this spot, and pilgrims still go there to make offerings even today.

Deeds of compassion live on forever.

## THE BRAHMIN AND THE GOAT

A Brahmin was preparing to make an offering to his dead ancestors by sacrificing a goat and had turned the animal over to his disciples for the preliminary bathing and garlanding. While this was going on, the goat suddenly acquired recollection of its previous existences and thereupon burst into a loud peal of laughter, like the breaking of a pot. But a moment later it fell into a fit of weeping. The disciples reported this unprecedented behavior to the Brahmin, who asked the goat, "Why did you laugh?"

"Long ago," replied the goat, "in a previous existence I was a Brahmin like you and I, too, celebrated just such a sacrifice for the dead. As a result of this act of killing I was doomed to be reborn as a goat for five hundred successive existences and in each existence to have my head cut off. I have already suffered this fate four hundred and ninety-nine times, and now when my head is cut off for the five hundredth time, my punishment will come to an end. Therefore in my joy I laughed."

"And why," asked the Brahmin, "did you weep?"

"I wept when I thought of the five hundred existences of sorrow which you are about to bring upon yourself by cutting off my head."

"Never fear," said the Brahmin, "I shall not sacrifice you and you shall escape the pain of having your head cut off."

"It will make no difference for you to spare me, my head must inevitably be cut off."

The Brahmin, however, gave orders to his disciples to see that no harm came to the goat. Once free, the goat ran over to a ledge of rock and stretched its head out to nibble the leaves on a bush growing there. At that moment out of the clear sky came a sudden bolt of lightning, which split off a sliver from the overhanging rock, and this sliced off the goat's outstretched head as cleanly as with an executioner's knife.

The Bodhisattvic vow to liberate all beings, not just humans, so central to the theory and practice of Buddhism, emerges clearly in two ceremonies unique to Buddhism: the rescue and liberation of nonhuman beings, and the rite of administering the precepts to them.

The rescue of nonhuman beings is scripturally encouraged. The Brahmajala sutra, a well-known Buddhist scripture, includes this admonition: "If one is a son of Buddha one must, with a merciful heart, practice the liberation of living beings . . . and cause others to do so." The practice of liberating nonhuman beings is said to originate with this scripture.

Among Indian emperors who have followed this injunction to liberate and protect beasts of every sort, one of the most famous was Ashoka (268–223 B.C.). In one of his Pillar Edicts he declared, "I have enforced the law against killing certain animals and many others, but the greatest progress of Righteousness among men comes from the exhortation in favor of noninjury to life and abstention from killing living beings."

In Japan, too, in ancient times, when Buddhism dominated the hearts and minds of the Japanese, animal liberation was decreed by the emperors themselves. For example, Emperor Temmu, in the year 676, having commanded a Great Purification in all the provinces of his country, ordered that "all living beings be let loose." Those freed included criminals not convicted of capital crimes, as well as animals. In the year 745, Emperor Shomu ordered that all falcons and cormorants be set free, with the double aim of liberating these birds and prohibiting hunting and fishing with them.

Such practices also flourished in ancient China. The Chinese emperor Hsu-tsung of the T'ang dynasty (618–906) dedicated eighty-one ponds for the liberation of living beings. And a well-known Chinese Buddhist monk, called the Cloud of Compassion, in the year 1032, made the West Lake in China a pond for liberating living beings. He held an assembly of the people of the district on the Buddha's birth date (April 8) and told them to let loose fishes and birds.

While Buddhism was still a viable force in China, up until the Communist revolution of 1949, the practice of releasing living creatures was common. Holmes Welch, who has written extensively on Chinese Buddhism, says that near the main gate of almost every large monastery there was a pool for the release of living creatures, into which the pious could drop live fish they had rescued from the fishmonger. Behind the monastery there were stables for the care of cows, pigs, and other livestock similarly rescued. Sometimes thousands of animals were set free or rescued from dinner tables in mass releases intended as offerings to the Bodhisattva of Compassion, Kuan yin.

A remarkable incident related to this (reported in the newspapers of China in May of 1936) concerns a fox whose every hair was snow-white. It had been trapped by a hunter, but appeared to be tame. Later, although not confined, the fox made no attempt to escape. The hunter gave the fox as a pet to a neighbor named Lim, who treated the fox as a member of his household, a position it readily accepted. One night Lim had a vision in which he was directed to take the fox to a Buddhist monastery called White Cloud and liberate it there. Accordingly, the next morning he took the fox to the monastery. The abbot at the time was the Venerable Hsu yun, who immediately took a warm interest in the fox. The abbot suggested that Mr. Lim open the basket in which he had brought the fox. The fox hopped out, and to the amazement of Mr. Lim and several onlookers, made what was unmistakably a bow to the holy images on the shrine table.

Hsu yun explained that he felt the fox was a reincarnation of a former resident monk who, having accumulated much negative karma, had been reembodied in this manner. The abbot spoke to the fox, asking if it would like to take the Three Refuges: refuge in Buddha, Dharma, and Sangha. And then, the Five Precepts, stated from the human standpoint: (1) to refrain from taking life, (2) to refrain from taking what is not given, (3) to refrain from improper sexuality, (4) to refrain from telling an untruth, (5) to refrain from taking liquors or drugs that confuse the mind. The fox seemed to understand. It bowed low before the abbot, who then recited the mantra of the Great Compassion, following this with the formula of the Three Refuges and the Five Precepts. Throughout the ceremony the white fox maintained a dignified posture and bowed when the ceremony was finished. The abbot gave the fox a Buddhist name meaning Toward Goodness.

Within a short time the animal became fond of a vegetarian diet. On several occasions when the cook mixed chopped meat with its food, the fox refused to eat. Thousands of devout Buddhists came to see the animal, which by now was known far and wide as the Buddhist Fox.

Once some mischievous boys chased the fox. It took refuge in a tree in the monastery gardens. The abbot, hearing the boys' shouts, went to the tree and beckoned to the fox to come down. At once it leaped onto the abbot's shoulders, taking great care not to scratch him. "A kitten could hardly have been more gentle," remarked the abbot. Observers reported that whenever Hsu yun sat too long in the cold meditation room, the fox would nuzzle his cheek until the abbot got up and went to bed.

Speaking from his enlightened wisdom, Zen Master Dogen has said, "Those who experience this communion [with Buddha] inevitably take this refuge [in the Three Treasures of Buddha, Dharma, and Sangha] whether they find themselves as celestial or human beings, dwellers in hell, hungry ghosts, or animals. As a result, the merit that is accumulated thereby inevitably increases through the various stages of existence, leading ultimately to the highest supreme enlightenment."

The purpose in administering the precepts to an animal, then, is to raise the level of its consciousness so that it may achieve a more felicitous rebirth and eventually attain full liberation. The ceremony of giving the precepts is not primarily directed to the discriminating mind, but to Buddha-mind, the Mind inherent in all creatures. In Mahayana Buddhism the precepts are more than guidelines delineating morally desirable behavior; they are an expression of ultimate reality, of the absolute Buddha-nature. On this level we cannot speak of high or low, moral or amoral, karma or akarma, birth or death, animal or human being.

Thus from the *absolute* standpoint of Buddha-nature, every creature, just as it is, is whole and complete, a perfect expression of Buddha, a term used in two senses: (a) ultimate truth or absolute Mind, and (b) one awakened to the true nature of existence. A mouse here is the equal of an Einstein. But from the perspective of the senses and the intellect, all things, animate and inanimate, are temporary transformations of the one Buddha—

or Essential Mind—names for the ever unnameable "it"—the substratum of Emptiness (perfection) underlying all existences. "Heaven and earth and I are of the same root, all things and I are of the same substance," affirmed a Zen master of old. On this level, each life, each thing, is causally related to every other, forming an indivisible whole. No creature, whether it walks, creeps, crawls, swims, or flies, ever falls short of its own completeness. "Wherever it stands, it does not fail to cover the ground."

Bodhi, the dog now lying at my feet, has been evolving and devolving in his beginningless and endless course of becoming through innumerable eras, now as a mineral, now as a plant, now as a fish, now as a reptile, now as an ape, now as a demon, now as a demigod, now as one like myself—I who am *what?* Yet, once again, if I look at him through eyes undimmed by relativity—by notions such as karma, morality, causality, Buddha, mind—he is not a dog. Furthermore, he never evolved or devolved, was never born, will never die. Suppose he were asked, "What are you? Where did you come from? What is your relation to your fellow creatures?" How would he respond? "Woof! Woof!"

Translated into the language of humans this reads: "Throughout heaven and earth I am the only One."

# Valuing Life
## (1974)

I am sometimes asked why Buddhism values life so highly when it appears to be a law of nature for all forms of life to feed upon each other. It is of course true, it's a law of life, that everything feeds on everything else. We see this throughout life from the smallest organism to the highest. Since this contention comes up most frequently in terms of eating and not eating meat, let us put the discussion in that context, as it may be easier to understand.

People will say, for example, "I understand that some Buddhists don't eat or serve meat or fish for spiritual reasons, because that would make them an accessory after the fact, so to say, of taking life. But what about the eating of vegetables? They also have a life. And especially in recent years, we've heard so much about plants and flowers being so sensitive."

The answer is that there are levels of existence. We exist on two levels simultaneously. One is the level of what we call, to use the philosophical terms, the "unconditioned" or "absolute." On this level of the unconditioned, we cannot make any distinction between high and low, better and worse. On that level, we can't say that taking the life of a cow is any worse than taking the life of a plant or that taking the life of a plant is any better than taking the life of a cow. This is the level of true equality. Here fish swim among the branches of the trees and birds fly deep in the ocean. There are no distinctions. On what we call a "relative" level, we do make distinctions; there is a hierarchy of events and values. Certainly on this level, the life of an Einstein is infinitely more precious than the life of a mouse. Similarly, to take the life of a cow is more heinous than taking the life of a flower.

Not long ago I was talking with a man in the meat business who's a large wholesaler, and we were talking about a book by Upton Sinclair, *The Stockyards*. It takes place in the 1920s and tells the horrors of how animals are killed in the stockyards. This man had read the book and I said to him, "Have things improved?" He looked a little shamefaced and said, "If anything, I think that they're worse." So that, while in many ways we seem more sensitive to these issues today, in reality that awareness has not penetrated to the core of our lives. To take the life of a cow is worse, karmically speaking, than taking the life of a flower because it takes far more effort and energy. The nervous system of a cow, too, is more developed. On this scale of development, certainly to take the life of a human being would be far worse than to take the life of a cow. So on this relative level we make distinctions and we do have a hierarchy of values. But, in actuality, we live at both of these levels at the same time, the relative and the absolute. It's just that most people are not aware of the absolute level, and so they simply believe that everything feeds on something. Killing then seems inevitable because the respect for this unity of life is unknown.

Then there is a second aspect, that everything depends on *how* we take life. Even the mind-state with which we take life determines whether an act is morally or spiritually reprehensible or not. Killing animals, hunting and so on, may be done mindfully with no thought of self and other, no intent to kill per se. When this is the case, the act of killing is not really a problem. If you must take life for food or health, even the life of such as insects that cause disease, it can be done with a mind of regret, apology. In traditional hunting-gathering societies, there is a genuine feeling of apology: "I'm sorry I have to take your life, but I need it for food. Please forgive me." This is also a way of indicating your oneness with life. More, there is typically a sense of the awesome responsibility inherent in any act of taking life. Traditional cultures know well that all life is interconnected and sacred. And so they do not hunt animals lightly. They know it is spiritually perilous to do so. Well, skeptics will say, "A lot of good that does the animal, to apologize." This misses the understanding of the absolute, unconditioned level on which everything is already joined, the recognition that all life, and all interconnections, are subtle, mysterious, sacred.

You'll find, for example, in Zen training, this whole problem of taking life comes at the very end of training because it is a profound thing to understand. There is one level, where to take any life under any circumstances makes you spiritually culpable. Then you go to a more comprehensive level, and there you can justify the taking of life for the greater good. For example, if a rabid dog was running down the street and might bite somebody, certainly you'd shoot it. But, spiritually speaking, a lot depends on how you do it. If you do it with hatred—"That damn animal! Let's get him"—or frenzy or fear and revulsion, you would be creating a problem. But if it's done with no hatred at all, as a necessary thing, with complete identification and even love for the animal, then it becomes something else again. There's a real transcendence of the relative distinction between me and the animal or whatever life is being taken. Even with taking a flower, if you have to pull up a flower, apologizing to the flower, saying, in essence, "I don't mean to hurt you," has its subtle, positive effect. A realm of oneness and of healing opens.

To a Buddhist, then, evil is separation and alienation from yourself and from others. In Buddhism there are the Ten Precepts or moral principles, all of which come out of this idea: not to kill, not to lie, not to steal, not to have improper sex, not to take liquors or drugs that muddle the mind and not to cause others to do so, not to praise yourself and put down other people, not to speak of the shortcomings of others, not to give material or spiritual aid grudgingly, not to give vent to anger, and not to put down the Three Treasures: the Buddha, the teaching (Dharma), and the community of people who practice together (Sangha). There are also three General Resolutions: to avoid evil, to practice good, to liberate all sentient beings.

Not to do evil really means not to separate yourself from your daily life, the world as it unfolds around you. Separation means the denial or negation of our True-nature, and it is in our

True-nature that all purity, all goodness, all virtue, reside. We have compassion and love as our birthright. We don't have to get them from the outside. Buddhism teaches that we are all inherently good, in the sense of being whole and complete, not separated. To avoid evil means to avoid doing the kinds of things that alienate or separate us, estrange us, from life. And to do good means to affirm in a positive way this essential unity of all existence.

The Ten Precepts, not to kill, not to steal, and so on, are given from the point of view of a fully realized Buddha. They are the expression of the way a *Buddha* would act. That is to say, such a highly spiritually developed being would not kill because there would be nothing to kill, there would be no sense of other. After all, anger, violence, and so on arise from a sense of frustration, a feeling of being separated, of being shut off. Even though the precepts are stated from the point of view of a Buddha, we try as best we can generally to follow them.

Now the question comes up: Somebody comes to attack you. What do you do? Do you have a right to defend yourself; do you strike back? Or to make the case even more intense: Suppose somebody is about to strike your child or has struck your child, completely unreasonably—what do you do? What would a good Buddhist do? The trouble is, people want a yes-or-no answer, a black-and-white answer. There is no such thing. One never knows what one is going to do, really. Nevertheless we have these precepts as a kind of general guide.

You may think, if you're struck, then you strike back. You're entitled to. But are you? This assumption is a kind of a conditioning. It's interesting to note that even the law says you can not use any more force than necessary to repel an attack. If somebody slaps you in the face, to take out a gun and shoot that person is certainly not justified by any kind of a legal code.

A child might thoughtlessly step on a bug. The mind-state of the child is that the life of a bug is not important. The bug has only crossed the child's path, but the child takes its life. Of course the child has seen grown-ups react with resentment, annoyance, or fear at insects. This sets up a kind of conditioning about reacting out of fear or annoyance. And so the habit of violence is carried on, generation to generation.

The whole idea of violence, either on the part of the person who's attacking or the person who's protecting, depends on your particular mind-state. At a certain stage you would probably react in one kind of way; in a more developed stage, in another.

In his biography, Gandhi talks about how when he was in South Africa he would insist on sitting in a seat that was reserved for white people. As a result, he would be attacked, but he never fought back. He would protect himself, just as nonviolent demonstrators do in this country, by going limp. Fighting back often only creates more violence.

A reverence for life that opens our hearts to those whom we regard as a nuisance (such as insects) or even as our enemies (such as oppressors) is cultivated and sustained through the practice of zazen. Fostering zazen and the attitudes that arise from it, a Buddhist community provides a refuge for practitioners from the larger culture that often encourages aggression for solving disputes and conflicts. Anyone can learn to be more mindful and more respectful of the unity of life. Even the knowledge that such an approach is possible can be valuable. In the end, the need to fight back, as natural as it seems to be, itself springs from separation and fear.

When all life is truly seen as of one root, interconnected and sacred, then even in a violent culture, new responses will arise and at last the old cycle of violence will end.

# Thanksgiving:
## A Life of Gratitude
### (1975)

Today, as you all know, is Thanksgiving. Of all our national holidays, none is more in accord with the spirit of Buddhism than this one. In our daily prostrations before the Buddha, in placing our hands palm to palm (gassho), when greeting each other, and in many other ways we are expressing our thanks and gratitude for a multitude of things, but mostly for our human body and the opportunity it affords to come to Self-realization. And while the holiday was originally an expression of thanks of the Plymouth colony for the first rich harvest after a winter of privation and starvation, it really symbolizes the spirit of gratitude that resides in the heart of all of us.

Of all emotions the feeling of gratitude is probably the most dignified; it lies at the core of a spiritual life. Even dogs and cats show it. Not to feel and express this most elevated of emotions therefore is to be lower than an animal. Until one has begun to feel real gratitude, to parents, to teachers, to family, children, and friends, to members of the Sangha, to all who have made it possible for us to know and realize ourselves, to realize the Dharma, one's practice is still deficient. Gratitude is really the language of the heart.

And yet when we look on the world with eyes dimmed with ignorance, hearts clouded with despair, we are bound to ask ourselves, What is there to be grateful for? Are we to be grateful for global starvation? For an environment that is terribly polluted? For the fact that one out of five Americans will die painfully of cancer? For the violence in our own country and elsewhere?

Nonetheless, as Buddhists, we can see a great deal for which we can be grateful. First, we can be grateful to our parents for having provided us with a human life that enables us to awaken to the most fundamental experience any living being can have. Not long ago I read an article that held that a man's most fundamental life experience is to be a soldier; a woman's, to have a child. But for the truth-seeker, the most fundamental life experience possible is to wake up to the real nature of life: ours and everyone's.

Those who are married can certainly be grateful to each other. Wives can be grateful to their husbands for enabling them to know all the emotions of a wife, and vice versa. Parents can be grateful to their children, without whom they could never know the joys and sorrows of parenthood. And really we need to be at least just as grateful for the difficulties as for the enjoyment and the pleasure, for it is through our sufferings that we have the chance to grow and enrich our lives.

How can we not be grateful to the Sangha, for its communal warmth and mutual aid, for the friendships based on honesty and love? Without working together as a community, a Sangha, how could we come to know the deep joy that opens to us through meaningful ceremonies? Is there anything more frustrating than to feel deep emotion and not be able to express it? This is why ceremonies and rituals, when they have genuine feeling behind them, are so vital and meaningful.

And, of course, we can be grateful to all Buddhas and Bodhisattvas, visible and invisible, who make it possible for us to hear the truth, to believe it, and to experience it in our lives.

We hear it said in Buddhism that really there is no one to feel grateful to and no one to express it to. In the most profound sense that is, of course, true. As we progress deeper into practice, so much of what we formerly took to be real vanishes before our touch and sight. Our cherished illusions and deluded notions of right and wrong cannot stand up to the light of the truth within us. Those whose minds are still clouded by fear and anxiety, at a certain point in their training when their old unreal world is slipping away and the "new" one has not yet entirely emerged, can find their fears increasing instead of diminishing.

But this is only a halfway point. I hope you know that as you persevere, you will achieve a rocklike steadiness, a joyous transparency, and an all-pervading freedom.

It is also said that in bowing down before Buddhas, there is actually nobody to bow down to and no one bowing. Who bows to what? In truth nobody bows to anyone, and yet there is this wonderful, free, gratitude-filled bowing down. In this subjectless, objectless wholehearted bowing, nothing is excluded. The whole world bows. All creatures—men, women, animals, insects—bow to one another in mutual greeting. Is this not true thanksgiving?

A less strenuous way to express thanks is to put the hands together palm to palm in what is called gassho. Do it often enough and you find the rigid outlines of a self-absorbed ego softened. Feelings of humility, respect, and gratitude emerge. In this lowering of the mast of ego it is impossible to have an egotistical thought or to speak an unkind word.

Thanksgiving is a deep sentiment and, for Buddhists, is not celebrated one day a year. For the spiritual-minded person, it is a way of life, embracing every day, every hour, every minute, a way of living that is truly life-affirming, filled with thanks for everything.

# Common Questions
## about Zen

(1974)

TAKING LIFE

Often in the summer, we hear a question that concerns the first precept. And this is the question of the taking of life, of killing little bugs, ants, mosquitoes, and so on. People who are working as gardeners can be very much troubled by this matter. When we talk about the first precept, "not to take life, not to kill but to cherish all life," we understand that we must avoid the taking of life wherever possible. Working in a garden, killing insects, is certainly not the best thing to be doing, if one is killing when one doesn't have to. If one is compelled to do so, though, as say when insects present a clear and reasonable danger of spreading disease to human beings or animals, that's another matter. When we are compelled by circumstances to take life—and the key word is *compelled*—then it should be done, not in a spirit of vengeance, not in a spirit of separation, but with a feeling of oneness and contrition, of regret. At such a time we gassho, place the hands palm to palm. The gassho in effect says, "I'm sorry I have to take your life."

Sometimes you see people mash a mosquito that has bitten them. I am reminded of the biblical exhortation to take an eye for an eye and a tooth for a tooth. The same people who speak of such Old Testament morality as archaic in its severity don't hesitate to kill a mosquito that merely stings them. That's surely an unjust exchange! Yet the biblical injunction itself may have more in common with the first precept than one might first think. It meant that even in one's grief or anger, one had to be careful and appropriate, taking no more than "an eye for an eye, a tooth for a tooth." It was a way of limiting violence and not an exhortation to it. Yet now often we thoughtlessly kill insects or other small animals, such as squirrels, that merely annoy us!

As we know, life is not inviolable. Something often has to die in order for another thing to live. But where it is necessary to take life for a greater good, then doing it with a feeling of contrition lessens the karmic consequences. As your Zen practice deepens, you feel a greater closeness to all forms of life: when a mosquito alights on the hand, you'll simply blow it off, and similarly with ants and other insects. You will not kill them.


## THE PRECEPTS

The precepts are an *ideal,* an expression of the way a Buddha would act and live—although of course a Buddha doesn't think in these terms. We must not become impatient with ourselves if we find we cannot immediately measure up to this standard. In this lifetime, we all follow certain pain-producing habits or patterns. We must realize that anybody who earnestly does zazen will experience a loosening and eventually a breaking of these patterns—in other words a movement in the direction of the precepts; but this is not a simple matter. The process may take many, many years. Even enlightenment doesn't immediately redirect these habit-energies or these habit-forces that have been going in a certain direction for so long. Again, we mustn't be too hard on ourselves.

Now there's one other matter that comes up from time to time relating to the precepts. People who find themselves breaking certain precepts again and again get discouraged. They feel somehow that they're lacking in virtue or are terribly weak. This leads to guilt feelings or feelings of inadequacy, all of which have an unfavorable effect on one's practice; they lead to disgust with oneself. When you get disgusted with yourself, you don't want to sit. You feel that there must be something wrong with yourself. You feel that you haven't made any progress, and that you're intrinsically inadequate. Such negative thoughts begin to assail the mind. Again, remember that you, me, all of us, are striving to realize Truth and develop compassion—and that includes compassion for oneself. No one becomes a full Buddha overnight. Be gentle with yourself yet do your best. Then there will be little cause for regret.

## EGO

Some practitioners wonder why Zen emphasizes transcending the ego. For some people, this idea has an unfavorable connotation. They say, "But aren't there some people who do not have enough ego? What about people who need to have the ego built up more before it's taken away?" First of all the word *ego* as used in Zen Buddhism means something altogether different from the word as used in psychology or psychiatry. I won't attempt to say precisely what it means in psychiatry, but in Buddhism it means the sense of oneself as a separated, perhaps you could almost say an isolated, being. "Here am I, and outside me there is the rest of the world, confronting me, even menacing me." Most people, no matter how strong their character, or adequate their functioning, suffer from that feeling. Do some people need to have their psychological ego built up? Of course. That is not the ego that is taken away. In fact, no ego is "taken away." The spiritual world, so to speak, and the ordinary world interpenetrate. They find completion in each other. Only delusions disappear. Sometimes, however rarely it might be, a competent teacher will find, because of schizophrenia or some other so-called psychotic illness, zazen practice is not to be recommended. Anybody who comes to me, as such people have, who is psychotic, I send to a psychotherapist. That person is not in a condition to practice Zen. And the person who is highly neurotic, in the sense also that he or she can't function in relation to the environment, or is constantly beset with hallucinations, (not of a psychotic nature) in the sense of what are called in Zen makyo, such a person, too, would find it difficult to do zazen. Makyo are certain phenomena—hallucinations, fantasies, visions, revelations—that one practicing zazen is apt to experience at a certain stage. They become an obstacle only if one is ignorant of their nature as distractions and becomes ensnared by them. A very high-strung, nervous person might be distracted by makyo, and could benefit if he or she wants to practice Zen by working with a sympathetic therapist either to establish a base for zazen or as an accompaniment to daily zazen.

I remember one time someone said, "Suppose you had a person who was suicidal, who wanted to commit suicide or had attempted it already, unsuccessfully. Would you try to take away that person's ego? Doesn't that person need more ego, to bolster self-esteem?" Well, from the Zen Buddhist point of view, again, there is in reality no ego to take away. This delusional sense of oneself as separate from, detached from, the whole living universe can be a difficult problem, though. The person who is contemplating suicide is a highly egotistical person, from a Buddhist perspective. That is, such a person is deeply deluded, terribly caught in the painful illusion of separateness. That he or she might need to further develop or strengthen what we might term the psychological ego, the ability to meet life on its own terms, does, however, seem quite reasonable.

In Buddhism, all of existence is seen as a Oneness, a multifaceted Unity. All beings, not only human beings, but all sentient beings, are seeking awareness of this unity. There are other names for this: love, compassion, and so on. There might be cases where, at a certain point, one might have to build up a person's ego. Later on, with an experience of Oneness, that person will see into the unreality of ego so that it, as a limitation, is transcended. One is truly oneself: It's just that there is a lot less ego-clinging, and so there is greater freedom in the deepest sense of all.

Still, in our culture, that sense of "me and my," of "I-ness," is so strongly emphasized. It's amazing, really, how often the word *I* is used in our speech. The English language is constructed in such a way that 90 percent of English sentences require the personal pronoun. There are other languages that don't require it at all; Japanese is one in which 90 percent of the sentences can be made without using a personal pronoun. In English, we would have to say, "I'm going downtown today." A Japanese would say, "Downtown going today." There's no personal pronoun; it's implied. The English language is structured this way because of our minds. If you teach your children, and yourself, to try to avoid the word *I* when it's not really necessary, not simply avoiding the word *I*, but avoiding the expression of self that the use implies, it can be helpful. In Zen practice, after all, we're trying to see through ego, and if we keep saying "I, I, I . . ." unnecessarily, it tends to reinforce an idea of a separate self.

But, let this be natural. There's no point in twisting yourself, or your children, or anyone else for that matter, into a mental or emotional pretzel trying to figure out how to communicate without using the word *I*. Zen emphasizes what is natural. As a basic guideline, just be aware of how you're using language.

## ATHEISM

If you are an atheist and do not believe in the notion of God, you *may* have a brilliant future in Zen. In a non-Buddhist tradition a great theologian said, "The true atheist is closer to God than the person who goes to church once a week. The person who goes to church once a week thinks of himself or herself as being a very holy person, although she or he may not think of God very much. The atheist, who says, 'I hate God!' can only hate God in the name of God, thereby affirming God." So the atheist is close to God.

Buddhism, of course, has no God concept, which is why many atheists are attracted to it. But you don't have to think of Buddhism in terms of atheism or not-atheism or anything else. In Zen the emphasis is on something so fundamental it transcends all that—the fundamental human need to know who and what we are. Certain Freudians talk of how important it is to express oneself sexually, how dangerous sexual repression can be to our mental and physical well-being. But the worst kind of repression is spiritual, the repression of the desire to know who and what we are, why we were born, why we have to die. If this desire is repressed, we can truly find no peace. The most beautiful experience will be soured by a gnawing that will always remain at the back of our minds. Once the desire to know who and what we are has been awakened, has come even slightly into consciousness, it can never be put down again without losing something vital. We can paper it over with all sorts of activities, running here and there, but eventually we must get down to really looking into our minds and finding the answer. Until then, we have no real rest. Only the real answer to this question brings deep, lasting satisfaction and peace.

## THE "ODDITY" OF ZEN

The reaction of parents to a child's emotional struggles can sometimes be strange. For instance, some parents may congratulate a child if he or she goes into psychotherapy. "Oh, that's fine," a mother or father will say. "My son really wants to help himself. He's seeing a psychiatrist." Or, "My daughter is working with a therapist these days. She seems to be benefiting a lot from it." But let those same parents discover a child doing zazen and they may say, "What are you doing, just sitting by yourself, while the suffering of the world passes you by? What are you doing to help? You're just gazing at your navel. Why don't you mix with people, with your family, and try to help?" Parents can find it hard to give high marks to a child trying to help him or herself by meditating. It can be threatening and seems to set off archaic alarms and religious anxieties.

But when family members are not critical, they may feel you should become a Buddha overnight. Americans are such idealists! And if you don't act like a Buddha, if your conduct isn't faultless, they may say, "See, you're just as bad as the rest of us. You haven't become an enlightened person. Why are you doing zazen? It's not helping you and it's not helping anybody else!"

This kind of thing comes up all the time. There are even parents who want nothing to do with their children because they practice Zen, which is just unbelievable. Given time, these attitudes will change. As one's zazen bears fruit, parents will see its benefits, if they haven't purposefully blinded themselves to what becomes quite obvious to others.

On the other hand, there are parents who *are* understanding. This is one of the really encouraging things. We had a parents' seminar not long ago that was very beautiful. It was an open forum, a real give-and-take right in the zendo (meditation hall), and at the end, many parents were really glowing. Many wanted to know when we were going to have another parents' weekend. So there are all kinds of parents. Be patient. If you act superior to your family members out of defensiveness—and why else would you act this way?—or to your friends, this won't help. One just has to be patient. As you change, have faith that your family will become aware. Mothers can be especially quick to notice how much happier and calmer you are. And they will trust what you are doing.

Some Zen practitioners have a mistaken notion of what it means to continue their practice wherever they are. So even at a party, you will see them go off into a corner, get into a lotus posture, and "make like a Buddha" while others are conversing, drinking, and having a wonderful time. No wonder some people think Zen meditators are weirdos. If you're at a party, get into the mood or don't go. My first teacher, Harada Roshi, was very much against drinking. And yet when there was a party in the monastery and temple supporters would bring liquor, he would take just a few drops to be one with the occasion. At other times he would never touch liquor, though he enjoyed smoking. Everything in its place.

PART II

꙳

# ETHICS,
# RESPONSIBILITY,
# PRACTICE

# On an Ethical Way of Life: Commentary on Some of the Buddhist Precepts

## (1975)

My teacher Yasutani Roshi used to say that Zen cannot be abstracted from the Buddhist precepts. The Way of Buddhism, he would continue, comprises three basic elements: the precepts, zazen, and satori-wisdom. To quote Yasutani Roshi:

> In fact these three are one, but if we were to divide them and give them an order, the precepts would be the foundation, zazen would be next, and satori-wisdom on top of both.
>
> This relationship can be illustrated with a simple example, namely, the building of a house. The precepts represent the building site, zazen the house itself, and satori-wisdom the furniture and appliances. We first must find a site, after which, for proper habitation, a house is needed. In an extreme situation one could live without a house simply by digging a hole in the ground and covering oneself with straw matting. But without ground one couldn't even do that. So the site is fundamental.
>
> Let me now explain these three from the standpoint of equality, or undifferentiation. As I have already said, the precepts, zazen, and satori are indivisible; the three are one and each one embodies all three. To pursue the image of building a house: bare ground takes on value when a house is built upon it, and a house becomes comfortable to live in only when a garden is added and the rooms furnished. Only then do the three become one complete living unit.
>
> Now, what are the Buddhist precepts? They consist of rever-

ence for the three treasures, namely, the Buddha, the Dharma, and the Sangha, or Buddhist community; the pledge to avoid evil, practice goodness, and strive for the salvation of every sentient being; and the ten cardinal precepts, which exhort one to refrain from (1) the taking of life, (2) theft, (3) unchastity, (4) lying, (5) selling or buying alcohol or mind-altering drugs, (6) speaking of the misdeeds of others, (7) praising oneself and reviling others, (8) withholding or grudgingly giving spiritual or material aid, (9) anger, and (10) blaspheming the Three Treasures.

These sixteen precepts are not rules of behavior that are extraneous and therefore a strain to observe. Rather, they describe conduct that is the natural outgrowth of Buddha-nature. These precepts, handed down to us from ancient times, are the same for monks as for lay people.

A correct attitude when accepting the precepts is to believe that they are a natural expression of harmonious conduct issuing from the Buddha-nature that all possess. For this reason everyone should make an effort to keep them. Observing the precepts is necessary for no other reason than that they are the foundation of the Buddha's Way. Just as it is impossible to build a house without a site, so is it impossible to progress in zazen without the precepts as a foundation.

Those who are undisciplined in their daily life—that is to say, lazy, weak-willed, self-indulgent, and/or immoral—will not be able to discipline themselves in zazen. A disciplined life is the foundation of Buddhism and the foundation of zazen. At the root of a disciplined life and zazen practice lie the precepts.

Should one ask, "What, then, is Zen?" the answer would be: Zen is the attainment of peace and tranquility at the very core of our being, that is, our Buddha-nature. Or to state it more succinctly, Zen is the realization of Buddha-nature.

Now the precepts and Zen are grounded in the same Buddha-nature—their content is one and the same. The only difference is that the precepts are rules that one accepts, that one believes, and that one makes an effort to keep, while Zen is a practice leading to the realization of one's Buddha-nature, the attainment of inner peace and tranquillity and the spontaneous acceptance of the precepts into one's life, which is to say, freely living by them. The more one practices Zen the more one becomes self-effacing, steady, agreeable, kindhearted, flexible, and virtuous—the more, in other words, one comes closer to one's Buddha-nature, which is the source and expression of true Zen Buddhism.

Though we use the word *precept*, a much better term—that is, a more Buddhist-like one—would be *item of good character*. So, rather than "the Ten Precepts" we might want to say, "The ten items of good character." (The word *commandments* is not appropriate. The implication of someone giving an order to someone else misses the mark. The phrase *the ten cardinal prohibitions* is also frequently used, but that, too, fails to hit the target.) After all, from the Buddhist perspective, these ten ideas are not fences placed around us to prevent us from straying into immoral realms, but rather, ten items that delineate the behavior of a highly spiritually developed person—a Buddha, Bodhisattva, or *arhat* (someone who has become deeply enlightened). They are the natural expression of the functioning of the mind of such a person. Since we are not Buddhas and Bodhisattvas yet, the best we can do is sincerely try to live by these items of good character. We uphold them and let them uphold us and the daily activities of our lives.

When we discuss morality in this context, we should perhaps think of it as Morality with a capital *M*. It's not the ordinary morality of good *versus* evil, right *versus* wrong. Rather, it is the way a person acts who is living a life in harmony with the Dharma, the natural order of things. The word *Dharma* fundamentally means "that which upholds the universe." It has many other meanings, but it refers principally to the natural laws that make it possible for the universe to function, and for human—and other—beings to live harmoniously together.

Traditionally, a life of Dharma for human beings is seen as resting on three things: the precepts as moral behavior; zazen; and *satori* or transcendent wisdom. All three are interrelated.

Without moral behavior (behavior that does not cause pain to oneself and others), it is not possible to really practice pure zazen and to reach a state of complete absorption or samadhi. And without zazen or this samadhilike state, there cannot be awakening and the transcendent wisdom that comes from it. Similarly, without a stable base of regular, daily zazen, moral behavior is all too often a patchwork, a hit-or-miss proposition of impossible ideals and failed efforts. And prajna wisdom without the other two is abstract, nonfunctioning or unusable.

One of the differences between the Theravada (literally, "teachings of the elders") form of Buddhism, common to Southeast Asia, and the Mahayana (literally, "great vehicle") traditions of Buddhism in respect to the precepts, or items of good character, is that in Mahayana the intention or the thought itself is as important as the actual act. Mahayana Buddhism, which evolved in China, Tibet, Mongolia, Nepal, Korea, Vietnam, and Japan, emphasizes compassion and the ideal of the Bodhisattva. Zen is a branch of Mahayana Buddhism that arose in China. The word *zen* comes from the Chinese *chan*, which comes from *dhyana*, the Sanskrit term for meditation. Zen developed from its Chinese roots to flourish in Korea, Vietnam, and Japan as well. In Mahayana, the thought is parent to the act.

In classical Buddhism, actions are not termed "good" or "bad," but rather "skillful" or "unskillful." Skillful actions are those that arise from an awareness of Unity, or nonseparation. Such actions, not overly bound by attachment to thoughts of self and other, are spontaneous, wise, and compassionate. Unskillful actions, on the other hand, grow out of the unwholesome roots of greed, hatred or anger, and delusion. As the primary delusion is that of self and other, thoughts and actions that arise from such a condition of separation, of separateness we might say, tend to be reactive and self-protective. They can hardly form the basis of a skillful—that is, creative and fulfilling—life. For example, think of the first item of good character: not to kill but to cherish all life. It is not possible to commit murder unless the thought to take a life has arisen. One must have already seen a person as separate from oneself and one's

74

own self-interest to conceive of him or her as someone to be killed.

Out of this seed of separation, this thought in the mind, the deed can happen. Killing is the outward expression of a mind dominated by separation, specifically by anger or hatred. Deeds are thoughts made manifest. From unskillful thoughts, unskillful or pain-producing acts arise. Almost all action proceeds from thought.

## THE SECOND PRECEPT

The second precept is to refrain from taking what is not given. Another way to put it is, not to steal but to respect all things. For someone who has achieved the highest spiritual state, there can be no sense in taking what does not belong to one. How can there be? Being selfless, all things already belong to such a one. But until one has actually reached this stage, it would be dangerous to rationalize the taking of things that don't belong to you and not bothering to return them. To misuse things is also contradictory to the spirit of this second precept or item of good character. To take a book, for example, and lay it down open so that the spine breaks and the book, in time, is destroyed is also a form of stealing. It shows a lack of respect for the ultimate value of the article. Fraudulent business dealings would certainly come under this precept, as would the underpayment of employees. But, more subtly, stealing time from oneself and from one's own deepest purposes, squandering resources, one's own and the world's, would also be a violation of this precept.

So, what may seem to be a simple and obvious relation to objects can really be approached from many levels. Traditionally, in Zen training, the precepts are explored from five distinct perspectives: (1) Theravada, (2) Mahayana, (3) Buddha-nature, (4) Bodhidharma, and (5) Dogen's teacher, Ju-ching. We've already defined the first two traditions. The perspective of Buddha-nature is the concrete expression of perfection, unity, completeness, that is intrinsic to all existence. Bodhidharma, the

Twenty-eighth Patriarch in line from the Buddha, was the First Patriarch of Zen in China. It is generally thought that he came from India to China by boat about the year 520 C.E. Bodhidharma upholds the determination, sincerity, and discipline of the realized mind. Finally, Dogen (1200–1253) is the Zen patriarch venerated as the founder of the Japanese Soto sect of Zen. Dogen's approach, which he received from his teacher in China, emphasizes absolute faith in the enlightened mind, One Mind. From this perspective, all things, just as they are Buddhanature, are highest truth.

So far we have been essentially working with the Theravada perspective, which is the more literal point of view. Moving to the Mahayana viewpoint, we may say that the second precept tells us that what is paramount is that which benefits the larger community, not just the individual. So, anything that helps the larger community, the greater good, as we say, takes precedence over the individual good. This is why even in our ordinary legal law, it is the right of the state to claim certain property to build a highway, for example. The priority of the larger community over an individual's rights is a natural part of life. Going further, from the point of view of Buddha-nature, there is no self that can steal from any other self. In this condition of absolute truth there are no selves, no me, no you, so how can there be stealing? And, in this profoundest condition of truth, there is nothing even to be stolen. "Who steals what from whom?" it may be asked. All phenomena are simply energy in flux. Nothing has an enduring self. Or to put it another way, the so-called self is constantly undergoing transformation according to causes and conditions. What we call an object is simply a temporary manifestation, so temporary in fact that its life is something like a millionth of a second. Everything is being born and everything is dying, constantly, instantaneously!

From this point of view, how could there be any stealing or, conversely, any giving? But again, a warning: Only when one has actually attained this state oneself is one entitled to act this way. Yet, incidentally, highly spiritually developed people, those whose understanding is at this deepest level, don't go around borrowing or taking things and saying, "It's okay for me to do this. I'm deeply enlightened." Highly developed people do not say—or do—such things. They are simply decent, ordinary people. They are human beings through and through. As a rose is a rose is a rose, such people are *people.* Their very ordinariness expresses what is best in human nature.

From the point of view of Bodhidharma, the great, ancestral founder of Zen, we have this statement about the second precept, taken from *A Survey of Buddhism* by Sangharakshita: "Self-nature is clear and obvious. In the sphere of the ungraspable Dharma, not having a thought of grasping is called the item of refraining from stealing." If there is no thought of grasping, then there is nothing to grasp.

Zen Master Dogen says, "Self and external objects, just as they are, are differentiated, yet one. The gate of liberation opens spontaneously." They are one, yet two. They are two, yet one. From the point of view of the Buddha-nature, there's no differentiation at all. However, from the relative point of view, which means from the point of view of the manifestation of this Buddha- or Dharma-nature, we do differentiate. There is a me and there is a you. And at the same time, as Dogen's words imply, there is no me and there is no you. Another way to say this might be that they're not two, yet they're not even one.

To come to this kind of fully integrated understanding, not just intellectually but in the deepest experiential sense, is to use objects as though not using them at all and to own things as though not owning them whatsoever. Each thing is now fully itself. Here they are, right before us, being used and cared for appropriately by us. Each thing—a piece of paper, a lightbulb, a car, a book—is now used without covetousness, without possessiveness, without grasping. *Using* is not even the correct word here. One simply enters the gate of liberation together with all things. This is to truly be free of objects, free of the pull of things as possessions. It is to be free and, simultaneously, it is to free all things.

## THE FOURTH PRECEPT

It can't be emphasized too often that the precepts are not rules. They're not commandments imposed from the outside, either by some supernatural being or by some outer force. The precepts express the highest truth of Oneness or indivisibility or unity underlying all relationships. While they do prescribe or delineate behavior that we call moral, the basic purpose of the precepts is to support and strengthen our practice. If we give the three basic elements of Buddhist teaching an order, we could say that the precepts are the foundation, zazen is next, then on top of both, growing up out of them like a flower, a lotus, would be satori-wisdom.

The fourth precept is "Not to lie but to speak the truth." Many people think that some of the other precepts, such as not to engage in improper sexuality, or not taking liquors or drugs that confuse the mind, are the really tough ones. But actually they're not. This fourth is one of the two most difficult to try to observe, the other being the sixth, "Not to speak of the misdeeds of others."

Lying has been defined as the telling of an untruth with the intent to deceive. Of course, making a misstatement of fact without knowing it obviously is not a lie. And there are people who normally exaggerate and can't speak without resorting to hyperbole. Everything they say gets magnified to the $n$th degree, injected with a certain emotional quality. What they do isn't lying; it's not even playing fast and loose with the truth, as the saying has it.

But there are certainly subtle shades. One example that comes to mind is what happens when people cross the border into Canada. The border isn't all that far away from our Center. Many members periodically travel back and forth. In general I think one would almost need a computer to determine the number of subtle shades of meaning, let alone outright lies, that end up being told crossing the border. We all know the situation. Customs people can be a strange breed. They're taught to be suspicious and they can certainly seem to "have it in" for certain types of people. The stories that one hears about the terrible hassles that customs people can give young people, particularly those who have beards and aren't dressed in a traditional way, are truly distressing. So there is the natural temptation to avoid all that by just saying, "No, I don't have anything in my bag," when you've, say, bought a gift for a friend. The thing that one has to remember is that one is setting up a pattern, and part of this pattern is a guilt feeling that is not easy to live with. If you are in spiritual practice, the more you practice the more sensitive you become, and the more these things will bother you. I've had people come to me and say, "You know, I said such and such at the international border. When driving here I was stopped and asked this and I answered in this way. I knew it was a violation of this fourth precept. What do you do in such a situation?" And usually that person gets a blank look from me. This is something that each person has to work out individually.

It should be stated that the telling of an untruth in any situation can be a pretty bad thing. From the Mahayana perspective, of course, the concern is always the greater good. If by telling an untruth you can save another person—that is, save them from a painful situation—then the white lie can be justified. But you've got to be pretty sure in your mind that it's not a selfish thing, not a rationalization that you're indulging. The damage that we do to ourselves, to our practice, and to others through unthinking lies can be considerable. So we should all make a real effort and train ourselves to refrain from the temptation toward indulgence in false speech.

THE FIFTH PRECEPT

The fifth precept, "Not to cause others to take substances that impair the mind, or to do so oneself, but to keep the mind clear," bothers a lot of people. People have come to me and said that they don't want to take the precepts as vows in the formal ceremony of Jukai, in which one becomes a member of the Buddha's family, because, they admit, "frankly, there's one precept that I know darn well I'm not going to be able to keep. It's the one about alcohol. I like a little wine with a meal and it's not only for the stomach's sake. And I like a beer when I'm socializing with friends. It's hard for me to reconcile this with the precepts."

First of all, notice that the precept says, "Not to use substances that impair the mind." And remember, too, there's a distinction between the Theravada and the Mahayana points of view. This precept, again, must be worked out in a way that makes sense in your life. Still, it would be a mistake to take this precept lightly; there's a story that you can find in *What Is Buddhism?* by Khantipalo, an English Buddhist monk living in Thailand, that raises a fundamental concern. It presents a Theravadin point of view. It goes like this:

> It appears that a man of that country had aroused the enmity of some demon. This being plagued him and told him that he would only leave him in peace if the man consented to break one of the five precepts. Now, this man was a sincere Buddhist layman who had successfully kept his precepts, and he thought, "I can't break the first, for to kill a being is a most terrible thing. And for the second, I've never stolen anything in my life and it would be a great crime to begin. For the third, I've always been faithful to my wife and we are happy together, so how can I break the third one? And then the fourth, if I break it is sure to make someone unhappy and bring myself a bad name. What about the fifth? Hmm. Hmm." And so he decided that one little drop of liquor would not do any harm and would at the same time satisfy that devil. He had never before tasted alcohol, and that little drop that he sipped intrigued him by its taste. And he thought, "This tastes good. Hmm. A little more won't harm me." And so, a little more, more, until he was rolling drunk.
>
> Passing a tinker on his way home, he stole some trinkets and, reaching his house, at last found his wife absent and noticed for the first time how pretty his neighbor's wife appeared. And then going to her, he gave her the ornaments and entered her house. After some time she proposed that they have some food, so he took an ax and hacked off a goat's head. Finally, the tinker came

up with officials to accuse him of the theft and he roundly denied it, declaring his innocence. And so all five precepts were broken.

All because of one little drop of liquor. From a Mahayana perspective this story is not without some holes, not because it is implausible, but because from the Mahayana point of view it is more essential to learn control, to learn not to become attached to liquor. From a Mahayana perspective the warning, we might say, is about excess. Practically speaking, the best way to know about the dangers of liquor could be to take some. Young children seeing their elders drink might want to try it, too. To say, "No, it's not good for you," or to give a preachy sermon about it might only make them more interested. But saying, "Sure, here's a whole glass. Drink it up!" could stop their interest *forever.* When children get sick on liquor or when they simply experience for themselves its bitter, burning taste, they may never want even to look at it again. And the same is true with smoking. "You want to smoke a cigarette? What, just one! Anybody can smoke one cigarette! Why not try a cigar!" Well, that might be taking it a bit too far. But surely for any child who has been intrigued by smoking, actually puffing away at a cigarette can be a vile and disillusioning experience.

When my teachers in Japan attended a party, they would invariably take a couple drops of sake, wine, or beer—nobody ever drank hard liquor, but usually there would be beer or wine. My teachers would put just one or two drops or so in a little cup, and when people would drink, they would take a sip, in order not to separate themselves from the party. Even in this they were teaching. After all, when you're at a party, to separate yourself from the situation subtly condemns others and isolates yourself. Not to take liquors or drugs that confuse the mind, and not to cause others to do so, means just that—not to confuse the mind or the mind of others. In the Theravada, it doesn't say not to cause others to drink. But in the Mahayana, it's literally part of the precept, not to sell or to buy liquor that confuses the mind. To take one or two drops of liquor is probably not going to confuse the mind. And there are drugs other than alcohol, cocaine, or marijuana, drugs like rapacious acquisitiveness or any of the other confusing addictions to which contemporary society so excels in habituating us; these, too, need to be examined in light of this precept. What is it that confuses the mind? We must look carefully and act appropriately.

Of course it's something else to get into the regular habit of drinking. Serious, habitual drinking is a real problem. But to take a little wine might not be harmful. In certain situations it could even be a positive thing. Eventually, though, you reach a point where you have no desire for it. You reach a point of sensitivity. It's the same with eating meat or fish. People who haven't eaten such things for years find that, after a time, even the thought of eating a piece of meat can make them feel sick. They have reached a point of such sensitivity. And the same is true with liquor. Just a couple of drops perhaps does something. There's a slight dulling of the senses, and a relaxation that takes place. But, after a time of practicing, even the lift that one used to get from that fades. You realize it's a kind of a pseudo lift because there's a dullness that accompanies it. There's not that wonderful clarity that you get from doing zazen. After that, there's no need for it.

## THE SIXTH AND SEVENTH PRECEPTS

The sixth precept, "Not to speak of the misdeeds of others," is for many people tough to uphold. It is so easy to find oneself, even after vowing not to, repeating gossip about people, even sometimes gossip with a little malice in it.

Often we may say things about a person with an absence of malice, in a way that does not demean or belittle the person. Maybe someone did something funny or a person is a true "character," and everybody enjoys the laugh. That kind of thing can seem innocent enough. But one begins to tread on dangerous ground to speak of the shortcomings of another. It's so easy to let this become a habit.

In speaking of the shortcomings of other people, consciously or unconsciously, there can also be a subtle desire to put the other person down or put oneself up. This idea also draws us into the next precept, which is not to praise oneself and condemn others. The two precepts go closely together. Telling jokes in which one person is constantly the butt is a kind of putting oneself up and the other person down and often expresses an unconscious resentment against that person. And what is that resentment? We must ask ourselves and try to see it, and if it's there, try to overcome it. One way to overcome it can be by focusing on positive, constructive things that the other person does.

In our zazen, too, we can think of that person before beginning a round of sitting, and we can send loving thoughts toward that person. Such efforts tend to overcome and erase negative feelings. Often, however, negative feelings are at a deep level. Then we must try to understand why a person reacts negatively. It would be a good idea to really look at it. Ask yourself, "Why do I really feel this way? Why am I dwelling on so-and-so's shortcomings? Why do I feel a need to put him or her down?" The results of such questioning can help free you from old, sticky habits. Of course, trying to elevate yourself and put other people down can often arise from a feeling of inferiority, an anxiety about your fundamental worth. In acknowledging this and working on healing it we can end the problem at the root. Sometimes, too, we may unconsciously be trying to get even with somebody who we feel has wronged us. Slander can enter in here, either open or concealed.

In our culture people tend to feel that frankness is an outstanding virtue. "If you've got anything to say about me," we feel, "say it to my face." But you can be frank to a destructive degree. Sensitivity is needed, as well as frankness, an ability to put yourself in another's shoes. In other cultures, frankness doesn't have quite the virtue it has in ours. Many other cultures prefer restraint and some delicacy to frankness. Of course we're not talking about parents or teachers disciplining children. But we're talking about openly denouncing another person, perhaps even a friend or spouse. This is a dangerous kind of thing. Some pop psychologists suggest that bringing quarrels into the open is healthy, that it clears the air, so to speak. While this may be true sometimes, it also can mean the end of a relationship. As always, it depends on *how* one speaks—what one's intention is. Everything depends on the basic respect one human being can have for another. If that fundamental respect is broken, if the essential dignity of a human being is violated, then the damage can be irreparable. And no matter how much either one pretends in the future, "Oh, well, I know you spoke your truth there. It's all right, I needed to be talked to that way," the pain caused, and the resentment, can be too much. And in many cases it's irreparable. So one must be careful about denouncing somebody openly. I think Dogen has a passage somewhere that in essence says, "To lose respect for a person's dignity by denouncing him is contrary to the spirit of Buddhism."

Of course there will be times when honesty and forthrightness *are* called for. But to maintain respect one must be sensitive. Sometimes one has to do things indirectly, other times directly. It's all a question of the mix, of being alert to the whole situation. At bottom, if there is real love and respect, it won't matter. If there isn't, then whether it's done directly or indirectly, whether it's done to the person's face or behind the back, the other person will pick up on it. And there will be pain, fear, anguish, resentment, and possibly even a growing hatred. And so the important thing is that we maintain our respect and a sense of our dignity and the dignity of the other person. If there is self-hatred, then there can hardly be love for anybody else. That's why it always starts with ourselves.

If one is always putting oneself down, in essence saying, "I'm inadequate," there will be resentment projected toward other people. When you get into that kind of mind-state, your energy gets caught in nurturing resentment. So it's a good idea, when you find you've said or done something wounding to another, to apologize as soon as you can. As the great Tibetan teacher Milarepa said, "The best thing is not to do any wrong. But if you have and can repent of it afterwards, that is also very good."

## THE EIGHTH PRECEPT

The eighth precept is "Not to withhold spiritual or material aid but to give them freely where needed." Sometimes we hear it said, in Zen, that the most important thing is spiritual aid. If you give food, this line of thinking goes, you've satisfied the stomach but you haven't done anything for the mind or spirit. But notice that this precept says not to withhold material or spiritual aid but to give *both* freely where needed. You can't teach the Buddha's truth to a hungry person. If the stomach is growling, the mind won't be at ease. The nourishment that person needs—as her body is clearly saying—is food. Until that need is met, all your fine words will bake no bread. She will not be listening to your words—and why should she? No. Naturally she's going to be listening to the rumbling of her empty stomach.

Today there are many homeless people living on the streets. They clearly need material aid, and if it is possible for us to give them the kind of aid they need, it is important to do so and not just sit back and say, "What's the use of giving material aid? That isn't really going to help. What I should be giving is spiritual aid." Don't deceive yourself this way!

Yes, the greatest gift is the gift of the Dharma. This is true enough. But so much depends on the person, the situation, and our own mind-state. Often, to get people interested in the Dharma, which is the path that leads beyond suffering, a path of happiness, we must first assure them of the necessary material supports. Take a simple example: a person has no robe and is sitting zazen in uncomfortable clothing. Probably the best present you could give such a person would be a robe, not a book on Zen.

## THE NINTH PRECEPT

The ninth precept is "Not to indulge in anger but to exercise restraint." Often people say, "How can you resolve not to become angry? Either you become angry or you don't, and no matter how much you resolve, if you're going to get angry, you're going to get angry." This may be true to a point. If there is still a strong feeling of self and other, there can easily be the kind of resentment that we already talked about, which would give rise to anger. Truly, then, no matter how much you resolve not to become angry, you're going to become angry. You won't be able to exercise control.

What this precept really means, then, is that "I resolve to find out why I become angry." This is especially important for dealing with habitual anger. "I resolve to find out why I become angry frequently, and I resolve to remove the causes of this anger." Of course, not surprisingly, the foundation of anger is most likely going to be rooted in a strong sense of me and mine. Enlightenment, then, is the most fundamental way to truly eliminate the cause of anger.

To be angry, one needs an object. There is a dualism between one's self and another, some person, some "other" who one feels has somehow wronged one. *"You* did this to *me."* Still, until we can get to the cause, and even when you are working on the cause, and certainly everybody doing zazen is working on the cause, it takes a long, long time to really root it out. One stopgap measure that can be taken is deep breathing. When you feel anger come up, begin drawing the breath in slowly and deeply, and exhaling. This can help calm the mind and at least bring a little more openness and space to the situation.


THE TENTH PRECEPT

The tenth precept is "Not to revile the Three Treasures—the Buddha, the Dharma, and the Sangha—but to cherish and uphold them." To revile the first of the Three Treasures, the Buddha, doesn't only mean Shakyamuni, the historical Buddha or Manjusri, the Bodhisattva of wisdom, or Samantabhadra, embodiment of calm, compassionate action. It can also mean one's teacher, who stands in the place of the Buddha. And it can also mean oneself and the fundamental aspect of *all* things— trees, animals, people. So, you see, this is a profound and all-embracing precept. Not to revile the Dharma of course means the teaching—not to put down the teaching. And what is the teaching? It is expressed in Shakyamuni's own great utterance at the time of his Enlightenment: "Wonder of wonders—all beings are Buddhas!" So, to accept one's own potential for wisdom, compassion, and enlightenment—as well as that of others—is also not to put down the teaching.

It can also mean not to feel that the Dharma is only for certain kinds of people, or even that all teachings are the same. Not reviling can be subtle and complex. On the face of it, saying that all teachings and traditions are the same can seem like a fine, reasonable, and generous statement. And to claim that only one's own religion has "the truth" is not only narrow but dangerous. Inquisitions and religious wars have sprung from such delusive thoughts. One of the great virtues of Buddhism has been that it has never had a religious war (in the sense of the holy wars of Christianity or Islam). There's no such thing as a holy war or crusade in the name of Buddhism. Yet, to give the impression that only Buddhism has the truth and other religions don't is, also, untrue. But to go to the other extreme and say that all religions are one, that all are the same, or that Buddha, Jesus, Moses, Muhammad, and Socrates—all great men—were all saying the same things, is, perhaps, to overlook quite important distinctions.

A number of years ago I was in a discussion in Japan where all the major world religions were represented. I wasn't speaking on behalf of Buddhism. I was just a listener. When the Hindu speaker presented his views, he said that in the view of Hinduism, Christianity is on the level of *bhakti* (meaning the path of loving devotion to God, recommended as the most effective path in Hinduism, the path of grace), and Jesus is a *bhakta*, or whatever the noun would be. And with that, the person representing Christianity got up and a terrific battle ensued! What do you mean by putting down Christianity? The Indian had explained that *bhakti* was the first stage of the Hindu path, the devotional stage. He was aghast at the reaction that he got; he didn't mean it as a put-down, although it could certainly have sounded very much like that.

But thinking about that afterward, certainly from the Indian point of view, this was absolutely true. If you take all of the stages, from the *bhakti* all the way to the *vijnana*, the highest stage, I think it can be seen how this is the way Christianity would seem to them. And of course it's awfully hard to avoid giving the impression that this is a put-down. Certainly any fair-minded person who compared a great Indian saint such as Shankara, for example—the subtlety of his philosophy growing out of the highest stages that he had gone to—and put him side by side with Jesus, could think that Shankara had evolved further, gone through many more stages. Clearly Jesus was a highly enlightened person. Had he lived longer—he died so young—perhaps the record of his life and teaching would have revealed equal depths. The point here is simply that it can be a put-down of the Dharma when you do not give it its due worth. And its due worth means knowing what it is, knowing its real value, and perhaps, where appropriate, saying so when it truly needs to be said. What's most important is clarity and speaking from your personal experience of practice.

Now about the Sangha. Not to put down, not to revile, the Sangha in one sense means not to put down the subtle interrelations, the vast web of connections that hold us all. It can mean, then, to uphold the environment itself, the fundamental, informal Sangha of plants, animals, watersheds, and the great wide earth; to help, not harm, our living planet. Of course it also means not to put down any person in the formal, literal Sangha. But you might say, "Why should one be any more observing of precepts number six and seven toward a member of the Sangha than anybody else?" Simply because at one level the Sangha is the community of people who follow the teachings of the Buddha. Our practice together sustains each of us individually and it sustains all beings. Accepting that we're on the Path together gives energy, that is, reality, to our desire to practice the Way. Reviling a member of the Sangha is like reviling your brother or sister. The whole family suffers.

Real respect begins in the family. One of the things that impressed me very much in Japan was how an older brother or sister would be called by a younger brother or sister. The word for elder sister is *nei-san*. In families where there was real love and harmony, I noticed that the children would usually put an *o*, which is an honorific, before the word and call the elder ones *o-nei-san*. The parents would also be given honorifics; the greater the love and respect, the more honorifics were used. In families that quarreled a lot there were fewer honorifics. Honorifics were a way of showing respect for the person. So the Sangha, being our spiritual family, is a group of people toward whom we should always speak with respect. In this way we all derive strength from being together, practicing together.

Of course, all the honorifics in the world won't solve tension and real problems in a family or in a Sangha. Respect, love, patience, tolerance, and a willingness to communicate honestly (keeping in mind the fourth precept), as well as respect for differing viewpoints, are attitudes that can help create an atmosphere in which honorifics come naturally to our lips. We have to work at it together.

If we were to compare the blood family and the Sangha family, the Sangha family might in certain ways be seen as going deeper than the blood family. This has been said by the Buddha. Of course, he was speaking about monks who had left home entirely and become Homeless Ones. But it could be laypeople just as well. Karmic roots go deep in Sangha. Given this, we should try as far as it is possible, and of course it's always *possible* if we are willing, to cherish one another, to uphold each other, to support each other, to give each other warmth and love and not put each other down. We may have annoyances and differences, but when they're over, we can try to make a consistent effort to support and uphold each other with whatever love we're capable of, with whatever respect we can command.

From the realm of practice, the realm of the realization of mutual Sangha, love and compassion fan out to others, blood family and friends and so on. But as has been said all through Buddhism, the Sangha deserves our highest respect and love. Why? Not only because it is the community of people who are doing the same kind of thing, but because the Sangha is the root of the society in which it functions. It's the foundation itself. By upholding each other as a Sangha, a community of equals on the Path together, we uphold society. Sangha is one of the gateways through which compassion and understanding flow into the society and culture. In our world today, so fraught with violence and tension, what could be more precious or worthwhile?

In Chekhov's *The Cherry Orchard*, there's a famous scene in which a character comes to a friend who is drinking and who lives a wanton life, and he says to him, "My friend, how badly you live!" That could be said of so many of us. "My friend, how badly you live!" At least in the Sangha we are trying to live an open, warm, and naturally human life. Some families seem naturally to do this, many do not. In the Sangha family this is the clear and conscious intent. We hear so much in our country about "the good life." On the radio and television, in newspapers and books, we hear about the good life. Having two or three telephones in the house, two or three color TVs, two or three cars, this is the good life. Being able to go away, traveling in a thoughtless, touristy kind of a way—this, too, is the good life. But truly, I think, the "good" life is nothing other than making a day-to-day effort to uphold the precepts, in what we think, what we say, and what we do. Letting awareness and love flow out into the world, mysteriously it returns to us. What a good, what a wonderful life!

# Commentary on the First Buddhist Precept: To Cherish All Life

(CA. 1960)

*The following section has been excerpted from the* Jujukinkai, *by Yasutani Roshi, translated from the Japanese by Ken Kraft.* Jujukinkai, *a book on the workings of the precepts, is given to Zen students near the end of their training and examines the Ten Cardinal Precepts from five essential points of view. Because I feel some understanding of this is crucial to Zen practice itself, whether it be the practice of beginners or "old hands," I have decided to include this commentary here, having read it in the zendo to my students many times.*

These days many voices proclaim the sanctity of human life. Human life should of course be valued highly, but at the same time the lives of other beings should also be treasured. Human beings snatch away the lives of other creatures whenever it suits their purposes. The way of thinking that encourages this behavior arises from a specifically human brand of violence that defies the self-evident laws of the universe, opposes the growth of the myriad things in nature, and destroys feelings of compassion and reverence arising from our Buddha-nature. The first precept of Buddhism advises us to cherish all life. The following five perspectives on this precept illuminate the ways in which it is understood in depth and subtlety through Buddhist practice.

## 1. The Standpoint of the Theravada

Regardless of the spirit or the reasons, taking the life of anything is considered in Theravada Buddhism to be a violation of the first precept. The precept of refraining from taking life means one must absolutely avoid killing the tiniest insect, even if it be harmful to people. All Buddhists, whether monks or laypeople, should uphold this precept. This precept arises from the compassionate and reverent mind of Buddha-nature, as does each of the Ten Cardinal Precepts. Stated another way, this precept is grounded in the principle of mutual attraction and rightness innate in all nature.

It is essential that laypeople and monks together conscientiously uphold this precept. Is it really possible for human beings to live without literally killing anything? Here I am setting forth the ultimate implications of the Dharma and not considering human exigencies. One must have faith that from the standpoint of the Dharma this is how one should act, then exert oneself to observe this precept to the best of one's ability.

## 2. The Standpoint of the Mahayana

According to the Mahayana tradition, the spirit of the first precept is to refrain from killing the mind of compassion and reverence—in other words, not to oppose the law of mutual attraction and rightness.

## 3. The Standpoint of the Buddha-Nature

Since the Buddha-nature is equated with the whole of the precepts, those who have not seen into Buddha-nature will be unable to fathom these Buddha-nature precepts. That is to say, only with full awakening does one perceive for the first time how the Buddha-nature precepts are upheld. Buddha-nature never dies, and the realm of Buddha-nature is completely without dualism. Consequently, killing cannot be opposed to not killing—there is no killing and no being killed. If one retains even the slightest notion of killing or not killing, one instantly violates the Buddha-nature precepts.

92

## 4. Bodhidharma's One-Mind

Self-nature is inconceivably wondrous.
In the everlasting Dharma,
Not giving rise to the notion of extinction
Is called the precept of refraining from taking life.

Each of the Ten Cardinal Precepts is preceded by the character *fu*, meaning "not," such as "not to kill." When we speak of the Patriarchs' observance of the precepts, this idea of negation is inappropriate, for they have achieved the degree of liberation in which body and mind are entirely dropped (and all dualisms transcended). It is in this spirit that one must approach Bodhidharma's One-Mind perspective.

## 5. Dogen's Teaching (Received from His Master)

"In refraining from taking life you allow the Buddha seed to grow and thereby inherit the Buddha's wisdom. Do not destroy life."

At this point we will examine the spirit of the first precept according to Dogen and in light of the Theravada, Mahayana, and Buddha-nature standpoints.

It is helpful to refer back to the sequence of the characters in the original Chinese (of Dogen's master). The first sentence literally reads, "Life is not-killing," and the last is "Do not kill life." "Do not kill life" illuminates the Theravada and Mahayana teachings, while "Life is not-killing" illuminates the Buddha-nature teaching.

How do we reconcile these different perspectives on refraining from taking life? Be careful here. If you assume that the Zen sect emphasizes the Buddha-nature over the Theravada and Mahayana, you are distorting things, for in reality the Buddha-nature precepts are the highest integration of the Theravada and Mahayana perspectives. And since the Buddha-nature precepts are none other than the active practice of Buddha-nature, you must accept, believe, revere, and practice them.

# Responsibility and Social Action

## (1974)

In Zen Buddhism, responsibility means responsiveness. Responsiveness is responsibility. To respond fully to every situation that comes your way, from a call for help of one kind or another to just talking with someone, and to give all of yourself to it—this is responsibility.

A developed, compassionate, loving person influences people unself-consciously, motivates them, and inspires them to act in similar ways. The whole community benefits. Even just doing zazen in the zendo has a powerful, invisible effect. People find it hard to believe that there can be social usefulness in just sitting and meditating. And yet the truth is that if you purify your mind, if even to a small degree, and transcend ego-attachment, you are at the same time purifying other minds. The effect on other people—on your family, on your circle of acquaintances—grows and grows.

Everything depends on your mind-state, and on what your conscience dictates. In Buddhism, compassion and wisdom are the qualities that develop out of your practice. Gradually you can act without being attached to the result and simply do what you feel needs to be done. Some people feel called upon to deal with social injustice and other inequities of life in an active way. The important thing is how you do that. If you're striving for particular results, then you're attached. If you're striving to be unattached, then you're committing another kind of subtle fault. When we get deeper in our practice, we give our all and at the same time simply spontaneously respond to the needs of the situation. Then we do what our karma, which means our whole pattern of life, dictates. And that's always changing. We must remember that karma is not a fixed thing. The relation between cause and effect is dynamic and it's constantly changing. The more we practice, the more we become aware of these things. The more we become aware of these things, the more our past karma changes. Gradually our future karma will be created from a different base—a base of Awareness.

There's really no distinction between "being" and "doing." Being is an aspect of doing, doing is an aspect of being. Without an awareness of being, there can be no truly meaningful doing. Any doing that lacks awareness of the being aspect becomes a frenzied thing, a do-gooding, that will often do more harm than good. Eric Fromm, in his book *The Art of Loving*, says, as I remember it, that in our Western culture, a person, to be active, must always be doing something. It is the active person who is always right. And to be active means to be working, to be studying or doing sports, and so on. He goes on to say that what's not taken into account is the motivation behind the acting. For example, somebody could be doing something out of tremendous ambition to make money, or for fame or position, or one could be driven for certain psychological reasons. There could be a compulsive driving of yourself, in which case the activity becomes a passivity because one is not the actor but rather, one is being acted upon, one is being driven. And so he says that actually the highest activity is zazen. (He used the word *meditation*.) Because, when it is done under the proper circumstances, the proper mind-state, it is a free act and therefore the highest kind of activity. And this is certainly true enough.

Sitting in this way, one develops a sensitivity after a while and one feels the pain of the world very strongly. One feels part of everything else. You find in Zen two feelings about this, side by side. There have been Zen masters who have encouraged social action, and in Buddhism as a whole there has been at certain times great social concern. We find it with the Buddha himself. But probably the greater weight of the evidence leans toward developing one's own self first, that is, before trying to do good works on a grand scale.

Until one develops compassion and sympathy, one is not

rightly attuned. Of course this doesn't come entirely through enlightenment. But certainly with enlightenment and the dropping away of habitual self-concern, feelings are liberated that allow us to become more deeply sensitive to every kind of situation. Some people, however, try to help others on a large scale before they're ready. Remember Milarepa, the great Tibetan Buddhist teacher, who says, "There will never be any end of people to help. Till the end of the world there will always be people to help." But to help people without hurting them at the same time, or hurting yourself, means that we must first work on ourselves. But certainly this does not exclude helping in emergencies or times of crisis or simply whenever you're asked. Nor does it exclude doing whatever might be useful or beneficial in general. If you can see it, then you can do it. This is a natural part of practice, but we must not become attached to it. In *The Three Pillars of Zen*, Yasutani Roshi talks about the difference between a Bodhisattva and a Buddha: a Bodhisattva, he says, is still attached to the idea of saving or helping people. *Attached* to the idea. Whereas a Buddha spontaneously does these things wherever he or she can. A Buddha is one who is constantly helping but has no self-conscious thought, no special intention, about it.

A middle way alternates between the life of inward meditation and the life of action-in-the-world, the twin poles of nirvana and samsara that are ultimately one. What we take in through meditation we must give out in love and action on behalf of our fellows on this earth—humans and nonhumans.

Social action is itself a kind of meditation and can be a great ripener of compassion and equanimity. It is also an act of giving what we can. This corresponds to the eighth precept: not to withhold material or spiritual aid.

The Buddha said, "Whoever nurses the sick serves me."

The object of gaining an insight into the inner truth of things is really to qualify oneself for greater compassionate action in the world.

A Zen master said, "Zen [training] is a preparation for life in the world, not the goal of life in the world." Buddhists do not take a fatalistic view of karma. Rather, Buddhist teaching has always urged practitioners to make every effort to remove disease and war.

In short, the relation to cause and effect is not fixed but constantly changing. Men and women make their own history, but they make it under specific karmic conditions inherited from previous generations, collectively as well as individually.

More than any previous society in human history, capitalist industrial society has created conditions of extreme impermanence, terrifying insubstantiality, and a struggling dissatisfaction and frustration. It would be difficult to imagine any social order for which Buddhism was more relevant and needed. Surely Buddhists should be sharp and active critics of all social conditions and values that move deluded and struggling humanity further to increase pain and suffering, greed and violence. At the same time they must remain compassionately responsive toward the individual men and women who drive others and are themselves driven by their own undisciplined impulses. Is not a Buddhism that lectures individuals on their delusions, but that has nothing to say about the deluding political and economic conditions that reinforce these, merely hypocrisy? Here again our way is the middle way, concerned with individual change but also with the context of social change, yet ultimately with something greater than either or both.

The Buddhist Way, with its compassion, equanimity, tolerance, concern for self-reliance and responsibility—above all, its Cosmic view—can be a model for society.

What are needed are political and economic relations and a technology that will: (a) help people to overcome egocenteredness through cooperation with others instead of subordination, exploitation, and competition; (b) offer to each a freedom that is conditional only upon the freedom of others, so that individuals may develop a self-reliant social responsibility rather than being the conditioned pawns of institutions and ideologies; (c) concern themselves primarily with the material and social conditions of personal growth, and only secondarily with material production.

"He alone can do good who knows what things are like and what their situation is," quotes E. F. Schumaker in his classic, *Small Is Beautiful*.

To a world knotted in hatreds and aggression, Buddhism offers a unique combination of an unshakable equanimity and a deeply compassionate practical concern.

> *He who clings to the Void*
> *And neglects compassion*
> *Does not reach the highest stage.*
> *But he who practices only compassion*
> *Does not gain release from the toils of existence.*
> *He, however, who is strong in the practice of both*
> *Remains neither in samsara nor in nirvana.*

A major task for Buddhism in the West, it seems to me, is to ally itself with religious and other concerned organizations to forestall the potential catastrophes facing the human race: nuclear holocaust, irreversible pollution of the world's environment, and the continuing large-scale destruction of nonrenewable resources. We also need to lend our physical and moral support to those who are fighting hunger, poverty, and oppression everywhere in the world.

To remain silent or indifferent in the face of the challenges in today's imperiled world is, in the end, to give aid and comfort to forces of reaction and bigotry, and to weaken the effectiveness of those seeking to combat such negative forces. Let your practice go with you out of the zendo and see what happens. Let the world's pain come into your zazen and see the great exertion that will emerge.

# Pain, Suffering,
## and Resistance to Practice
### (1971)

*This talk was given at a time when Zen practice in the United States was still centered very much in life at a Zen center. Things have changed and Zen today is very much in people's actual daily lives. Still, so many fundamental points are examined here that I feel its usefulness has not been outlived.*

Sometimes, after practicing Zen for a short time, people feel that they are not getting out of Zen what they expected. While they admit that their personal problems have been alleviated to some extent, they still feel restless, impatient, irritable. And often this state of mind is accompanied by the statement that "somehow I feel I'm not helping people by staying here at the Center; I feel that there's something very selfish about my being here. I want to go out and help people in the world, where there's pain and suffering. And I want to try as far as I'm able to help relieve it." This, in substance, is the way this statement comes to me. This is not an uncommon reaction, and I want to talk about it, and also about the whole question of pain and suffering . . . why people suffer.

Often, what brings people to the Center is a feeling of constriction, of frustration, of a lack of control and the need for some kind of structured discipline. Time and time again people will write to me, or write on their membership application, "I want to be a member of the Center because I need the discipline of the Center. I need to be working with people who are more advanced in practice than I am, who will help me to achieve what I'm trying to achieve, to get rid of my personal problems, the blind drives and frustrations and inner conflicts."

And then they come here and work for a short time and there's a noticeable improvement, an improvement that they themselves feel. They're more stable, less distracted, and not squandering their energies as they used to. Nevertheless, they reach a point where they begin to feel they're not helping to relieve suffering. Certainly any impulse toward compassion is good. However, in almost all cases, this kind of statement, when made at an early stage of practice, is really a rationalization, a kind of self-justification or excuse to try to get back to old patterns of thinking, feeling, and acting, the old pain-producing patterns that scatter one's energies and ultimately lead to an aimless, futile, and painful kind of life.

It is fundamental that we can't help anybody until we first help ourselves. Until *we* have enough, we have nothing to spare. This is so fundamental that it's hard to see how anyone could say that they want to go out and help people when it is obvious even to themselves that they still have so little control over themselves, so little stability, so little joy and freedom in their own lives. And of course, it's never an easy thing to help other people without at the same time doing harm.

Recently one of our young members told me that she had taken a job as a nurse's aide because she thought it would help her practice in that it would bring her into contact with people who were suffering. And she felt that it would help her practice by bringing out her compassion. But having taken the job, she told me it turned out to be just the opposite. It was most distracting to have to deal with sick people. She's discovered that her ideal "sick people" can, in actuality, be annoying, irritable, demanding. Sickness does not necessarily make people spiritually inclined. Many people, of course, can and do discover a deep spirituality in times of confinement and illness. But many can be self-centered and understandably want, more than anything else, simply to relieve their pain and boredom. During their healthy life, perhaps they never "got enough," never healed enough, or developed enough in and for themselves. And now in their sickness it all comes out with an edge of desperation as well. All of which makes it extremely difficult to try to help them effectively.

Of course professional nurses are concerned with relieving pain, and if there is a natural sympathy about them, they can help those who are suffering with an illness. But even when helped in this way, people will, of course, become sick again. If not from the same illness, then from another. If not from a specific illness, then, at last, from old age. It's just like feeding people, the whole economic problem. As the Marxists say, or as many people say in the name of Marxism, this is the fundamental problem of life, the economic one. But it isn't, really. Because when you've supplied people with food, with the necessities of life, you still haven't resolved the basic anxiety. The Scandinavian countries are said to have one of the most advanced systems of social security, yet they have one of the highest suicide rates, too. And it's a fact that when there is no struggle in life, when things are provided, then a deep boredom can set in, a real inner dissatisfaction. There's nothing to strive for anymore and this provides its own pain.

If we analyze a little more the condition of people who express this dissatisfaction after a comparatively short time of practicing Zen, we see that the pattern is common and that almost everybody goes through it. When one is exposed or subjected to the discipline of a spiritual training center—and it really is a minimal discipline—one can, after a time, begin to resent it. One is used to scattering one's energies and being distracted. Previously one was much more subject to whim and caprice, like a weather vane blown in different directions by every kind of emotional wind. Yet strangely, often as soon as one finds oneself in a position of relative freedom from this kind of thing, one begins to resent it. Old habits want to reassert themselves. We start to feel the ancient pull of our old haunts. Not only do we begin to resent the place, but we resent the people, too, who we feel are responsible for our being here and for putting us in this situation. This could happen at sesshin (intensive meditation retreat) for someone who is normally "out in

the world" or to someone who is living at the Center in a training program or even on staff. And this is a vital point reached in
practice; this is a crossroads. If one gives way to this feeling of
wanting to escape and does, well, it means that one has to start
all over again some other time and some other place. The basic
problem has not been resolved.

On the other hand, if despite our wanting to run away we
continue to struggle with the discipline and with our practice,
then suddenly we find there's a turning around. The old craving
for this and that, the desire to run away, to do this and that, suddenly becomes quiet. A real stability and a great deal of energy
come up. In the deepest sense, there's peace, a deep tranquility
and a clarity, and this gets deeper and deeper. Here again, it's a
question of time, of one's karma, of how strong these blind
drives are in one. But people who are practicing—and again, it
need not necessarily be at a center, it can be people who go off by
themselves in the woods or in a desert or even in a hut or a
house to do zazen—are subject to one degree or another to this
same phenomenon. Since, however, in such situations there
isn't the discipline of a regular program, and the support of others on the Path, few people can carry it on. Usually it's people
who are experienced in their practice who are able to get a great
deal out of that kind of a setup or regimen. The reason that we
have a center, the reason that there are centers with a structure,
a discipline, is precisely this.

There are of course centers and ashrams in this country that
operate on an entirely different principle. They're really communities of people who want to follow a certain lifestyle. What
we're talking about right now, though, is religious discipline and
not simply people who come together to "do their thing" in
what they find to be a congenial atmosphere. I'll talk about that
a little later. So it's important to distinguish between a center such
as ours, where there is religious discipline and a teacher, and many
other types of centers where the discipline, if there is any, is usually much more unstructured. There can be rapid turnover at such
places, or if there isn't such swift turnover, then people can easily settle into a comfortable kind of rut, and one's basic problems,

that is spiritual or religious problems, the basic anxieties of wanting to know who and what we are and what the meaning of our life is, become papered over with a comfortable style of living. And it could be just as comfortable if you're eating organic foods or making crafts. This can become another kind of "good life," as it has indeed become for many people in this country today. Different, of course, from the country-club version of the good life, but in many ways, just as stylized, just as—given your personality and interests—comfortable. Many things, of course, many positive things, can be said for it, but at the same time we must recognize that it is different from places where there is genuine religious discipline with an emphasis on Realization.

Now, on the subject of suffering: perhaps it would be well to distinguish between pain and suffering. Pain, as the Buddha said, is a condition of life, whereas suffering is the discontent and disappointment about our experiences, especially about those experiences that we consider to be negative. Buddhism, I think it is fair to say, deals with this problem of suffering more than the other great religions, although they all respond to it, perhaps not as centrally as Buddhism.

In Buddhism, the Four Noble Truths make clear the fact of suffering, the origin of suffering, the extinction of suffering, and the path that leads to the extinction of suffering. The Buddha laid out this formula, and the path to the extinction of suffering is of course the Eightfold Noble Path of Right Understanding, Right Mindfulness, Right Speech, Right Action, Right Livelihood, Right Effort, Right Attentiveness, Right Concentration. I don't want to go into a full discussion of these now, but just to say that when we have Right Concentration, all the others come along with it or emerge from it.

The point is that pain and suffering, the manner in which people interpret pain, the manner in which people stand outside pain that leads to suffering, is something that has occupied the minds of all thoughtful, sensitive people. We see so much pain in the world, how can we *not* question it? In our own time, the sufferings brought about by the Second World War, and the period preceding the Second World War, and then Korea and now Vietnam, are, in total, unimaginable, truly enormous. The enormity, the evil of this pain, especially that of World War II, was probably greater than at any other time in the history of mankind. Millions and millions of people were put to death, were forced to endure all kinds of sufferings, the kind of suffering that the mind cannot begin to cope with, terrible suffering and pain. As former chief court reporter at the Nuremberg trials, and then, later, at the Tokyo trials, I heard testimony that was almost unbelievable. Hearing of such horrors, who would not ask, "Why is there so much pain and suffering in the world? Why is man so inhuman to man?"

And if one is a Buddhist, and we read that the Buddha says that inherently we are loving and compassionate, inherently things are whole, things are complete, things are harmonious, there is a fundamental unity, a fundamental love, how can one reconcile these two views? And then since the Second World War, our own country, which took such a leading part in the Nuremberg and Tokyo trials, is itself now imposing tremendous pain and suffering on people, both here and abroad. How can people who profess to be, and actually were, so concerned about pain and suffering in the world now turn around and do such terrible things? Not quite the same thing, of course, but certainly we have inflicted a great deal of pain and suffering with what is happening in Vietnam. How does one explain this? How can one believe that human beings are inherently loving, wise, and compassionate when those who profess to be morally superior simply turn around and when their time comes act in an utterly inhumane way?

To grapple with this is the beginning of a spiritual or religious life. We have the Buddha's explanation of pain and suffering, but we must remember that this came out of his own deep experience and was not something he theorized about. As he says himself, his understanding arose out of his great enlightenment. In Christianity, this problem comes up as "Why would a just and loving God create so much pain in the world? Why would a just and loving God send down his only son, who was innocent and pure, and cause him to suffer so much pain?"

People find it hard to believe the Buddha's statements that suffering comes from three conditions—namely, greed, anger, and delusive thinking. Can they really encompass the hatred and greed and wrong thinking that have brought so much overwhelming suffering in the world, especially the enormity of pain of our recent past and present? And then, too, people will say, well, all right, we can see how it is quite possible that greed, anger, and delusive thinking truly cause man's inhumanity to man, but what about nature's inhumanity, or nature's pain-producing earthquakes, epidemics, and fires that often have no seemingly human origin. Why do they have to happen?

I think that people who truly accept the law of karma aren't compelled to ask these questions. This word *acceptance* is really a difficult word because it has the implication of passively taking, accepting something, being willing to go along in a kind of resigned way. But this isn't what acceptance necessarily means, at least not as it's being used here. Here it means a concurrence in, a seeing clearly through, through, that is, to the very bottom, a means to see the law of causation as it operates, and the primary and secondary causes that arise, and the effects that they create. In other words, seeing through the whole concatenation of causes and effects and our own participation in it all, seeing ultimately how all our thoughts and actions produce an effect, which we cannot disaffirm. Seeing all of this, one is not impelled to ask "why" questions.

It may seem strange to some people that one could accept even the worst kind of suffering, such as war, in this spirit. But again it does not mean that one condones such things at all but rather that one is not completely thrown by them. A person who is completely thrown becomes neurotic, and it is quite possible for people who have no kind of religious or spiritual base not only to become neurotic, but to become quite a bit more profoundly disturbed trying to understand human suffering on any level.

Those who do see into it can help, in their own way, and we must never forget that there are many ways. And we must not, out of a kind of religious exclusivity, feel that political, economic, or social solutions are useless. They do help. But anyone who understands the fundamental, root cause of suffering knows these can at best be peripheral remedies, albeit necessary ones. Anything, any political action that can stop a war, is a tremendous thing, obviously. And we must support all such efforts. But the problem of suffering still remains in the world and will remain in the world so long as greed, anger, and delusion on both the individual and collective level remain. For they will build up until, like a huge swollen river that breaks through everything that seeks to hold it, they rush out again to engulf all in their path. This is what happens when the individual self-clinging ego, the rigidified outcome of long-held habits of greed, anger, and wrong thinking, builds up and then crashes out, destroying everything in its wake.

The suffering of the world always begins on the individual level. This is why the Buddha said, "Verily I say unto you, in this fathom-high body is the world, the waxing thereof and its waning away." In the long run if you want to really have an effect on the world's anguish, learn to work ceaselessly on yourself even as you continue to strive, on a daily basis, to do the best you can for others.

# The Artful Use of Pain in Zen

## (1992)

I want to make clear at the beginning that, for reasons which will become obvious as this essay progresses, my experiences with pain in a Zen monastery in Japan were unique. Of course, in one sense everybody's case is unique, given that people have different karmas, and my karma in this respect was certainly different from that of other people. The fact is that a number of unusual circumstances came together, with the result that I was propelled to go to Japan and enter a Zen monastery. I should also point out that I never was, nor am I now, an "Iron John," able to endure any kind of pain. I persisted because I was sick of the "joyless pursuit of pleasure" that characterized my life at the time, and I desperately wanted out. This painful mind-state was the engine that drove my efforts.

Just consider: If you wanted to become a champion swimmer or a concert pianist, you would have to train, and train hard, wouldn't you? You would have to practice self-denial and endure pain and discomfort. If you didn't practice for long, tedious hours, how far would you get toward achieving your goal? The fact is, no real training under a competent teacher in any discipline is without pain and sacrifice if you work at it seriously. Zen is no different.

To awaken to the true nature of existence in this lifetime; to find out why we are born and why we must die; to bring light into a mind that has been cloaked in darkness for who knows how many lifetimes; to cleanse the mind of its accumulated waste of ignorance and deluded thinking, gathered since time immemorial; and to redirect and transform a life so that one knows and lives from the truth of human existence—compared

107

to such an immense undertaking, why, even Hercules's feat of cleaning out the Augean stables in one day by diverting two rivers—stables that held three thousand oxen and had remained uncleaned for thirty years—pales by comparison.

I was forty-two years old when I returned to Japan in 1953 for monastic training in Zen. This was my second trip to Japan (my first having been in 1946, as a member of the International Military Tribunal that tried General Tojo and other Japanese charged with conspiracy to start a war). Before going to Japan for the first time, I knew nothing about Zen or Buddhism. My intellectual understanding of Buddhism actually began when I met Dr. D. T. Suzuki in Japan while I was a member of the Tribunal. From time to time he would informally lecture American Occupation personnel about Buddhist philosophy and Zen when they came to visit him in his cottage located in the compound of Engaku-ji (Engaku Monastery). I soon became a frequent visitor. Although much of what Suzuki said was above my head, the sparks of Zen he occasionally emitted lit up long-dormant spiritual longings in me. But since I had never done any kind of zazen—and zazen was hardly Dr. Suzuki's forte (he never spoke about it)—the opportunity to learn about zazen from either him or the Engaku-ji monks was lost to me.

My first contact with practical Zen came when an American professor friend who was teaching in Japan on an exchange professorship and I contacted Nakagawa Soen Roshi, the abbot of Ryutaku-ji (Monastery of the Swamp Dragon). We had written him asking him for his permission to visit his monastery with a view possibly to training there for a while. He wrote us that before he could permit us to train in his monastery he would have to see and speak with us. He therefore advised us to come for three days only. At the end of that time, during which my friend and I talked with the roshi and struggled with cross-legged postures by ourselves in the main hall, he said that I could stay for a month, but advised my friend to continue his teaching and come to the monastery only on weekends.

My training at Ryutaku-ji during that month was hardly the traditional kind. The roshi instructed me to continue to sit in the main hall (not the zendo) and to sit any way I wished and as long as I wished before getting up for kinhin (formal walking meditation). Neither he nor the monks during that first month showed me how to sit in zazen or how to do kinhin, nor did they formally teach me anything else about Zen. Each day I swept a portion of the monastery grounds; other than that, I had no regular duties. The one discipline imposed was that I eat at the times regularly prescribed for the monks, but I did not eat with them. Apart from that, I rose and went to bed when I wished. The roshi also encouraged me to exclude every kind of reading except books that dealt with the lives of the masters. "Devote your extra time," he told me, "to zazen or else to walking about the extensive grounds of the monastery while trying to absorb the beauty and atmosphere of the place." Though this training, if it could be called that, may have provoked dismay, if not chagrin, in another serious Zen aspirant who had come from abroad at great sacrifice, oddly it never worried me at all. I had good reasons not to complain. During that month the roshi, who had good friends in all walks of life—innkeepers, artists, actors, musicians, poets, and sundry "far-out" characters— introduced me to many of them, either when they came to the monastery to see him or, more interestingly, when he took me with him to visit them in their studios or places of business. Since he was only a few years older than I and we had many artistic interests in common, we often hiked around the countryside like buddies. In fact, he often referred to us as "two Zen hoboes."

Besides taking me to visit his fascinating friends, the roshi also asked me from time to time to accompany him to art exhibitions of paintings by famous Zen artists, such as those of the Japanese Zen masters Sesshu and Hakuin and the Chinese Zen monk Mu Ch'l (Mokkei in Japanese). These paintings were all Japanese national or cultural treasures. Not only this, but he occasionally took me to a musical concert, as we were both fond of classical music, especially that of Beethoven. Speaking of music, one of my biggest surprises at Ryutaku-ji came at the beginning of my stay there when I learned that the roshi was fond of the Beethoven last-period quartets, music that musicologists have described as the most subtle and refined of all Beethoven's works. One day the roshi asked me if I would like to meet his mother, who had a cottage on the grounds, and hear some classical music there. "Sure, I'd love to," I told him. After introducing me to his mother, he began playing a recording of Beethoven's Opus 132, from the last-period quartets.

Although, as I've said, the month's stay could hardly be called training in the traditional sense, I later came to see its great value. It provided me with an unparalleled introduction to the style and atmosphere of Japanese Zen. I saw Zen functioning in the lives of sensitive, cultivated Japanese as well as in the lives of ordinary Japanese. Equally important, I was forging a karma with an uncommonly generous and accomplished Zen master. As a matter of fact, my serious Zen training might never have gotten off the ground had it not been for my stay at Ryutaku-ji, strange as that may seem.

Was there a plan, a method, to the roshi's seeming "Zen madness"? I'm sure that the roshi, with his perceptive eye, sensed that I had been a self-centered, pleasure-seeking person with little self-denial. He must also have sensed that beneath my casual manner a genuine desire for Awakening existed. Had I at the beginning of my stay in Japan been thrust into the lion's den of tough Zen training, I'm not sure I would have survived; I might easily have packed my bags and fled back to the States. In addition, having developed a warm relationship with Nakagawa Roshi, having been the beneficiary of many of his kindnesses, I now knew enough about Japanese culture to know that if I summarily quit my next abode, the monastery of Hosshin-ji, he would be placed in a most embarrassing position. After all, he himself had personally assured Harada Roshi, my next teacher, that I was ready for the hard training I would receive at Hosshin-ji and would not quit it prematurely.

At the end of the month, my stay at the monastery was upped to three more months. Now my training took on more traditional aspects. I was permitted to sit in the zendo with the monks and was told I had to follow their schedule. Still, the roshi said nothing about my participating in sesshin, and I didn't ask to do so.

My hard training didn't really begin until I came to Hosshin-ji to work with the then eighty-four-year-old Harada Roshi. How I got to Hosshin-ji is an interesting story in itself. It shows how roshis work together their wonders to perform. One day Nakagawa Roshi said to me, "The *rohatsu* sesshin [which celebrates the enlightenment of the Buddha] will soon take place at Hosshin-ji. It is the hardest sesshin of the year." And then he added, as though to himself, "I wonder if you are ready for it." He looked intently at me, smiled, and said, "If Harada Roshi is willing to accept you for that sesshin, Kapleau-san, would you like to go?"

"Sure, why not?" I answered in an offhand manner, not having the slightest idea of the pain and struggle the sesshin would entail.

"Before I consult with Harada Roshi about your case, I want to think further about this whole matter." Two days later Nakagawa Roshi announced with an enigmatic smile, "I've made up my mind. Come with me," and he led me to his inner sanctum, where he proceeded to the altar and took from it a letter. "Do you see this letter? It contains wonderful news, for the person who wrote it, for you, and for me."

"What's the letter all about?" I asked impatiently.

In his near perfect English, the roshi slowly explained, "The man who wrote it is a practitioner of Zen, an old friend of mine, and he writes about a deep enlightenment he has just experienced. His letter made me decide to take you to Hosshin-ji for the *rohatsu* sesshin—provided, of course, that after you meet Harada Roshi and he has had a chance to talk with you, he accepts you for the sesshin and for further training. I should also tell you that Harada Roshi is a much better teacher for you than I am. That's why I want you to begin serious training under him." A wave of respect and love for Nakagawa Roshi engulfed me, for this man who for all his accomplishments—he was a writer of fine haiku poetry, a skillful amateur actor, and of course a respected Zen master—was at heart a man of great humility.

111

A week later the roshi told me that Harada Roshi and his attendant-secretary were staying at an inn in a town not distant from Ryutaku-ji, and that we had an appointment to see him that afternoon. When we arrived at the inn, we were led into a room where Harada Roshi and his attendant-secretary, both in long johns, were doing a variation of hatha yoga, physical exercises for stretching and harmonizing the body-mind. There was the famous roshi sitting on the tatami mat with his legs extended out at right angles to his body and his chin touching the mat in front of him! "Wow!" I exclaimed to myself. "Eighty-four years old and still flexible enough to get into such a posture! Here I am only forty-two, yet I can't begin to extend my legs that way!

When Harada Roshi and his attendant had finished their exercises, Nakagawa Roshi introduced me to them. Harada Roshi then did an unusual thing: he came toward me and extended his hand in a handshake, a most unusual gesture for a Japanese of his generation. And accompanying his hand was a large smile.

The long and short of our meeting was that he accepted me to the *rohatsu* sesshin. It turned out to be the most painful ordeal I had ever experienced in my life, and at the same time the most rewarding. Having never crossed my legs or even sat in a chair in meditation before I came to Ryutaku-ji, nevertheless during the sesshin I had to follow the rigid schedule of getting up at 3:30 in the morning and doing whatever zazen I could manage until 9:30 P.M., and then, under the constant prodding of the monitors, continue far into the night.

The pain was excruciating. I started with the so-called Burmese posture (legs uncrossed with knees resting on the mat), but because of the pain switched to the Japanese kneeling posture (*seiza*, kneeling with feet under the buttocks), encased in a multitude of cushions of every type to lessen the pain. But the pain hardly diminished. During that first terrible day I flipped and flopped from one position to another ceaselessly as I battled the fierce pain, trying in every way I could think of to get on top of it, without much success. Harada Roshi had

112

Another revealing event occurred during this crucial sesshin. On the fifth day, I think it was, Nakagawa Roshi, during a break, took me and my American professor friend (who had come into the sesshin just as it was beginning) into one of the side rooms. In a hoarse voice he whispered, "Two of the monks at the sesshin have just had kensho. If you"—looking at me intently—"work harder, you can surely come to Awakening."

"What are their names?" my friend suddenly asked the roshi. With that the roshi swung at him; my friend ducked just in time. The roshi walked out without a further word.

The sesshin provided other surprises. I remember two participants wearing only loincloths, diving into the ice-cold pond on the monastery grounds, evidently in an effort to dispel a persistent makyo. A woman, also at her first sesshin, climbed into the arms of a tall, metal, seated Buddha and did zazen there for most of the night. For me, the most painful surprise came on the sixth day of the sesshin. I was doing zazen in the bathhouse late at night in my rickety chair when suddenly I found myself being whacked on the shoulder with the *kyosaku* stick—the "encouragement stick," which assists one in concentrating the mind—wielded by Tangen-san, one of the four monitors. He had silently crept up behind me and was doing the hitting. This was a compassionate urging, for the stick arouses energy through stimulating acupuncture points in the shoulder-blade area. He continued for what must have been a couple of hours, without letup, surrendering his own sleep to do so. When he finally did stop, I tried to stand up, but the pain in the back of my knees where the corners of the chair had wedged into them was so intense that I collapsed. When I came to, Tangen-san was standing over me with a bowl of raw eggs. "Eat them," he commanded. "You feel better." Greedily I swallowed all the contents of the bowl. When I had finished, he said, "You have one hour to rest before morning sitting begins. Come to zendo on time, Kapleau-san."

During the bull session after the sesshin I said to Tangen-san, referring to the whacking in the bathhouse, "You were taking a great chance. Suppose I had died from a heart attack as a result

of that beating. Can't you see the newspapers in Japan and the U.S. reporting: 'Middle-aged American dies from severe beating in Zen monastery.' Zen in Japan and America would have suffered a great setback."

All Tangen-san said was, "You stronger than you think, Kapleau-san."

What motivated me to subject myself to such harsh training and, more importantly, persist in it for the three years I trained at Hosshin-ji? That was a question I asked myself many times. No one was forcing me to stay; I could have left at any time. Why didn't I? The answer, I think, is simple: I stayed because I needed the treatment given me. At a deep level of my being I knew that, given my karma—and, as you have heard, everyone's is unique to himself or herself—only through this kind of tough training could I hope to begin to dissolve the oversize lump of ego I called myself. So I take no credit for what I did. As I said earlier, I never was, nor am I now, an Iron John. The fact is, I was "on a road I knew not of, going to a place I knew not where," driven by a desperate need to liberate myself from the binding chains encasing me, the result of my having lived for many years an ignorant and irresponsible life.

It might be helpful to point out some of the obstacles that slowed my progress. One of the worst was my impatience to get kensho as fast as I could and then to return as fast as I could to the United States. Keen observer that he was, Harada Roshi, sensing this mind-state, would bait me with these words: "Kapleau-san, if you get kensho this sesshin, I personally will pay for your plane ticket back to America. And you don't even have to finish the sesshin. You may leave the next day." Impatience, of course, is a common American failing. For us, everything typically has to be instant: instant Zen, instant enlightenment, instant progress. The "quick fix" is the hallmark of our culture. If results don't come fast enough, we soon tire of the work and look for something else, or get discouraged and give up. This impatience, I believe, is a manifestation of the inner restlessness that keeps us constantly on the move. We are alienated from ourselves inwardly and from nature outwardly.

As Americans we face another obstacle: our insistence on comfort. That's why sitting quietly, in silence, while trying to concentrate the mind is psychologically and physically painful for us, in the beginning at least. The comment by a onetime president of Stanford University, speaking at commencement, that "our aim at Stanford is not to make you students comfortable but to make you strong" is foreign to most of us. Comfort! How we insist upon it in all circumstances and how we refuse to put up with its absence, even for short periods! But physical discomfort is only really distressing, as someone has said, when the mood is wrong. When faith in what we are trying to accomplish is strong, faith in ourselves, the teaching, or the teacher—the three really being inseparable—then all discomfort becomes unimportant.

What did I learn from the pain I endured in Japan? That, when one is in the wholehearted pursuit of an ideal, pain is not resented; it can provide an unparalleled opportunity for growth and maturity. Pain is the fire in which the dross of our personality—the loathings, desires, doubting, and fears—is burned away and the mind tempered and strengthened, not unlike brittle metal annealed into steel. Moreover, when pain, which the Buddha proclaimed as a condition of existence, is courageously accepted, it is a means to liberation in that it releases our natural sympathies and compassion and thus enables us to experience pleasure and joy with new depth and purity.

Let me conclude by citing an incident that occurred while I was living in Japan that illustrates the truth of the dictum "No pain, no gain." A troubled middle-aged, well-to-do American had been the patient of several psychiatrists and was looking for help from Zen Buddhism. He had come to Japan to learn about Zen firsthand. Japanese and American friends of his in Japan brought him to the monastery in Kyoto of a retired Zen master. I was also invited to the meeting. As we sat on cushions on the floor of the roshi's living room, the roshi asked this man a number of questions about himself and why he wanted to come to Japan to learn about Zen. After this man gave various reasons, the roshi unexpectedly asked, "Can you do zazen with your legs in any of the lotus postures?"

The man replied, "I don't know. I've never tried meditating before."

"Try to sit in the half-lotus position." The roshi explained how to do it.

"I don't know if I can, but I'll try." The American visitor easily edged his left foot over his right thigh.

"That's good. Do you feel any discomfort or pain?"

"No, none at all."

"Now try to put each foot over the thigh of the other, in the full lotus."

"I've never done it, but I'll try." Without any difficulty the American got into the full lotus.

"You have no pain or discomfort?"

"No, not so far."

This middle-aged man's performance blew my mind. I had been in Japan for more than a year, training in a Zen monastery with a famous roshi, yet I was still struggling to get into the half lotus. Yet this man who had never done any zazen, was not athletic (in fact was somewhat corpulent), could easily do what was so hard and painful for me. Why? Was there something wrong with me? I pondered the question again and again, finally dumping it into the lap of karma: he had "good" karma, I had "bad" karma.

Now, one would suppose that a person blessed with such fortunate karma would surely go far in Zen. Actually, this man didn't even begin zazen. After diddling around Japan for a month, he gave up on Zen and returned to the United States and never practiced there either. A year later he died of a heart attack.

What is the moral of all this? That when you experience pain and discomfort, do not resent it but become one with it. Pain can be a brilliant spur to continued effort and growth and, eventually, to Awakening.

# Diet and Zen Practice

## (1969)

*When I first began teaching, many new students of Zen in the West were deeply concerned about the relationship between food and spiritual life. They wanted to eat in a way that would help them gain greater clarity and ease of mind. Many had deep attachments, too, to concepts of a spiritual diet. My interest was in helping them find freedom, not another fad. And so I gave this talk.*

When Shakyamuni, not yet a Buddha, seated himself under the bo tree for his supreme effort and resolved that "though only my skin, sinews, and bones remain and my blood and flesh dry up and wither away, yet never from this seat will I stir until I have attained full enlightenment," he had behind him six years of the most fearsome austerities. Of these, prolonged fasting and the consumption of but one grain of rice a day were two of the milder forms. Yet he failed to gain emancipation through these harsh means. One day as he lay in a faint half-dead from hunger and exhaustion, tradition tells us he clearly perceived that such self-torture could only lead to death and that without a body the inner freedom he desperately sought could not be won. So he eagerly drank the rice milk a concerned village maid offered him, gradually regained his strength, and thereafter determined to steer a middle course between self-mortification and self-indulgence.

The futility of punishing the body as a way to enlightenment, so dramatically conveyed to us by the Buddha, is clear enough. What is less clear is the point where legitimate self-denial leaves off and actual asceticism begins.

119

Asceticism, obviously, is a relative term. One man's meat turns out to be another man's poison. During my stay in a Buddhist meditation center in Burma many years ago, we were told by our monk-preceptor not to meditate in either the half- or the full-lotus position as both were unnecessarily painful—had not the Buddha himself taught the Middle Way, which eschewed the path of asceticism? The posture urged upon Westerners and Burmese alike was sitting with legs folded one in front of the other. A Westerner inquired whether the solid wood-plank bed without bedding of any sort on which we all were required to sleep did not constitute a form of self-torture. He was told in all seriousness, "Not at all, it is the most natural thing in the world once you get used to it." Upon my return to Japan I described the Burmese sleeping accommodations to several of my Zen monk friends, who normally sleep on a thin quilted mattress placed on two-inch-thick tatami straw matting. "Why, that's mortification of the body, which the Buddha rejected!" they exclaimed. Upon being told that the Burmese labeled the lotus position harsh and ascetic, they laughed and replied, "No, once learned it is perfectly natural."

What is even more grueling for Westerners to adapt to is the meal of rice served three times a day in Japanese monasteries and twice a day in the Burmese, where solid food is not taken after noontime. To an Asian monk, however, for whom rice has virtually a mystique, the consumption of such quantities—and the whiter the better—is only "natural." Of the three or four Americans I know who have lived in a Japanese monastery for six months or more and who regularly ate the standard diet, not one escaped either anemia, beriberi, or chronic constipation or all three. Their bodies, unaccustomed to such great quantities of rice and miso (fermented soybean mash), had to labor to extract even the barest nutrients from them.

Rice—this time brown—is now being used by Zen students in the United States to torture their bodies. In this case it is under the prodding of George Ohsawa, a Japanese who has promoted it as the "perfect food" in connection with what he unabashedly calls a "Zen macrobiotic [i.e., long-life] diet."

(Ohsawa, by the way, died several years ago at the age of seventy, ten years short of the span he had predicted for himself.)

"In Japan," Ohsawa has written in his book *You Are All Sanpaku*, "those who live longest as a group are the Buddhist monks. The traditional ways of eating and drinking, which still survive intact in the Zen Buddhist monasteries, continue to confound the scientific seekers after long life and eternal youth." As it turns out, brown rice is not the perfect food—whole-wheat and whole-rye flours are both richer in protein, vitamin B, and minerals. Further, brown rice is not eaten in Zen monasteries. Ordinary Zen monks, as distinguished from Zen masters, are not especially healthy or long-lived; their diet is not based on the yin/yang principle, as claimed elsewhere by Ohsawa; nor is the macrobiotic diet part of Zen practice. Given the widespread interest in Zen today, it is highly improbable that the macrobiotic diet would have lasted as long as it has had not Ohsawa gratuitously linked brown rice and the macrobiotic diet with the fruits of advanced Zen practice.

One of the few crises that occurred in the monastery where I stayed involved brown *gohan*, the Japanese word both for rice and a meal. One day the roshi surprised everyone by having brown gohan served instead of the customary white. Then a rare thing happened: the monks deliberately violated the stringent rule against wasting food by eating a couple of mouthfuls of the rice, as though to satisfy themselves that it was as bad as they thought it would be, and then leaving the rest. The next day the brown gohan was again served, and the same silent drama played out. On the third morning white *and* brown rice were placed on the table. All except the roshi and I reached for the white, which was consumed with the usual speed and gusto. The following day not a grain of the brown appeared, and it was clear the monks had won the battle of the rices. Though one could not doubt the genuineness of the roshi's concern for the health of his monks, it was obvious from the start that this was a crusade for which he had little stomach, for with the resumption of white rice (mixed as usual with barley) the roshi, as if to say, "Now that's over with, let's enjoy our customary gohan," ate his with as much relish as the rest.

In *You Are All Sanpaku,* Ohsawa has written, "In Zen Buddhist monasteries the most superior disciples are always selected for the singular honor of becoming cooks. . . . They are selected so that their superior knowledge and experience in the selection and preparation of food, according to the teaching of the Unique Principle of Yin/Yang, may support and sustain the developing judgment of the other disciples. . . . In Zen Buddhist monasteries this traditional manner of selecting, preparing, and serving food is called *shojin ryori.* The closest translation would be 'cooking which improves the supreme judgment.' "

Shojin ryori would correspond to what the Hindu scriptures call *sattvic,* or pure foods. In the Hindu spiritual tradition, milk, butter, certain cheeses, fruits, vegetables, and grains are pure, since they bring a feeling of purity and calmness to the mind and at the same time nourish the body. On the other hand, such foods as spices, meat, fish, eggs, and alcohol are called *rajasic,* or stimulating, because they stimulate the nervous system and excite the passions. For the Japanese, however, who had little taste for milk, butter, or cheese until World War II, shojin ryori foods are seaweed, miso, sour plums, mountain potatoes, black beans, mushrooms, salted radishes, the root of the lotus, and of course rice, but not dairy products.

The shojin ryori foods most frequently served in the Zen monastery are rice, miso soup, salted radishes, and potatoes, while the others are eaten only occasionally and sparingly. The monks could hardly maintain their minimum health and perform the hard work required of them, however, if this slim fare were not buttressed by feast days celebrating the Buddha's birthday, Bodhidharma's death day, the monastery founder's day, and the like, when all manner of vegetarian meals are served. The monks are further fortified by dinners of fish and meat, rice, vegetables, fruit, cake, beer, and sake wine provided on those frequent occasions when they are invited into the homes of believers to chant sutras in memory of the family dead.

Even so there is much sickness among the monks. Stomach disorders are common, as they are among the Japanese population as a whole (Japan has the highest incidence of stomach cancer in the world), and TB and other pulmonary diseases have always been rampant among the Japanese, Buddhist monks included. Those who live longest are not the ordinary monks and priests but the Zen masters. This is due not to their diet (which in any case is not better than that of the monks), but to their years of zazen meditation and the deep inner calm it brings them. Those masters who have passed on at a comparatively early age—Dogen at fifty and Bassui at sixty—were believed to have been victims of tuberculosis.

In the thirteen years I lived in Japan, mostly in and around monasteries and temples, I never heard it said that monastery food was selected on the basis of the principles of yin and yang. Indeed, how could it be when much of the food is donated and the monks are trained to accept gratefully and without preference whatever is given them? It is true that the job of chief cook in the monastery is entrusted to the monks most advanced in their practice, but not for the reason given by Ohsawa, namely, that they have superior knowledge of the "Unique Principle of Yin/Yang." The reason is simpler and at the same time more profound: their minds are purest, i.e., most equable. For if one preparing food is angry or resentful, fearful or anxious, the mental vibrations resulting from this impure state of mind are communicated to the food and "poison" it, so that a sensitive person eating it may experience stomach upsets, headaches, or other illness. This is why only the most developed monks are selected for this important job.

There is much to be said for a simple diet. Most people overeat, and Seneca's observation that men do not die naturally but kill themselves with their knives and forks is as true today as it was in his time. Zen cannot be practiced effectively by anyone troubled by indigestion, chronic constipation, and kindred ills resulting from eating too much or the wrong kind of food. A safe guide is not to eat more than two-thirds one's capacity. Especially if one has a sedentary job, exercises little, and meditates long, to eat little is better than to eat much. A sparse diet helps zazen in yet another way by muting sexual desire and the fantasies that it spawns. As one's practice advances and samadhi is gained, the body-mind acquires such a keen sensitivity and subtlety that there is a natural preference for "pure" foods and an aversion to the "coarse" variety (such as meat). Indeed, during the deepest states of samadhi the body requires little or no food but seems to extract a different kind of nourishment from the atmosphere. Until this point is reached, however, it is unwise if the body is accustomed to meat and fish and eggs to suddenly give them up, as the resultant strain may bring about illness and put an end to zazen. Whatever dietary changes are made should be introduced gradually, giving the body's chemistry time to adjust.

There need be no fear of dispensing with animal proteins. In his book *A Turning Point in Nutritional Science*, Dr. Ralph Bircher, of the Bircher-Benner Clinic in Switzerland, writes, "If you start with a natural diet containing a sufficient amount of fresh food, green leaves, and cereal germs, then mankind can not only exist without animal protein, but it can attain a much higher level of health ... full health is attainable without animal food." To which may be added that there is greater stamina, a sense of buoyancy and purity. Despite this, it may be better not to give up meat and fish but to wait until they give one up.

Before Americans decide to adopt either the shojin ryori food of the Japanese or the sattvic foodstuffs of the Hindus, they would do well to ponder the fact that these diets grew out of the spiritual needs of peoples molded by a climate and terrain unique to themselves, and that their minds and bodies were formed by a way of life different from our own. Even if the Ohsawa macrobiotic diet followed the regimen of the Zen monks (which it does not), it would be unsuited to Americans, based as it is on the dietary preferences of an older generation of Japanese.

The truth is, there is no such thing as a Zen diet; there cannot be, for it is a contradiction in terms. The minute one proclaims *the* perfect diet beside which all others pale, he enslaves himself to it. This is not Zen, which teaches perfect freedom to accept or reject without compulsion or remorse. Every ism—whether it be vegetarianism, meat-ism, brown rice–ism, or even Buddhism—is a hang-up, a limitation on our inborn freedom and therefore not Zen. The serious practitioner of Zen will find that as his subconscious fears evaporate and his compulsive habits disappear, his built-in body wisdom will naturally select the kind and quantity of food necessary for his physical, mental, and spiritual growth, just as a small child will instinctively eat the foods right for it if its instincts are not thwarted by the arbitrary will of its parents.

It may be helpful to conclude this article with some statements about the dietary habits of the monastics and myself. Needless to say, it does not involve a "perfect" diet. Wherever possible, we avoid canned or processed foods. The sugar we use, sparingly, is natural brown, and our bread, whether it is baked by us or bought, is whole wheat or rye. Other kinds of donated bread are gratefully eaten. Seasonal raw fruit and vegetables are favored over cooked, but we do not make a fetish of raw foods. Only two meals a day are served, breakfast and lunch. However, on heavy workdays a light supper will be served. Once a week, on Sunday, no food is served, but liquids are taken, or perhaps an orange or apple. We do not eat with chopsticks or use Japanese-style lacquer bowls, nor do we eat kneeling. We use American-style knives and forks and dishes and sit on chairs at mealtime.

Neither meat nor fish is served at the Center. In the beginning we did eat fish and meat, most of it contributed by members. However, as our desire and need for animal foods diminished, we stopped preparing it. Members who had contributed fish and meat dishes out of a genuine but misplaced concern for our health soon caught on and switched to vegetable casseroles. There is a widespread notion that one cannot eat meat or fish and practice Zen. If this were true, there would be few Buddhists in the world. I know many enlightened monks and laymen in Japan who eat fish and meat. The classical Buddhist prohibition against eating meat seems to refer to eating meat from an animal killed specifically for one's own food. The Buddha himself is said to have died from eating a piece of rotten meat (some scholars claim it was a mushroom) at the home of a follower. Though he normally ate only sattvic foods, his sense of gratitude would not permit him to refuse it. Still, in the end, the development of compassion will most likely mean that, as one's practice matures, one will abhor foods that require any unnecessary killing. Surely, these days, in this culture, we can get protein in many other ways.

Breakfast at the Center begins with fresh fruit followed by a bowl of raw wheat germ to which is added a teaspoon of dried torula yeast, sesame seeds, yogurt, and buckwheat honey. (In cold weather a hot cereal such as cream of rice or oatmeal is added.) Not only is this mixture nourishing, but what is equally important, it is tasty. While decaffeinated coffee is occasionally available, the liquids usually served are raw milk (furnished by one of our members), roasted-barley tea, or herb tea.

A typical lunch consists of a potato or rice casserole (both brown and white rice are eaten) or buckwheat groats, a cooked vegetable, and a salad of raw lettuce and spinach, tomatoes, and cucumbers or other seasonal vegetables. Dessert is mostly fresh fruit. If donated, it may be a cake. We do not eat between meals.

To sum up, certainly for Americans unaccustomed to large quantities of rice, an exclusive diet of this food, whether brown or white, can be harmful. "Pure" food diets, whether Japanese or Indian, are keyed to the available foods and tastes of those countries and not our own. American Zen students will find their practice aided by a dietary regimen more in accord with their own food tastes and habits. Animal proteins can safely be dispensed with if done gradually. Substituting whole grains, nuts, and vegetable proteins brings a gain in stamina and lightness—and many books can teach us how to make a smooth and well-assured changeover. To make a categorical imperative of any diet is contrary to the spirit of Zen, which teaches freedom and not attachment.

In the profoundest sense, health is more than a matter of eating the right kind and quantity of food. We are nourished or depleted just as much by our thoughts as by proper quantities of proteins, calories, and vitamins. A mind feeding on lust or greed or revenge or despair or anger will poison the most nutritious food, leaving the body-mind vulnerable to disease. In the end, without zazen, which purifies the heart, clarifies thought, and invigorates the body, macrobiotic diets, sattvic diets, *all diets*, are deficient.

# Mind-Altering Drugs:
## Commentary and Reflections
### (1969)

*As actual Zen practice began to take hold in the West, all teachers, myself included, discovered that many of our young students owed their initial turn toward Zen to an experience with mind-altering or mind-manifesting drugs. This created a unique set of circumstances for Zen practice, with unique problems. I felt that an in-depth clarification was in order. Hence this talk given almost thirty years ago. Its fundamental points still apply. While the whole issue of psychedelics or entheogens ("sacred-manifestations"), as I've now seen them called, and the spiritual life has been with humanity a long time and is complex, for me, what is most important about them is simply that they have led people to genuine spiritual practice.*

Let me say at the outset that I do not propose to explore the matter of whether psychoactive drugs do or do not cause damage to the chromosomes, the brain, or health generally. This is really a medical question and can be left to the doctors and researchers—the intelligent and fair-minded ones, that is. Nor do I propose to dispute the view advanced by many that psychedelic or illegal drugs have religious significance. The questions to which I shall address myself are: Can these drugs bring true peace of mind as well as genuine clarity and vigor of mind? Do they free the user from the bonds of ego? Do they enable the user to *live* in the truth of Oneness? In other words, do pot and acid, even when taken under ideal conditions and not abused, bring the wisdom and strength to live with zest, compassion, and inner freedom in a world that appears joyless, unloving, and violent? Lastly, what is the nature of Zen enlightenment, or satori, and how does it relate to zazen or meditation?

Before going further, let me say that I have never "dropped" acid, smoked pot, or taken any of the depressants or stimulants—in fact I can't remember the last time I took even an aspirin. What I say to you therefore about drugs derives not from my own use of them but from what Zen students at the Rochester Center say on their membership applications to the question, "If you have ever taken hallucinogenic drugs, or are now taking them, explain fully"; from what they tell me privately in dokusan about their use, abuse, and disuse of the hallucinogens; from my own observations of students who have taken them in the past; and from some reading of the statements of those who have extensively experienced the hallucinogenic drugs.

Significantly, nowhere in the teachings of the masters of the three great Asian religions of Buddhism, Hinduism, and Islam do we find mind-altering drugs advocated as a means to enlightenment. This is all the more remarkable when we remember that hashish has been known and used for centuries in the Middle and Far East. No doubt individual teachers themselves have smoked hashish on occasion—for a specific purpose. But the weight of religious traditions is against drug use. In Buddhism the fifth precept forbids the selling or buying of liquor or drugs (i.e., causing others to partake of them or doing so oneself), for obvious reasons. Hinduism likewise inveighs against their use. So does Islam.

Two and a half years ago the Sufi master Sidi Abdeslum, of Morocco, visited the Rochester Zen Center during his first trip to the West. A few nonmembers with a known interest in Sufism had been invited to hear him, and in the question period one of them asked, "Do the Sufi masters ever prescribe hashish or other mind-expanding drugs to those on the spiritual path?" "Absolutely not!" he replied with some heat. "Everywhere I go in the United States I am asked this question. It is ridiculous to suppose that any teacher would prescribe a hard course of training if true spiritual emancipation could be had by comfortably smoking hashish or swallowing drugs. Only because they know from their own arduous exertions that there is no easy road to liberation do the masters compassionately advocate the hard but sure way."

Speaking as a Zen teacher, I regard the psychedelics as *upaya*— i.e., an expedient device for bringing to the path of genuine Self-realization many who would never get there by any other route in our drug-saturated, materialistic culture. I say "drug-saturated" because America's reliance on drugs is unequaled in the history of mankind. "We take pills to pep us up, pills to calm us down, pills to gain pounds, more pills to lose them, pills to avoid conception, other pills to help it. Millions of Americans can't sleep, wake up, or feel comfortable without drugs," reports *Look* magazine. So why not drugs to try to break down the walls of ego for a glimpse of the world beyond?

What lies behind the search for a chemical solution to the problems of life? Clearly, millions of Americans in the latter half of the twentieth century are so painfully tense, fearful and anxious, unfulfilled and estranged, that life can be made bearable only by the swallowing of a pill, the gulping of liquor, the downing of a saturated sugar cube, or the smoking of a piece of hemp. The desire for escape from this world of stress and trial to one of greater harmony and meaning underlies most drug use. Resorting to hallucinogens represents for many a desperate, almost compulsive attempt to *feel* at the deepest level, to overcome the deadening passivity and inability to love stemming from our computerized, fear-ridden, dehumanized society with its perpetual accent on consumption.

For the great majority the reliance on drugs is totally in keeping with the American ideal of comfort and ease. From "the gentle blue pill" that assures social success to the "relaxing" effect of a highball, the use of drugs is presented and swallowed as a means to an easier, more comfortable, more secure, and more sociable life. One need only listen to the seductive cooing of a TV announcer urging us to bask in the pleasures of additional phones upstairs or a new second car because "you owe yourself this extra luxury" to realize that the "good," the "sweet" life is the luxurious life, the one affording the greatest amount of pleasure. Underlying this attitude is the notion that it is senseless, if not downright masochistic, to endure even small amounts of pain and discomfort when ways can be found to escape or mitigate them.

For a lesser number of young people drugs are an alternative to the "American way"—an alternative that holds great attraction in its immediacy and even its romantic aura. The use by this segment of the populace of drugs such as LSD and pot also has the advantage of not requiring faith in an "establishment" that is regarded with little if any trust as respects its ethics, morality, and basic sanity. The mistrust of all who profess to know or teach is undoubtedly a major selling point of such drugs. And while there is no insistence on personal comfort among the drug subculture—in fact there is a studied avoidance of it—yet here, too, the idea that struggle and pain are pointless is implicit.

More than twenty-five hundred years ago the Buddha declared that pain was a fact of human existence, that when we try to deny or avoid it, we condemn ourselves to a shallow, joyless life, for pain and joy are actually two sides of the same coin. Pain when not resented frees the natural sympathy and compassion of our True-nature even as it enables us to experience pleasure and joy in a new depth and purity. Zen Master Dogen has pointed out that anxiety, when accepted, is the driving force to enlightenment in that it lays bare the human dilemma at the same time that it ignites our desire to break out of it. Without anxiety as a spur, says Dogen, we are left to flounder in a shallow life, forever trapped in the dungeon of our compulsive drives and subconscious fears. One has but to read the lives of the masters and lay disciples of Zen who have come to satori-awakening, and of those who have found God in other traditions, to realize that few have had genuine enlightenment without having suffered considerable discomfort and even pain. The spiritual heights can no more be scaled by smoking pot and dropping acid than a mountain can be climbed by looking at a map of it while reclining in an easy chair drinking beer. It is the climbing that brings joy and strength—joy in the release from the bondage of self and mountain, top and bottom, and the strength to *live* in this realization.

That the "mountain" may be glimpsed in that rare acid trip that can truly be called religious, i.e., transcendental, I do not contest, but what disciplines do pot and acid provide for ascending it, or indeed for coming down (i.e., integrating the awareness into daily life)? When the glow of the "beautiful," even transcendental, trip fades, as fade it must, what alternative does the habitual tripper have but to take yet more LSD and more marijuana when faced again with the hard realities of life, but now with less energy, less ambition, and greater indifference? Cut off from the genuine spiritual struggle that brings strength, a passive observer seeing only what a trip will allow him or her to see, the acid tripper can all too easily lose subjectivity and a sense of involvement and may finally reach a state of total passivity. Like a person who, when needing money, won't earn it but will pawn valuable possessions until he or she goes broke, the man or woman who gives his or her life over to hallucinogens eventually dissipates hard-won spiritual resources. Habitual trippers naturally hope for the liberative or at least beautiful trip, one interlaced with lovely fantasies and bliss. But sooner or later, as in Russian roulette, the tripper hits the live bullet: the terrifying hallucinations, the depressions, and the fears bordering on panic.

What about zazen? How does it strengthen mind and body? How does it satisfy spiritual aspiration? It does so *not* by making life comfortable but by making one strong. Zazen is a dynamic practice, an intense spiritual struggle. It is a reveille and not a lullaby by which the normally unruly mind and restless body are purified and forged into a single instrument to penetrate the barrier of the five senses and discursive intellect. Zazen demands energy and a finely honed mind—requisites for effective zazen and at the same time by-products of it.

The cross-legged lotus posture is desirable but by no means indispensable, for zazen is much more than sitting in the proper way. It involves using the mind with perfect awareness, cleansed of all random and idle thoughts. Performed this way, work, too, becomes a form of zazen, a path of ever-deepening absorption. Sitting zazen and mobile zazen are thus mutually reinforcing. One who sits daily in zazen finds it easier to relate totally to daily tasks, and one who performs every job with total attention finds it less difficult to empty the mind during zazen-meditation. By gradually banishing the notion of a separate ego-I, the source of all our griefs and sufferings, zazen in time brings the indisputable Knowledge of who and what we truly are and of our relation to our fellow humans, the earth, and all living things. This is true enlightenment.

Zazen is difficult to begin but deeply satisfying to carry on. Drugs may be comforting at the start but can become sheer hell in time. In zazen body and mind are unified and energized, the will strengthened. With habitual use of hallucinogens, the body can be weakened, the mind dulled, and energies drained. In time, the life force itself may be threatened. Of course none of this is necessarily so. I have, however, seen enough instances of this to take it seriously as a real cause for concern.

To be fair, I should mention that at one stage of practice the Zen student may also experience illusory visions, fantasies, and weird sensations. These are known as makyo, the literal meaning of which is "diabolical phenomena." They may range all the way from simple, intensified visual and auditory sensations, feelings of sinking or floating, or experiencing of one's body as a melting substance, to penetrating insights, visions of God or Buddha, or clairvoyant powers. But the dull, uncomprehending look, the glassy stare, the zombielike gait, the feelings of insanity and suicide of the bad trips—these types of makyo are virtually unheard of in Zen. Furthermore, students who have dropped much acid in the past tend to have more gruesome makyo that last for a longer period and recur more frequently than do those with little or no history of drug use.

A competent teacher will calm a student's mind when makyo arise by pointing out their nature and significance and how to control and constructively channel the vast amounts of energy released during them. With acid, however, the sudden release of energy seems to leave the tripper with a feeling of utter help-lessness in an environment over which he has no control. For as long as the drug's effects last, he must simply "go with" or endure whatever occurs. Not understanding what is happening, the drug user can easily panic.

At the beginning of my own training in a Zen monastery years ago, I , too, went through a period of makyo, which were mainly visual. They grew from the paintings of Paul Klee, many of which I had studied earlier in my life. It was not merely the intensity of these fantasies that overwhelmed me. *I* was the cosmos dyed with unearthly colors of Klee. *I* was unity, *I* was love, *I* was joy incarnate! Utterly convinced that this was satori, I waltzed into my teacher's room at dokusan, elated and tri-umphant. Hardly had I begun my prostrations when he rang me out of the room. After two such traumatic appearances, I humbly asked why I had twice been summarily dismissed with-out having even been given the chance to describe my mind-state. "Too much ego," was the laconic reply. Even the ecstasy arising from feelings of oneness with my fellow man were dis-missed by the roshi as nothing more than makyo. If I attached myself to them, he warned, they would block my progress toward true enlightenment.

Zen teaching has always insisted that a purported enlighten-ment be tested and confirmed by a master whose own enlight-enment has in turn been sanctioned by an enlightened teacher. This is because of the great danger to the personality resulting from self-deception. The truth is, it is all too easy for a novice to mistake visions, trances, hallucinations, insights, revelations, fantasies, ecstasies, or even mental serenity for satori. Masters of old lashed out at those who claimed to be enlightened yet refused to be tested, calling them "earthworms living in the slime of self-validated satori." Since even a genuine enlighten-ment generates the subtle pride of "I am enlightened," the per-ceptive teacher's job—and it may be a long one—is to help the student wash away this "smell" of enlightenment through work on subsequent koans or other practice.

Consider, then, the massive ego swell of those who loudly

boast of an "instant" chemical satori. And how ridiculous some of them look trying to act like liberated Zen men—running scared but trying to appear otherwise. The ancient Zen "zanies" were a different breed. Apparent simpletons, they were actually profoundly enlightened men. Some of them even died standing on their heads to show their scorn of death. Yet they had the deepest affection for all living things and were full of tears for their fellow men.

So far we have said little about the nature of Zen satori and drug-induced enlightenment, so called. Now let me try to point out the difference. Timothy Leary and other spokesmen for the psychedelic movement have used the term *expansion of consciousness* to describe the mind-state resulting from LSD and other hallucinogens. In a paper entitled "The Religious Experience, Its Production and Interpretation," which seeks to justify the drug experience as a transcendental one, Leary speaks of consciousness as a biochemical process located in the nervous system. The way to expand consciousness, according to him, is to activate dormant brain cells through hallucinogenic drugs and foods, thereby attaining the transcendental vision, or religious experience.

Satori-awakening, however, is *not* an expansion of consciousness. True awakening occurs when both the conscious and subconscious minds—or the eight levels of consciousness, to use Buddhist terminology—have been thoroughly transcended, or "broken through." The Mind's eye is opened when *all* fantasies, hallucinations, images, ideas, thought-forms, and feelings have been "gone beyond." "If the mind is attached to any form or feeling or engaged in conceptual things," says Zen Master Bassui, "it is as far from true realization as heaven is from earth."

To illustrate the difference between expansion of mind and satori, let me use my wristwatch. The face of it would correspond to our life in time and space, to birth and death, cause and effect, karma, ego. The back of the watch, which is void of all marks, represents the changeless or equality aspect of our life, and of this nothing whatever can be posited. It is "void" of all limiting characteristics. One whose awareness extended no further than the senses and the discriminating intellect would be like a person who was ignorant of the back of the watch while recognizing only the face. Expansion of consciousness would be comparable to "stretching" or extending the face farther and farther, if that were possible, but no matter how much you extended it, you would still be dealing with "the face." Satori is like the sudden flipping over of the watch. Here's the back! Now for the first time you realize that a watch actually consists of a face *plus* a back. And that this has *always* been so.

Or to take another example. Consider the sun just before it comes above the horizon. Streaks of light appear at dawn, but the basic condition is still darkness. The darkness would correspond to ignorance or ego or delusion, the streaks of light to insights, visions, psychic powers, or "expansion of consciousness." But the prevailing condition is still darkness. Once the sun rises above the horizon, however, a complete reversal takes place. Now it is truly light, though not as bright yet as at noon. The sun corresponds to our True-nature and sunrise to a first, usually shallow, enlightenment. With continued Zen practice more and more light enters our life and the shadows vanish, as the sun of our True-nature rises to the fullness of noon.

Curiously, many people believe satori is the same for everyone. They seem unaware that there are shallow satori, deep satori, and full satori. A hundred candles lit in a pitch-black cave obviously give off more light than one or two. It is therefore pointless to ask, as many do, "How would *the* enlightened person act in such and such a situation?" as though every enlightened person would respond in the same way. *The* satori person is an abstraction. There are only individual people of satori, or enlightenment, whose character and personalities vary according to the depth of their insight and practice. Zen masters have said, "It is not the quality of the enlightenment that makes the person, but the quality of the person that makes the enlightenment." Enlightenment does not automatically confer perfection. It is merely the foundation of an edifice whose many-storied superstructure would correspond to the perfected character and personality of the spiritually developed individual.

135

Such a structure can only be erected by years of dedicated zazen upon the solid base of the inner Knowledge that enlightenment confers. In Dogen's words, "There is no beginning to practice and end to enlightenment; there is no beginning to enlightenment and end to practice." Practice means zazen. Zazen is the actualization of our inherent Bodhi-mind. Through zazen this Wisdom-eye is opened, and through continued zazen the defiling dust that clouds this Vision is removed.

The aim of Zen training is not ecstasy but Knowledge—of the meaning of birth and death. This Knowledge brings tranquillity, equilibrium, and a joyful freedom from self. In Japan I knew an old woman who had practiced Zen for some twenty years. Her friends called her "Sun face," so radiant was her smile, so selfless her presence. Can pot and acid produce such people?

# Repentance and Problems of Sex:
# The Third Buddhist Precept
## (1975)

*Certain precepts require us to look carefully at the most chal-*
*lenging territories of our human-nature. The third precept, on*
*not misusing our sexual nature, is one such. In addition,*
*because sexuality and problems of guilt, shame, and abuse are*
*so entwined, this precept and its related issues require greater*
*discussion than some of the others.*

What do confession and repentance mean in Buddhism? We are
confessing our past misdeeds. What are these misdeeds? We are
confessing our misdeeds that arise out of our separation. Separation from what? Separation from our True Self. Separation
from our True Self means separation from others. It means setting up in the mind the notion of self and other. And it is by this
step of postulating one's self as apart from others that the whole
concept of ego arises in the mind. And the larger the ego the
larger the separation; the larger the ego the greater the ignorance, the greater the darkness. And so in confessing, we are at
the same time saying to ourselves or expressing the desire to
want to overcome this split, this alienation. There can't be any
kind of repentance unless there is first a confession and an
acknowledgment that we are ignorant.

There's an old saying that the greatest of all sins is to be
aware of none. In the Buddhist sense sin means, as we have said,
separation. And there is no one in that sense who does not suffer from sin. So after there has been acknowledgment or confession, then there must be repentance if the process is to be
completed, that is to say, the process of putting ourselves, in tra-

ditional terminology, in the arms of the Buddha. This means to walk the path of Unity, of Oneness, of brotherhood and sisterhood. Repentance doesn't mean merely being sorry for what one has done, to oneself or to others. Very often the feeling of regret is rather a superficial one. It has a way when it is done insincerely of not really casting off troublesome and unwholesome thoughts and actions. So true repentance also means once and for all affirming this fundamental Oneness through Insight. It also means identifying ourselves completely with the true state of things. Or to put it another way, with the Buddha, the Dharma, and the Sangha.

Some may question, How is the Sangha the true state of things? Of course the word *Sangha* can be understood in many senses. We take it in its ordinary sense of meaning those who practice the Buddha's teaching. And to walk in the way of the Buddha's teaching, in the way of Oneness, means to bring out the underlying emptiness that is the substratum of everything. This emptiness does not mean a negative kind of void. Emptiness means the moon, the sun, the stars, our bodies, our minds. It also means our struggles, our pains, and our joys.

In addition to confession and repentance, there is the taking of the Refuges. The Three Refuges are: "I take refuge in Buddha and resolve that with all beings I will understand the Great Way whereby the Buddha-seed may forever thrive. I take refuge in Dharma and resolve that with all beings I will enter deeply into the sutra treasure whereby my wisdom may grow as vast as the ocean. I take refuge in Sangha and in its warmth, wisdom, and never-failing help and resolve to live in harmony with all sentient beings."

Here are some moving passages from *Entering the Path of Enlightenment,* a translation of *The Bodhicaryavatara* of the eighth-century Buddhist poet, monk, and Bodhisattva Santideva. "I go to the Buddha for refuge," says Santideva, "until enlightenment is reached. I go to the Dharma for refuge, likewise to the host of Bodhisattvas. With folded hands [in gassho] I implore the perfect Buddhas stationed in all places, and likewise the great compassionate Bodhisattvas. Whatever evil on the endless wheel of rebirth or simply right here whatever evil was considered by me . . . or caused to be committed or whatever was enjoyed foolishly ending in self-destruction, that evil I confess, stricken with remorseful feeling. Whatever wrong I've done to the Three Jewels (Buddha, Dharma, and Sangha) or to my mother and father or to praiseworthy teachers by abusive deed, speech, or thought, by many dark offenses, by the evil wrought by me, whatever violent evil was done, all that I confess. How can I escape from it? I am eternally fearful. Let death not be soon because of my despair that my evil has not diminished. How can I escape from it? Rescue me with haste. Death will come quickly and my evil is not diminished."

Finally he says: "Whatever evil which has been accumulated by my foolishness and ignorance and whatever of my speaking and teaching is objectionable and whatever is evil by nature, I confess it all. Fearing sorrow and with folded hands prostrating myself again and again. That which was not good will not be done again by me." That last line is important. The Buddha says somewhere, unless there is this determination not to repeat what was done, one will continue to do the same painful things over and over again.

THIRD PRECEPT

The third precept, or item of good character, concerns the proper use of our sexuality. It does not deny sexuality but asks us to respect it. As we know, there is a difference in the lifestyle of the monk and householder, the layperson in society. For the monk, every kind of sexuality is improper sexuality. For the layperson, improper sexuality chiefly means adultery. However, other practices come under the head of improper sexuality: sexual relations with an animal, or bestiality; sexual relations with a person who is not of age; sexuality with an insane person. These are obviously improper types of sexuality. We can also speak of other types of improper sexuality, most of which spring from egotism. These would include all forms of abusing one's partner, of using one's partner to satisfy one's own egotistical, selfish desires.

We will talk about celibacy and other issues, but let us begin with homosexuality and lesbianism. It's hard to find anything substantial in the traditional literature on these two subjects. Homosexuality is mentioned in relation to monks—for whom sexual relations would be off-limits, period. To my mind, for laypeople, homosexuality, as sexual expression, is simply a certain type of karma. Heterosexual expression is also a certain type of karma.

In the Buddha-nature there are not, properly speaking, two sexes. We can't speak of men or women for, in doing so, we are making a separation that is artificial. Conveniently, in order to talk about it, we are separating men and women from their Buddha-nature. The Buddha-nature of a man is to be a man. The Buddha-nature of a woman is to be a woman. What does it really mean to be a woman? What does it mean to be a man? Some well-known figure in ancient Japan said, "O man, be a Man! O woman, be a Woman!" Shakespeare has a line somewhere in which he says, "He was a man. Taken all in all, I shall never look upon his like again."

What does it mean to be a woman? To be a Woman with a capital *W* means also to be a man, and to be a Man with a capital *M* also means to be a woman. We may speak of certain qualities that have traditionally been associated with women, a certain gentleness, for example, a certain strongly sympathetic or even empathetic nature, a certain recessiveness. But surely, these qualities are just as valid for a man as for a woman.

What does it mean to be a Man? What does it mean to be a Woman? Ultimately it means to be so truly One with whatever activity you are engaged in as to reach a point of self-transcendence. Now you are simply yourself, beyond names, beyond man or woman. Now we are Man. Now we are Woman. In *Wuthering Heights,* one of the characters says, "I am you and you are me." Yet you are also you, and I am I, and the two of them must go together. Men and women, too, each express fundamental aspects of True-nature. And men and woman, for all their struggles to be

140

themselves and uphold significant gender differences or, shall we say, styles, deeply need each other. They are each aspects of a Whole. Let us never forget that.

What one was in previous lifetimes, that is, one's past karma, comes into play here and makes things yet a bit more complex. Let's say one is a man in this lifetime. That doesn't mean one was always a man. Indeed, a woman in a previous lifetime might well have formed a strong desire to become a man. Not because being a man is somehow better. Rather, it could have been because in certain countries, the cultural condition of women is so painful a woman might decide to become a man. In many Asian countries it used to be said that being born a woman is really a way of expiating painful karma, that if a human lives a so-called good life, then she'll be born a man in her next. That will be her reward. Imagine that! That will be her reward! As if, in reality, Buddhahood were not resplendent in the feminine form! Nonetheless, this was strongly believed in Asian countries, culturally conditioned perhaps, because it was so painful to be a woman in those cultures compared to being a man. Still, this is a kind of chicken-or-egg game, the question of which came first, the attitude or the cultural condition. We can all be glad that such stifling and destructive attitudes are disappearing. When one gender is denigrated, our own True-nature, our own innate Wholeness and Completeness, is sullied.

From the point of view of the Buddha-nature, it doesn't matter whether one is homosexual or heterosexual, male or female. To the degree that one allows one's Buddha-nature to express itself, to the degree that one overcomes the duality of self-and-other, which also means male and female, there can be no improper sexuality, no "right" gender. Improper sexuality must, by definition, spring from egotistical self-seeking, from selfish concern with one's own desires. To have any relationship at all, one must have a certain concern for the other. But if one is primarily seeking only to satisfy oneself, this is improper sexuality.

Whether one is homosexual or heterosexual, one need not feel any shame. If one fails to feel a Oneness, or Unity, and to express it in daily life, this, spiritually speaking, is alone cause

141

for shame: one should not understand oneself *only* as a homo-sexual or *only* as a heterosexual. In that sense neither term would be a compliment.

The third precept, from the point of view we've already stated, means to refrain from adultery. And adultery, too, although it may be defined legally, means that while one is living in a viable relationship with one person, one does not sully that relationship by concomitantly having a relationship with another person. But even here, we get into certain subtleties. There are many kinds of intimate relationships. One could be legally married, and yet not really have an intimate relationship with a partner. And one may be legally married to one person whom one is not living with and have a truly loving relationship with another person.

From the point of view of the Mahayana, one can do certain things sexually speaking if they are not ego-motivated and if they will help another. Once when I was working on a certain koan, Yasutani Roshi told me an interesting story that happened in the Middle Ages in Japan. There was, in Buddhism then, nothing but celibacy for an ordained monk, and the head monk of an important monastery near Tokyo was widely known as being pure-minded and pure-acting. Not far from this monastery was a large geisha house. One evening one of the geishas received a letter that her mother was seriously ill, and that the only doctor who could cure her commanded a high fee. The geisha didn't have the money, but that night she was visited by her rich patron, who was under the influence of liquor, and she told him about her mother and asked if he would lend her, not give but lend her, this huge sum for her mother's treatment.

The man thought about it and finally said, "I won't lend you the money, but I'll tell you how you can earn it. Not far from here is a temple. A monk who's supposed to be very pure-minded lives there. You're a beautiful woman. Seduce him and I'll give you the money."

The girl was desperate. So she said, "All right, I'll do my best." She arrived at the monastery on a stormy night and said, "I've gotten lost in this storm. I'm soaked and I'm cold. Could I please come in and use your bath?" It's a custom in Japan to invite in strangers on a cold night to use the bath. The monk said, "Of course, come in."

And so she went in. When she came out of the bath, she looked lovely. A professional courtesan, she now tried with all her skill to seduce the monk, but nothing would work. Finally she broke down and began to cry. She told him the whole story of how this patron had offered her the money for her sick mother. Would he please forgive her? The monk responded, "If that is the case, let us go to bed."

The next day the abbot called the head monk to his quarters (nothing is ever secret for long in a monastery) and said, "What is this I hear! It can't possibly be true that this geisha slept with you in your quarters last night!"

The monk said, "Yes, it is true."

"How could you do such a thing? Just think of your influence on all these young monks under your care, who look upon you as a model of virtue and purity!"

And the head monk didn't argue. He just said, "It had to be done."

"It had to be done!" repeated the abbot in disbelief. "Then it has to be done that I must dismiss you. Your influence on the monks could never be positive anymore. I must ask you to leave."

And without much ado the monk said, "In that case I will certainly leave."

Now the monks got wind of why the head monk had slept with the geisha, and they saw him leaving the grounds with his few belongings. They formed a delegation and went at once to the abbot. And they said, "We hear that you sacked the head monk. Is this true?"

The master said, "He slept with a geisha, right here in his room. So I had to ask him to leave."

"We know about the geisha."

"Well, you don't think I could keep him on after that, do you?"

"We certainly do."

"What! What does this mean?"

And then the spokesman for the monks said, "We feel that this monk has taught us a lesson in compassion." They told the abbot about the geisha's sick mother and added, "Unless you bring him back and reinstate him, we will all leave. He has revealed to us the meaning of true Mahayana compassion." Then of course the abbot reinstated him.

So, relating to this precept of sexuality and the Mahayana, Dogen says, "To refrain from defilement. Let the three wheels of self, objects, and actions be pure." Being pure means being unified, not separated. "Desire nothing. One goes along together with the Buddhas."

Bodhidharma says, "In the precept of refraining from improper sexuality, Self-nature is clear and obvious. In the sphere of the unstained Dharma, not yielding to attachment is called the precept of refraining from improper sexuality."

Recently during the last training program, one of the trainees came to me and asked, "Could one become enlightened and still engage in sex?"

"What prompted the question?" I asked.

"I was sitting with another spiritual group. One time I asked the teacher this question, and he answered, 'If you truly want to become enlightened, you must give up all sexuality.' At the time I had been recently married. Hearing that sort of killed the relationship, and not too much later the marriage ended. Now I've been living a celibate life, but I just don't feel right. I think it was a mistake and I'd like to meet a woman with whom I could share the joys of life and half the pains," he put it poetically. "Would it be proper for me to try to find a woman and get married?"

"It would be improper for you to *try* to find a woman."

He seemed confused and asked, "What do you mean?"

I told him that he probably wasn't ready for a celibate life or the question wouldn't have come up. In addition, I told him that the idea that mere abstention from sex would lead to enlightenment struck me as at least somewhat unperceptive.

Now he was really getting confused. "You mean *not* to seek a woman or to *seek* a woman would be improper sexuality?"

144

"Yes, the very act of seeking, of thinking—*I want a woman, I need a partner*—is already wrong. There's too much ego there. It's that kind of seeking that is itself wrong. Just cease clinging to the idea that one must be celibate in order to come to enlightenment. Let go of that idea, that's all that's necessary. Becoming open, selfless, and nonseeking, you will surely meet a person with whom you will be able to form a meaningful love relationship."

And then I told him about that old saying in which somebody asked a rabbi, "How does one find the right person to marry?" And the answer given was, "It is more important to *be* the right one than to find the right one." This is absolutely true. When we become selfless, nonseeking, we become the "right" person and then we become attractive, not only to members of the opposite sex, but even to one's own sex. Any person who is selfless is an attractive, appealing figure. We are drawn to such a person. So that's all one needs to do, and if one does zazen correctly, then one will certainly be able to meet someone and fall in love.

I also told this student, "What you were told by your teacher was not essentially wrong. It was just told to the wrong person at the wrong time." It's true that to reach the absolute highest states, sexual energy must be transmuted. We find this in the literature of all traditions. This is true for laypeople as well as monastics. However, this doesn't mean that one cannot become enlightened, and deeply so, while still in a sexual relationship. But the development of one's full potential is about much more than just having an enlightenment experience. To be able to act selflessly and spontaneously, to be just naturally oneself and naturally help others in one's daily life, obviously requires a high level of development. If we carefully study the lives of those who have reached this level, we find that eventually they evolve into nonsexual relationships. This doesn't mean that they necessarily have to part from loved ones. The relationship might still exist and even become more deeply loving. They just no longer expend sexual energy or get caught up in the clinging and attachment that so often characterize romantic affairs. After all, any kind of clinging has behind it some degree of self-love. "I love you because you make me feel so good." That's the

145

implication there, really. Because you make *me* feel so good, that's why I love you. Of course romantic love can also free a person up, to be open to a wider, vaster, more mysterious world. So, it's always a matter of being attentive, responsive, alert, and sensitive, of learning to trust what now constitutes the right, deepest Path for oneself.

Perhaps we can end by giving a koan. An old woman, highly developed in Zen, had on her property a little house in which lived a Zen monk. He'd been there for several years. One day, when her granddaughter came to visit, the old woman decided it was time to test this monk to see how far he'd gotten in his Zen training. And so the grandmother, who had been accustomed to bringing a meal to this monk once a day, said to her grand-daughter, "Today I want you to take the tray of food to the monk. And when you do this, put the tray down, nestle up close to him, put your cheek next to his, and then very sweetly say, 'How does this make you feel?' And then I want you to come back and tell me exactly what he does and says."

Well, the girl said she didn't want to do this. But her grand-mother insisted. At last she finally consented. She went and did what her grandmother had told her; she put the tray down, snuggled up to the monk, and said, "Now how does this make you feel?"

In a haughty manner the monk drew himself up and said, "It makes me feel like a cold tree leaning against a large stone in the middle of winter."

The girl went back to her grandmother and reported it all. And the grandmother exclaimed, "That no-good monk! He hasn't learned a thing!" And she ran out and burned his hut down!

Now this is a koan that is traditionally given in a monastery to monks. Yet it touches on something truly deep in human nature—sexuality, sexual expression, and repression, as well as wisdom and compassion. All are explored. And there are other koans that deal with sexuality. There are so many sex stories if you're living in a monastery. And they're not silly or lewd. They touch on truths we all know, all must live with. Let me give you one final example.

One time a young roshi was traveling in the countryside giving Zen talks. He stayed at the home of some devout people, and he noticed that his hosts had an attractive daughter.

After he'd been there a few days he went to the father and said, "I've been observing your daughter; she's a very lovely girl and her manner is both intelligent and refined. I would like to ask for her hand in marriage."

Her father was amazed and overjoyed. This was a famous teacher. That night the father said to his daughter, "A great thing has happened to our family, our house. The roshi who's staying with us came to me today and said he would like me to give your hand in marriage. You must agree. This would honor our house very much."

The girl's response was interesting and showed some real depth: "I'm flattered, of course, but I don't understand. Why would he want to get married? Getting married and having children would be a responsibility. How would he then carry on his teaching?"

Her father said, "Never mind that. Just tell him that we accept." In those days, in that culture, daughters were trained to be obedient, and so she went to the roshi's room and knocked on the door. He was doing zazen, and right next to him was another cushion. She started to say something, but he said, "Please, let us sit together first." She knew how to do zazen and so she sat down beside him. She did zazen and she did zazen. Finally she fell asleep. When she awoke, light was streaming into the room, the roshi was gone, and his few belongings were gone, too.

The story is told by monks, and the question naturally comes up, "Well, what really happened?" I remember one time when this was told in a monastery, ten or twelve different answers were given. Many temptations and repressions were explored. It opened up much hidden monastic territory. So sex, so much at the core of each of our lives, of life itself, is obviously something that has to be dealt with in koans and Zen talks (teishos), and in other ways by the teacher. Such koans are not easy to demonstrate, to give the right kind of answer to. They force us to examine the difference between narrow interpretation of the third precept and the Mahayana point of view. Interestingly, in some Theravadin traditions a monk has absolutely nothing to do with a woman, won't even ride in the same car with her. But in the Mahayana, it is the spirit of compassion, of nonattachment, of nonclinging, that is really most important.

# Buddhist Ethics
## and Abuses of Power
### (1984)

*In the mid-eighties, Zen communities around the country faced a new and unexpected problem—abuses of power, sexual and otherwise, by persons in leadership positions. Many communities—and lives—were torn apart. Ethical behavior and spiritual practice can never be separated. Failures to live up to the precepts cannot be hidden under labels of Bodhisattvic "crazy-wisdom." Let us be careful about this.*

Recent disclosures of the lamentable behavior of the heads of three large Zen Buddhist centers in this country—including harassment of female students, ongoing affairs with married women, alcoholism, and for lack of a better word, a plush lifestyle—have shaken Zen circles and brought into question the whole teacher-student relationship. Besides other painful fallout, these scandals have brought about the forced resignation of one roshi and the departure of trustees and many senior students from the other two centers.

Along with cries of betrayal by disenchanted students and much head-shaking by friends of Buddhism came two anguished questions: "How can a roshi, presumably sanctioned to teach by his own roshi, be guilty of such behavior?" and "If a sanctioned roshi—a Zen 'master' in the eyes of many—is not master of himself and is so consumed by his cravings as to be indifferent to the effect of his behavior on his students and others, what good is the seal of approval of a teacher and what good is Zen?"

Some blame the abuses of power on what they describe as the extension into American Zen of an authoritarian structure embedded in Japanese Buddhism, a model said to be at variance with democratic American ideals. Most disillusioning for many is the fact that the sexual transgressions were not by monks who had taken vows of celibacy and were feeling the strains of those vows, but by married roshis living with their spouses and children—priests who had pledged to uphold the Buddhist precepts and to make them the moral basis of their lives.

Fully to answer the two questions raised by troubled Zen students would call for a lengthy, detailed article on such arcane subjects as what lies behind teacher sanctioning today, who exactly is a Zen master, what the proper authority of a roshi is, and why the behavior of many teachers in the Japanese and some other Buddhist traditions is so at odds with the skillful actions set forth in the precepts. A short answer, however, to the questions of how roshis can so abuse their positions is simple: "These teachers are not actually Zen masters but roshis with obvious defilements." *Roshi*, meaning literally "venerable teacher," is a term of respect given to a Zen Buddhist teacher of long experience who may or may not be a master.

In his book *Points to Watch in Buddhist Training*, Zen Master Dogen defines a master as one who is deeply enlightened, who lives by what he knows to be the truth, and who has received the transmission from his own master. By these criteria can any of the roshis in question—or indeed any other roshis these days—be considered Zen masters? One with deep enlightenment knows good from evil and through the power of zazen translates this wisdom into daily actions. Deep enlightenment, however, requires years of persistent zazen grounded in observance of the precepts. And if the mind is constantly being disturbed by wanton behavior, pure zazen is impossible. Actions delineated by the precepts show us the way a spiritually developed person, a master, behaves. The truth is, a genuine Zen master does not con female students into having sex with him or break up families (his own as well as others) by having extramarital sex with married women. Nor does he drink and carouse to such an extent that he becomes a problem to himself and his followers.

Neither, for that matter, does an authentic master spend large sums of his center's money on an extravagant, self-indulgent lifestyle. Zen, as the stories of the masters' lives reveal, has always blossomed most fragrantly in an atmosphere of simplicity and frugality. Chuang-tzu, whose wisdom infuses Zen teaching, affirmed that "simplicity makes for perfect health and vigor." One can imagine Zen Master Dogen, who refused the gift of an honorary robe from the emperor, turning over in his grave at the thought that a roshi given to lavish spending on himself would claim a place in his Dharma lineage.

The transgressions alluded to here have created for American Zen a heavy karma that we must all expiate, a shame we must all share, for we rise and fall as one body. Truly, this is a time for collective reflection and repentance. It is particularly distressing to see some of Zen's contemporary exemplars brought low by such difficulties. Yet each of us needs to take personal responsibility for his or her actions.

The repercussions of these unhappy events have been felt in many Zen communities. Those with an immature practice may feel disillusioned and betrayed and may want to quit Zen. Such persons need to reflect that they have not been let down by Zen, only by would-be exemplars unable or unwilling to uphold Zen's most fundamental teachings. Isn't it clear that we need to reaffirm by our actions the ethical values of Buddhism, with their emphasis on proper human conduct? For too long have Zennists (or would-be Zennists) mouthed the dictum that "Zen is above morality," conveniently ignoring the other half of the equation: ". . . but morality is not below Zen." As a step in the right direction we can do no better than to ponder these words of Tung shan, the founder of the Sōtō Zen sect in China (quoted by Thomas Cleary in his book *Timeless Spring*):

> How could it be permissible to . . . gather followers and associates, toil in pursuit of dust for love of fame and profit, *neglect the rules of ethics and destroy proper conduct*? Grasping one lifetime of ease becomes myriad aeons of pain; if you develop like this, you are calling yourselves Buddhists in vain. [emphasis added]

Beginning some twenty-five hundred years ago, the waters of Zen have washed away the grime of ignorance and despair of millions of people in India, China, Korea, Japan, Vietnam, and more recently the West. Sometimes these currents have flowed swiftly, sometimes they have meandered. For thirty years, starting in 1950, they gushed at flood tide in America. Today that tide has receded. But as the tensions of fear, frustration, and anxiety in our Western society continue to mount, so will the calming waters of Zen rise again to high tide. The more our inborn freedom and creativity, the wellsprings of our spiritual life, are smothered by the material comforts generated by technology, the more our physical well-being is threatened by ecological disasters, by the gap between wealth in some countries and poverty in others, and by the ever-present prospect of nuclear doom, the greater will be the appeal of Zen. For in an ultimate sense, Zen will cease to attract only when human beings no longer seek release from their sufferings and when every man, woman, and child has stopped asking the fundamental questions that first surfaced with the dawn of human consciousness: To what end was I born? Why must I die? What is my relation to my fellow creatures?—in short, when human beings no longer need to know who and what they really are.

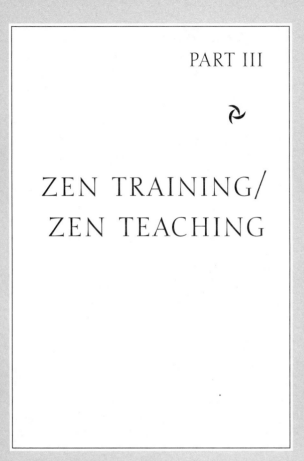

PART III

ZEN TRAINING/
ZEN TEACHING

# Dokusan:
# A Private Encounter
# with the Roshi
## (1986)

## DOKUSAN: ITS HISTORY AND CHARACTER

The private encounter with the roshi (dokusan) is one of the three pillars on which Zen training rests, the other two being zazen and the roshi's commentary (teisho). No English word conveys the precise meaning and spirit of *dokusan* (literally, "going alone"), only because no such mode of spiritual training has existed in our culture until recent times, but the words *encounter* and *confrontation* perhaps come closest. The private encounter is not an "interview" in which a would-be student answers personal questions, explains why he or she wants to practice Zen, and perhaps asks a variety of questions unrelated to practice. Nor is it a simple, friendly meeting. Neither does it involve a discussion of Buddhist doctrine in the manner of the classroom. Still less is it a counseling session during which a student seeks advice on matters of personal relationship. Depending on the student's aspiration and level of spiritual development, dokusan may be a confrontation, a deep, liberating encounter, or a simple matter of practical, individual instruction. In all cases it is, in Zen jargon, an intimate, "eyeball-to-eyeball" moment in which the roshi can probe the student's understanding and realization, if any, and give pointers for future practice. With a more advanced student it is a "testing" in which the roshi seeks to evoke a demonstration of spiritual understanding, not unlike the insertion of an irritant into an oyster to cause it to produce a pearl.

Such individual instruction is a teaching method of Buddhism said to go back to the time of the Buddha, when monks assembled in caves during the three-month rainy season for intensive training. Later in China a more open form of encounter between teacher and students developed. In Japan, and in Korea, too, the Zen masters continued and further refined this new and vigorous dimension in which dokusan became less a matter of didactic instruction and more a probing, challenging, and testing. It is this style that is most common in Zen centers in the West today with modifications that reflect our cultural and psychological characteristics. Before discussing these inner aspects, let me describe some of the outer, formal procedures that have been adopted in our centers in the United States and abroad.

Upon entering the roshi's room, the student, with hands palm to palm, first makes a standing bow and then proceeds to a mat in front of the roshi, where, as a sign of respect and humility, he or she prostrates once. Although prostration is traditional among Asians, I do not insist upon it in our centers. Yet I know that eventually most students, even those in whom such a gesture raises the hackles of resistance at first, do come to see its value as a "horizontalizing of the mast of ego" and perform it spontaneously and willingly.

Dokusan is announced in the zendo with a clanging of the roshi's handbell. Those who wish to go before him—and this is optional—quickly leave their seats in the zendo to get a place in the waiting line. They proceed to mats lined up before a small bell suspended from a wooden frame. The first person to reach the head of the line goes into the roshi's room without striking the bell. When the roshi rings his handbell, signaling an end to the first person's encounter, the student at the head of the line strikes the bell in front of him or her twice with a padded wooden mallet and then enters the roshi's chamber. The whole line then moves up one place. When the dozen or so sitters lined up have seen the roshi, the monitors in the zendo signal the next group to line up. And so on until all who wish private instruction have had it.

These procedures are more than ceremonial. Besides preserving a sense of order, they aid the roshi in determining the mind-state of the student. Has the student hit the bell firmly or with a glancing blow? Is the striking hasty or sluggish? Has the bell been struck too loudly or too softly, or is one strike noisier than the other? In short, *how* the bell is struck tells the roshi, who can hear the sound in his room, whether the student is a beginner or a more advanced student and what the condition of his or her mind is.

How long does an individual's meeting with the roshi take? It varies. Sometimes it may be only a minute or two, at other times as long as fifteen minutes or half an hour. The length is determined not by any arbitrary time limit but by the needs of the student. Much depends, too, on whether the meeting with the roshi is the student's first, which is usually lengthy, or whether the student is working on a first koan or is investigating subsequent koans. Since the number of participants at a seven-day sesshin is limited to about fifty-five, and since most of them want to avail themselves of every opportunity for private instruction, the roshi cannot, in fairness, entertain questions extraneous or irrelevant to a student's practice without penalizing other participants having pressing practical questions, who may thereby be prevented from going. Too, should the roshi become lax, some will take advantage of the opportunity to bring up personal matters (which are more appropriate for special counseling periods), while others will raise theoretical questions, perhaps like "What is the difference between such and such sutras?" or "How do the Sōtō and Rinzai sects differ?" They have drifted from the Great Matter at hand.

THE TEACHER-DISCIPLE RELATIONSHIP IN ZEN

While everyone is free to practice zazen and listen to the roshi's commentary, the essential nature of dokusan is the forming of a karmic bond between the roshi and a student, the significance of which is deep in Buddhism. So the personal encounter is not a frivolous matter, something to be taken lightly. Since what passes between the roshi and the student concerns matters of a deep and ultimate nature, only the truth must be spoken between them. For these reasons, only one who has become a personal student of the roshi (and later perhaps a disciple) may have private instruction with him. And because the relationship is karmic, it implies that the student will not lightly seek another teacher.

Ideally, training in Zen involves a master and his disciple, a bond much deeper than that between a teacher and a student. Strictly speaking, a student is associated with a teacher, a disciple with a master. In the ideal teacher-student relationship the student respects the teacher as the possessor of a certain body of knowledge or of a skill he would like to acquire, while the teacher values the student for his eagerness and his ability to absorb the knowledge he is trying to impart to him. Their relationship may be impersonal and limited; what sustains it is their common interest in this study. The master-disciple relationship, on the other hand, is personal and deep because it is grounded in a karmic affinity. What moves the disciple in the direction of the master is not the latter's knowledge but his compassion and enlightened wisdom plus his character and warm personality, the result of long discipline and training. The disciple senses that it is through these qualities that he or she will be able to develop fully and eventually come to deep awakening. At its highest level the relationship between a master and a disciple is even deeper than that between a parent and a child. In this bond the roshi assumes responsibility for the disciple's spiritual development, while the disciple undertakes responsibility for the roshi's economic and general well-being.

The roshi *gives* private instruction, the student *receives* it, but the latter gets nothing he or she did not already have. The disciple cannot boast of increased knowledge as a result of contact with the roshi, for nothing at all has been gained. Rather, much has been lost—chesty opinions, sticky notions of how things should or should not be, rash judgments, evaluations, deluded ideas, preconceptions—in short, all manner of mental hindrances. In general, then, Zen training can be described as an emptying or cleansing process in which if one's aspiration is high, faith strong, and determination and exertion persistent, one can no more miss awakening than miss the ground with a stamp of the foot, as a master of old put it. It is in the private encounter, however, that this whole process is intensified and speeded up, especially during sesshin (literally, "unifying the mind")—the seven-day seclusion.

The direction a student's meeting with the roshi takes depends primarily on the student's aspiration. Does he or she want to train in Zen to eradicate mental confusion and frustrations and the bodily pains that often spring from them? Is his or her interest in Zen philosophical or literary? Is the motivation to cultivate samadhi power, perhaps, for the practice of a martial art? All those worthwhile objectives can be accomplished through zazen properly practiced. From the standpoint of Zen Buddhism, however, these aspirations are, as yet, immature. Only when one aspires to enlightenment itself and yearns to help all beings be free of suffering has the aspiration become truly spiritual.

At a new student's first appearance before me I question carefully about aspiration. If it is to awaken, does the person have the conviction that he or she can do it? Do they have a determination to do so? Are they willing to dedicate themselves to achieving it? If the answer to each of these questions seems clear and positive enough, then I assign a koan, one with which I feel the person has an affinity. It would be a great unkindness, however, for a roshi to assign a koan simply because the student has answered these questions in the affirmative. As preparation for this important step, a student should first do breath practices: several stages of counting the breath and then of following, or experiencing, it. The aim of these practices is to help the student calm and discipline an impatient mind, hone concentration, and essentially learn to sit deeply and quietly, with stability and equilibrium. In short, these simple but effective practices teach the student how to loosen the hold of unruly thoughts and to acquire what in Zen is called a seat, the ability to "sit"—i.e., deal calmly—with all the vicissitudes of life. Until one reaches this point, it is usually futile to try to grapple with a koan. If koan practice is attempted without this preparation, the student can quickly become frustrated or bored and give up on the koan and often on Zen itself. And keep in mind these are not negligible or simply preparatory exercises. Shakyamuni Buddha himself, it is said, came to his deep enlightenment while following the breath.

## DOKUSAN IN THE CONTEXT OF ZEN TRAINING

Of the three facets of Zen training already mentioned, namely zazen meditation, the roshi's commentary, and the private encounter, this last offers the greatest opportunity for personal growth and spiritual awakening; that in fact is why it is held three times a day during the seven-day seclusion while the commentary is given only once daily. Although the three are not unrelated, they have different functions and purposes. In zazen, the practice of looking into one's mind, the student is on her or his own, seeking to penetrate beyond all thoughts. Facing a wall or divider, symbolic of our stubborn attachment to ego, neither the roshi nor anyone else can substitute here for the student's own efforts. In this solitary, silent voyage into the vast hidden world of mind, all of one's inner resources must be brought to bear by oneself on oneself. This process I have previously described as "a lonely trek through winding canyons of shame and fear, across deserts of ecstatic visions and tormenting phantasms, around volcanoes of oozing ego, and through jungles of folly and delusion in a ceaseless struggle to gain that oneness and emptiness of body and mind that ultimately lead to the lightning-and-thunder discovery that the universe and oneself are not remote and apart but an intimate, palpitating whole."

In the commentary, the roshi takes center stage for a solo performance. His talk of approximately an hour facing the *butsudan*, "place of the buddhas," if truly Zen-like, is less a sermon on Buddhist doctrine or a lecture on the meaning of the koan or a philosophical discourse on the nature of ultimate reality than a vivid, straight-from-the-gut *demonstration* of Reality itself. Charged with all the energy of his liberated mind, it inspires, instructs, and points the way to future effort. In the private encounter the student comes onstage in a contrapuntal duet with the roshi. Often dreaded by the beginner yet eagerly sought by advanced students, dokusan is the long-awaited confrontation with the roshi, a time to shine or simply to make oneself like a sponge, soaking up the truth the roshi is thrusting forth. The juxtaposition of postures suggests confrontation— though in the mild sense of the word. For while they face each other with no more than two feet separating them, their relationship is not adversarial. The roshi usually sits in the lotus posture on a round cushion placed on a square mat, while the student kneels on a mat, perhaps with one or two cushions between his buttocks and heels, in a comfortable posture. Zen rejects asceticism, and apart from encouraging the student to keep a straight back, the roshi does not insist on a prescribed position that may turn out to be painful for the student. Yet an erect posture is not without significance. With the back straight and the body-mind's center of gravity resting in the region two inches below the navel (the *tanden*), the student's mind is freed of attachment to random thoughts. The student can then more easily and quickly respond with his or her total being and not simply from the head to the roshi's guidance.

More specifically, this one-to-one meeting provides the newcomer with the chance to clear up doubts and frustrations and obtain teaching uniquely relevant to the particular physical, mental, or spiritual problems being experienced or explored. The intimate yet formal structure of this personal encounter, the fact that a number of students are lined up to see the roshi, precludes long-winded discussion; at the same time the roshi encourages uninhibited honesty. Any question may be asked that concerns the student deeply and is connected with his or her practice, but small talk and social pleasantries are usually excluded. The roshi likewise is frank and speaks always to the point. The focus is on the quest for, and realization of, Truth!

A Zen student in training is constantly being tested, but in this one-to-one encounter the roshi utilizes specific modes of testing, all of which have different purposes. One kind, for example, involves a student who insists that he or she has had an awakening and asks to be tested. "I've had an enlightenment experience. Please test me," such a one demands of the roshi. Although such an assertion already has a "smell" to it, it cannot safely be ignored. One who has had a valid awakening, even if shallow, doesn't say, "I am enlightened." Nor is enlightenment an experience to be grasped among other experiences; it is the ground of *all* experiences. Despite the student's attitude, the roshi will usually comply with the request; otherwise the student may believe that Realization has occurred when it has not. Or if something has, indeed, happened, then it can be clarified, its limits tested, its depth defined.

## THE TEACHER AS SPIRITUAL MIDWIFE IN DOKUSAN

If it is common to believe mistakenly that one is enlightened, it can also happen that one has an enlightenment experience yet is unaware of it. That is why Dogen could say, "Do not think you will necessarily be aware of your own enlightenment." This is because there may be understanding on a subconscious level that has not yet found its way into consciousness. So this is another reason why testing is vital.

The testing questions a roshi uses to establish whether a student has had a genuine awakening are traditional, and there can be quite a few of them. A faltering, uncertain reply to any one of the questions or even a simple "I think" can vitiate an entire answer. To be acceptable, the student's response must be spontaneous, sure, and radiate understanding from the eyes and body as well as from the mouth.

Sometimes a student who fails to give satisfactory responses to these questions will protest, "You're asking me Zen questions and I don't know enough about Zen to answer them. But I know I've become enlightened."

162

With such a student I will say, "All right, tell me what happened." He or she may reply, "I felt as though everything disappeared and I was the only one in the universe." Such a statement can be persuasive if it carries conviction and is accompanied by telltale signs previously mentioned, but only testing can verify it. When asked, "Who is it that knows you are the only one?" few can meaningfully respond. Where there is a deep penetration into truth, most people experience tears of joy, and that circumstance, if not simply an emotional reaction, may eliminate the need for testing. Yet a student can easily be deceived. Blissful states, hallucinations, oceanic feelings of oneness, trances, or the sudden cessation of thought, all of which can induce tears of elation and gratitude, especially in a person with a strong emotional nature, can easily be confused with genuine enlightenment. Testing is vital for another reason: to determine the depth and clarity of the awakening—if indeed there has been one. This calls for a different set of questions. If after more thorough questioning I feel that a student has not had even a "tip-of-the-tongue taste" of enlightenment, I honestly tell them so, for nothing can be more detrimental to one's personality than to believe one has had a valid enlightenment when in fact it is merely an insight, valuable though this latter may be on a psychological level.

The feeling or awareness that "I am the only one" appears in the accounts of many Zen students, both those who mistakenly believe they have become enlightened and those who have actually had an insight into truth, perhaps because it is attributed to the Buddha himself. Tradition tells us that when he was born, he took seven steps and uttered, "Throughout heaven and earth I alone am the honored One." This is not the place to discuss the metaphysical implications of this paradoxical remark.

Instead let us see how a great Zen master dealt with a monk who sought to bait him with this "one." Approaching the redoubtable Joshu, the monk asked, "If all the myriad things in the universe return to the One, where does the One return to?" Very likely the questioner was referring to a passage in the Gandavyuha sutra that says, "All things of the three realms are reduced to the One Mind." The monk's question is like asking, "If everything returns to God, where does God return to?" or "What was God doing before he created the world?" When St. Augustine was asked this last, he quipped, "Creating a hell for a person who asked the question!" That was clever, but had Augustine said it in dokusan, he would instantly have been rung out.

To understand why, one needs to savor Joshu's response: "When I was in Sei Province, I had one hempen shirt made weighing seven pounds." What a seemingly irrelevant reply! But Joshu is actually right on target. Obviously the monk is trying to twist the lion's tail, to get Joshu to say something like "Emptiness" or "Nothingness," but the master avoids the trap and gives the monk a faultless demonstration of the truth of Zen.

Let us probe the question and the reply. Philosophically the question is unanswerable, of course, as Joshu and the monk both know. By responding as he does, the master not only avoids a meaningless abstraction but brings the questioner down to earth, to the concrete and the real, where Zen operates. What could be more real than this hempen shirt weighing seven pounds that can be touched, worn, and experienced through direct contact? Notice, too, how Joshu equates oneness with the seven-pound shirt. "All myriad things" are in fact this one, this shirt: one equals seven, seven equals one, one equals all. Try to elaborate Oneness, though (as I am doing right now), and you fall into concepts and abstractions. But fondle the shirt, wear it—become "one" with it—and you know it directly, concretely, intimately. Ultimate truth can be grasped only through direct experience, not by abstract thought.

This fact is dramatically illustrated in a well-known koan in the *Mumonkan*, case 28, "Ryutan Blows Out a Candle." The flash that touched off a conflagration in the monk's still-deluded mind was, appropriately enough, the master's lighting a candle and then suddenly blowing it out. This dramatic climax had been preceded by a long discussion on the Diamond sutra between Lung-tan (Ryutan in Japanese), the master, and Te-shan, a scholar-monk. We can only speculate what they talked about, for the koan doesn't say; but since Te-shan was considered an authority on this scripture, lecturing widely on it, we can presume he questioned the master about it at great length and received the sort of responses that left him suspended in midair. When Lung-tan finally said, "It is getting late, you had better leave," Te-shan's mind was emptied of all the concepts he had been harboring. Peering out, he said, "It's dark outside." Thereupon the master lit a candle and handed it to him. As he went to take it, Lung-tan suddenly blew it out. With that, Te-shan was enlightened.

What prompted the master to blow out the candle? Was it the sudden eruption into his conscious mind of Lao-tzu's observation "When darkness is at its darkest that is the beginning of all light"? Or did he intuitively sense that Te-shan was in a state of absorption to the point of self-forgetfulness and needed only a jolt to precipitate his mind into Self-awareness? Literally it was a "shot in the dark" that struck home. Te-shan was clearly ready. Yet, without the presence of the teacher, Lung-tan, his "day" might not have come. So, you see, in Zen, the meeting with the Teacher can be of paramount importance.

# Pilgrimage as Training and Practice
## (1983)

*This essay is excerpted from an article originally published in* Zen Bow, *the newsletter of the Zen Center of Rochester, New York. It was the final installment of a detailed account of a pilgrimage to China made in 1981 by a number of senior Zen students and myself.*

Pilgrimages have been part of the formal practice of Buddhism from the time of the historical Buddha until the present. Indeed, it is said that the Buddha, in a discussion with one of his closest attendants, Ananda, spoke about the spiritual significance of pilgrimage just before his (the Buddha's) entrance into nirvana at the time of his death. At that time he said that four places would hold special power for those on pilgrimage. These sites were (1) the place of his birth (Lumbini), (2) the place of his supreme enlightenment (Bodh Gaya), (3) the site of his first teaching of the Dharma (Sarnath), and (4) the place of his final death (Kusinagara). These holy places in India have been the destinations of numberless pilgrims over the centuries.

China is where a zazen-based Buddhism, brought by the wall-gazing patriarch, Bodhidharma, took root as Ch'an, or Zen. The comments and evaluations that follow are the result of my observations and conversations on a pilgrimage to Zen's birthplace, China. They also include reflections from my reading of accounts by Western journalists who have recently visited China, and my research into Holmes Welch's authoritative books, *The Buddhist Revival in China* and *Buddhism Under Mao*, as well as Arthur Wright's *Buddhism in Chinese History*.

WHAT IS THE SIGNIFICANCE OF A PILGRIMAGE?

Although it has been described as a devotional trip to some holy place for the purpose of purifying and sanctifying oneself, a pilgrimage implies a certain mind-state. One must bring to it a measure of grace—that is, an eager heart and, most importantly, a felt need to discover and reaffirm one's spiritual roots.

In the same way that many devout Christians and Jews yearn to travel to Jerusalem to soak up the rich lore of the holy places out of which their religion grew, and Moslems yearn to make at least one pilgrimage to Mecca in their lifetime, we, too, can be restored and inspired by the rejuvenating experience of returning to the living roots of our Buddhist heritage. These roots, of course, are to be found in many countries of the East: foremostly in India, where the Buddha was burned, experienced supreme enlightenment, and where he taught, but also in China, Tibet, Japan, Korea, and Vietnam, as well as Burma, Thailand, and Sri Lanka. Though seemingly outward bound, a pilgrimage is really an interior journey.

One of the most intimate of all families is Buddha's, a royal family without beginning or end. Entrance to it is gained not through nobility of birth, money, or position, but through commitment and intense endeavor. The living symbols of this family and the most vivid manifestation of its ideals and spiritual goals are Buddha figures. Among other things, they reveal to us our own most deeply human possibilities for wisdom, compassion, and wholeness. When we first encounter such figures in a Buddhist temple or center in the West, with their strangely calm features and exotic dress, they can strike us as foreign, remote, and utterly inaccessible. Even though we try, we might not be able to identify with them. At best they seem like solemn personifications of vaguely felt superbeings; at worst, like tribal idols. Is prostration before them an act of propitiation or supplication? we ask ourselves. When does the gratitude we are supposed to feel from such devotions emerge? we wonder.

A pilgrimage can profoundly change all that. In venerating ancient Buddhas and Bodhisattvas in temples, caves, and grottoes, their original homes, in a timeless atmosphere of reverence and awe, prostration before them becomes spontaneous. And because in this unpremeditated, unself-conscious act of total absorption our Buddha-nature shines brightly, doubts lose their grip and faith is restored. Quiet joy and gratitude flow forth. At least that is what many in our group reported. The value of venerating Buddhas was pointedly expressed by Zen Master Dogen in his greatest work, the *Shobogenzo:* "There has never been anyone who has realized Buddhahood without having venerated at least one Buddha, for therein lies the origin of Buddhahood."

Some followers of the Buddha's Way dislike labeling themselves "Buddhist" or identifying with Buddhist iconography. "Isn't our essential nature beyond all names and forms?" they ask. Yes and no. "The Dharma, without form, informs all forms." What is objectionable is not name and form but *clinging* to names or forms. Buddha, Shakyamuni, Amitabha, Bodhisattva, Kuan yin, Kannon, Mahayana, Theravada, Dharma, karma, nienfo, nembutsu, kung-an koan, zazen, dokusan—these are all names, descriptions of our essential nature (also a name) in action. Their content and spirit is peculiarly Buddhist.

Devotions have many aspects. One cannot make offerings or prostrations to a chemical formula, worship a hypothesis, commune with a process, or hold love or fellowship with a law, as someone put it. We humans have a deep need to relate to concrete, tangible prototypes of the highest states of wisdom, virtue, and compassion attained by humanity. Shakyamuni Buddha was one such model of perfection, and Kannon (Kuan yin), the epitome of love and compassion, another. It can therefore be meaningful and deeply satisfying to make obeisance before such figures, with whom we thereby establish a karmic rapport that serves as a powerful impetus to practice.

There are other rewards. In paying our respects at Buddhist sites we are requiting the immense debt of gratitude each of us owes the Chinese masters and ancestors, even as we are forging another link with the past, the better to extend the chain of Buddhism into the future. In China today, the repressions of the Maoist era are still felt, and so many still accept the dogma that religion is an otherworldly superstition at odds with science and modern progress. So, for a group of twenty-two Western Buddhists to affirm the worth of Buddhism by making offerings before Buddhist works of piety was bound, I think, to give aid and comfort to our Chinese coreligionists, who are still a beleaguered minority, though perhaps less so today than previously. Also not to be overlooked is the unique impression we made on the crowds of people who watched—awestruck—as we performed these devotions.

On a less personal level, we discovered even on our limited pilgrimage that China is a cornucopia of Buddhist sculptures, paintings, shrines, and holy mountain sites. In number, scale, and magnificence the artifacts that remain even after the despoliations of the Cultural Revolution are mind-boggling. We tend to forget that Buddhism gripped the hearts and minds of a large segment of China's population for almost two thousand years— from B.C.E. 68 until 1950—and that it has been a powerful stimulus to Chinese spiritual and aesthetic creativity.

For Zen Buddhists, a pilgrimage to China can have tremendous significance. After all, that unique flowering of Buddhism we call Zen was nurtured in the soil of China, where it developed its distinctive form and flavor. The most widely used books of koans revolve around the lives of the Chinese Zen masters. And in China, Bodhidharma, the First Patriarch of Zen, "faced the wall" for nine years. To walk, literally, in the footsteps of these spiritual greats, to do zazen and chant in their temples, to ascend the mountain leading to Bodhidharma's cave and express gratitude for his heroic labors on our behalf—this is to bring the whole pantheon of Buddhist heroes stunningly alive.

WHAT HAPPENED TO BUDDHISM DURING THE MAO ERA, AND WHAT IS HAPPENING TO IT TODAY?

Under Mao, as we know, Buddhism was persecuted and suppressed. Land holdings of the temples and monasteries were confiscated, Buddhist schools and publishing houses shut down, and scriptures and other Buddhist books burned. Monks and nuns were expelled from temples and monasteries, laicized, and forced to labor on farms in remote agricultural districts. During the Cultural Revolution (1966–76), when Mao's Red Guards ravaged and terrorized the country, Buddhist temples, images, shrines, and monuments were openly desecrated and destroyed. Concomitantly the government instilled the belief in the people that Buddhism was a feudalistic anachronism that oppressed the masses and kept them in a state of ignorance and superstition.

Also during Mao's rule, according to Arthur Wright, the nationwide organizations of Chinese Buddhists, originally set up for the propagation and defense of the faith, became part of the complex network of organizations through which the government controlled the people of China. The great monuments of Buddhism were systematically restored, not as centers of worship but as shrines to the "cultural creativity of the Chinese people under the feudal empires of the past."

Harder to assess is the state of Buddhism in China today. In spite of Mao's having tossed it onto the trash heap of China's body politic, Buddhism has survived. The present Beijing government acknowledges that a large number of Buddhist believers remain, more than thirty years after the Communists' rise to power, and that its avowed goal of "scientific atheism" cannot be achieved by "compulsory or administrative measure."

The Communist authorities have allowed many Buddhist temples and more than one hundred Christian churches to reopen and be repaired with state funds, according to reports by Western newsmen. A lengthy article in The Denver Post, dated November 1980, on the state of religion in China describes a memorial service the writer witnessed at Hua Chen Temple, on Jiu Hua Mountain, conducted by eight monks. A decade ago, the writer says, such religious ceremonies, rooted deep in China's two thousand years of Buddhist belief, would have brought dozens of screaming Red Guards charging into the temple to end what the Maoists regarded as feudal, superstitious practices. Last year, he continues, 150,000 pilgrims came to Jiu Hua Mountain once the temples and monasteries had been reopened and repaired with state funds. This year, he says, the number of pilgrims is certain to be more than 750,000, perhaps almost a million.

The services in the temples on the mountain include morning and evening prayers, scripture readings, and memorial services for the dead. The chairman of the Jiu Hua Buddhist Association, which administers the temples, is quoted as saying that some of the pilgrims are Chinese from Hong Kong and Southeast Asia, but that most are now from China itself. "Everyone is now at ease about religious beliefs and coming to pray, and many are coming because they have not been able to do so for so long," he added.

In spite of these reports, our conversations with abbots and our observations of the functioning of their temples persuaded us that all is not gold that glitters. We felt that the abbots are not masters in their own houses. At several temples and monasteries they freely admitted they are controlled by the government, sometimes through the mediation of the Chinese Buddhist Association, sometimes through the Cultural Relics Preservation Bureau. We were also told that while China's constitution grants citizens the freedom to *believe* in religion, religious beliefs cannot be propagated nor religious activities carried on outside the premises of religious institutions, a circumstance confirmed by Holmes Welch. Several famous temples we visited that possess outstanding Buddhist figures and relics are nothing more than museums, with no religious services or Buddhist training available.

What we are witnessing in China today may or may not be the beginning of a religious revival. If indeed it is a revival, the crucial question is, what kind? One with tight restrictions on the activities of monks, nuns, and Buddhist laymen, denying them real power, or a spontaneous outbreak of religious feelings that reflects the yearnings of the Chinese for spiritual fulfillment and at the same time represents a rejection of Marxist material values? Nobody is quite sure.

A MAJOR TASK FOR BUDDHISM IN THE WEST

A major task for Buddhism in the West, it seems to me, is to ally itself with religious and other concerned organizations to forestall the potential catastrophes facing the human race: nuclear holocaust, irreversible pollution of the world's environment, and the continuing large-scale destruction of the nonrenewable resources. We also need to lend our physical and moral support to those who are fighting hunger, poverty, and oppression everywhere in the world. In our own country we must help preserve our Constitution and protect our pluralistic way of life. This means working with similar-minded groups in defending the civil rights of all Americans. We must utilize the ballot, letters to congressmen, and other means to preserve our religious liberties and the constitutionally decreed separation of church and state. With the example before us of the horrors of the Cultural Revolution and the trampling on human rights and dignity by military dictatorships and extremist regimes in numerous other countries, it behooves us in the West to be vigilant to protect our liberties from the encroachments of elements on either the extreme right—the greatest danger in the United States—or extreme left.

# The Enlightened One

## (1996)

In what ways is an enlightened person different from one who isn't? This is a question that people contemplating Zen training often ask.

One who has thoroughly mastered Zen is totally involved in whatever he or she does. Such a one is, in the words of Zen Master Dogen, "not bound nor does he bind," a statement often misunderstood. This doesn't mean that an enlightened person simply acts as he or she pleases, indifferent to the consequences of those actions on others. Nor does he or she deliberately flout conventional laws in the name of freedom. Rather by identifying with them completely, such a person transcends them and thus is no longer obstructed by them.

Although they may ignore conventionality, the awakened do not flaunt their behavior. Neither do they put people into a bind by imposing shoulds and oughts on them. Their lives are simple and unpretentious. They are full of gratitude and compassion.

Those truly enlightened do not boast of their enlightenment. Just as a truly generous person doesn't say, "I'm a generous guy, you know," so one who has integrated into life what she or he has realized in awakening will not wear enlightenment as a badge and shield. The fully awakened are modest and self-effacing. While they do not hide their light under a bushel basket, as the saying goes, at the same time they are not pushy or aggressively self-assertive. They know that in truth there's nowhere to go; they are there already.

Those who are fully awakened do not hate either themselves or others since they know that the all-embracing, nothing-lacking Essential Nature is common to all; thus they see others as fundamentally no different from themselves.

The truly awakened are not argumentative, for they know that all statements are only half-truths, a looking from one side at that which has infinite dimensions. And because the enlightened know that this present moment embraces all time and space, they do not regret the past, do not hope in the future, and are not dissatisfied with the present.

Looking into a face, the truly enlightened can readily see into the heart and mind. Though they are sensitive to the pain and sufferings of existence, they are not depressed by them, for they know that beneath the violence there is beauty and harmony, just as they know that there are many ways to overcome suffering. And so, wherever they are, they simply, naturally bring help.

The enlightened know the true nature of existence, that everything is impermanent, never the same from one moment to the next, that things are constantly arising and disappearing according to causes and conditions.

The fully awakened know that life and death are like the waves of the ocean, waxing and waning, and that underlying all phenomenal existence is That Which Never Dies because it was never born. Thus they have no anxiety about death, their own or others. They know that all are reborn according to the workings of karma.

What is it really like to be enlightened? There's one certain way to find out: wake up yourself!

# Discipline and Naturalness

## (1973)

Many people wonder about the benefits of a disciplined life of doing zazen, of planning for certain regular activities. Many people look upon this kind of thing as unnatural. It seems to be taking away from the enjoyment of life. To live a disciplined life seems perhaps egotistical. "Well, I should do that. I shouldn't stay up beyond such an hour because I find it hard to get up in the morning. I shouldn't go out with these people because they love to talk," and so on. Or: "I shouldn't go out and do such and such, it may lead to such and such a result." What fun in life is there then? To practice Zen seriously seems to make for a joyless, antisocial life. Life isn't celebrated with love, drink, and laughter. Besides, zazen seems to have an ego trip of its own— an uncomfortable, painful damming up of the joy of life instead of its bursting forth in fullness. This sounds terribly unnatural.

The trouble is that most of us today lead such unnatural lives to start with that we don't know any longer what naturalness really is. This seems to be true of our culture as a whole. If we take natural to mean spontaneous, free-flowing, without compulsiveness, without regret or remorse, then we begin to see this. What is it like not to be driven by the ambition, perhaps, to do certain things or to achieve certain goals. "I must make so much money" or "I must get such and such a degree." Most people *are* driven. Yet, it is quite true that every should, ought, and must is a limitation on our inborn freedom.

At the same time, we cannot say that "if I give up these various things, then certain mind-states will naturally follow," because this is looking at things dualistically. It also implies that laxness might somehow be of benefit on the Path. It is not. As the Buddha told a musician who had begun to sit in meditation: "Just as with your instrument, the strings of your patience must be neither too tight nor too loose. Then the music will come." So, all we can say really is that in order to get rid of many bad habits, many wrong ways of looking at things and ourselves, of squandering our precious energies, there is a certain basic way we need to live—neither too tight nor too loose. This may sound like a must or a should and, in a sense, it is. In the beginning there's no way to get around this because we've already gone so far away from our True-nature, from living spontaneously, creatively, and flowingly. We've gotten so far away that it takes an effort to get rid of the accumulated habits, the unnatural patterns of thought and behavior. To mobilize or utilize our natural creative force requires some strain in the beginning, to get beyond the strain. This is what practice and discipline mean.

Once our practice has matured, things change. There is a natural ease to everything. At an earlier stage, though, we have this must or this should. The judgments, the evaluations of ourselves and others, will continue to come, even though we know they are splitting us apart from people and things. You can't make a judgment without stepping back and looking, holding the thing at arm's length and deciding it's "this" or deciding it's "that." Sometimes it's easy to rationalize an unwillingness to exert oneself by saying, "It's an ego trip," or something similar. Sometimes it's not a rationalization but a confusion, a genuine, honest confusion that exists.

Especially when sitting, for example, we find it painful in the beginning, and one wonders, "What's natural about all this pain?" And yet, when one has learned how to sit properly, the back erect, with our energies centered in the hara, our whole relation to the world, to reality, is entirely different. This is exactly what the so-called lotus posture of the Buddha is portraying. It is embodying our True-nature: free from strain; compassionate and all-embracing. It has equanimity, with no sense of opposition, and gives off a feeling of centeredness, unity, knowingness. All of these qualities are the qualities of the enlightened mind. Just as in the sutras we get these extravagant phrases trying to portray the unportrayable, so, too, the Buddha figure is trying to reveal to us that which can never be fully revealed, but only hinted at, or partially indicated—the fullness, the essential joy and harmony of our own truly natural Nature.

In the same way, living the kind of life that is in accord with our inner nature paradoxically calls for a greater expenditure of energy in the beginning, at least until we have reestablished our ancient, innate rhythm, equanimity, and unity. It's not easy to do. It can't be accomplished overnight. We must be steadfast and patient. And we must remember that a fundamental law of the universe is that to get energy from our zazen, from our practice, we must first be willing to put energy into our practice. Energy begets energy. No energy exerted is ever lost. Once the body-mind is accustomed to this new, positive habit-pattern, then the energy flows ever more fluidly. Faith deepens, awareness sharpens, conviction strengthens, and our determination becomes a dynamo of inner energy benefiting us and, as Zen Master Dogen makes clear, all others as well.

Here are Dogen's inspiring words on exertion. Let us keep them in mind as we together face what might at first seem like the unnaturalness of the exertions before us:

> The great Way of the Buddha and the Patriarchs involves the highest form of exertion, which goes on unceasingly in cycles from the first dawning of religious truth, through the test of discipline and practice, to enlightenment and nirvana. It is sustained exertion, proceeding without lapse from cycle to cycle. Accordingly it is exertion which is neither self-imposed nor imposed by others, but free and uncoerced. The merit of this exertion upholds me and upholds others. The truth is that the benefits of one's own sustained exertion are shared by all beings in the ten quarters of the world. Others may not be aware of this, and we may not realize it, but it is so. It is through the sustained exertions of the Buddhas and Patriarchs that our own exertions are made possible, that we are able to reach the high road of Truth. In exactly the same way it is through our own

exertions that the exertions of the Buddhas are made possible, that the Buddhas attain the high road of Truth. Thus it is through our exertions that these benefits circulate in cycles to others, and it is due only to this that the Buddhas and Patriarchs come and go, affirming Buddha and negating Buddha, attaining the Buddha-mind and achieving Buddhahood, ceaselessly and without end. This exertion, too, sustains the sun, the moon, and the stars; it sustains the earth and sky, body and mind, object and subject, the four elements, and five compounds.

This sustained exertion is not something which men of the world naturally love or desire, yet it is the last refuge of all. Only through the exertions of all Buddhas in the past, present, and future do the Buddhas of past, present, and future become a reality.*

Exertion, then, is the nature of reality itself. What could possibly be unnatural about it? In the end it is as impossible to undermine or second-guess the wisdom of a disciplined life as it is to avoid the joy we discover in the experience of its merits.

*Quoted in William de Bary, *The Buddhist Tradition* (Modern Library, 1969).

# Impatience in Practice
## (1974)

Some of you may know the story of the Zen master who was asked by a student how long it would take him to get enlightened. The master said, "About fifteen years."
The student said, "What! Fifteen years?"
"Well, it might take twenty-five years in your case."
"It would take twenty-five years in my case!"
"On second thought, it would probably take fifty years."
How vividly this illustrates a fundamental point. Pains and pressures often come up because of an overeagerness in practice. Not an overeagerness for the Dharma, but an overeagerness to get something out of Zen. And get it very quickly. To get it and run, so to say. "If I can only get this kensho business, then I can really settle down and do everything I've always wanted to do. I've got to get this first, because otherwise I'll never be happy. Besides, I'll never have the power, the strength, the insight, to do all the things I would like to do." This is in the back of the mind and is a common ailment at the beginning of one's practice. But basically it springs from the separation between ourselves and this imagined kensho (enlightenment experience). We're postulating kensho outside ourselves. Kensho is a goal, and every goal implies something standing outside ourselves. There's a duality there, a dichotomy. And it is this very duality that causes more tension and a kind of grasping overeagerness.

You remember Dogen says, "There is no beginning to practice or end to enlightenment; there is no beginning to enlightenment or end to practice." It is this steady, rocklike sitting that really triumphs in the end, this ever-deepening of our practice. And this can only come about if we get rid of these impure

179

(errant) notions about kensho, enlightenment, and so on. It is difficult for beginners (and you're a beginner for at least the first three years of your practice) not to develop a self-intentional attitude that becomes an effort, a strain. No matter how often people hear that there's nothing to strive for, everything is already here, nonetheless they feel that without some kind of striving or struggling they're not accomplishing anything. If you're sitting comfortably, that is to say with a feeling of flow going through, a person might think, "Well, this isn't right. If I continue to feel this good, nothing good will come." And before you realize it, there is a certain attitude, what we're calling here a self-intentionality. And the consequences of this kind of thing can be considerable. One develops tensions in the body or one develops headaches. In trying to push too hard, one can develop pains. Lower-back pains often grow out of this kind of thing.

It is important in our practice that we use our energies completely and directly. Many people use a lot of energy, but it's used in the wrong kind of way. It's squandered. So many people thrash around in their zazen rather than directly and completely and single-mindedly applying themselves to their particular practice.

Now, what do we mean by this squandering and thrashing around? Some people thrash around or wallow in negative reactions to their feelings, to the feelings of other people either in relation to themselves or quite apart from themselves. Wallowing in negative thoughts. This is a common tendency; we all have this. Something happens, the ego has been hurt, we thought we didn't have much ego, yet we find that we do. This consumes a great deal of energy, far more energy than just the ordinary, run-of-the-mill, random sort of thought-arisings where there are no resentments, either directed against oneself or toward other people.

Other people use a lot of energy through indecisiveness. They can't make up their mind what they want to do. One master says, "Whatever you do, don't wobble." This doesn't mean that the person who is practiced in Zen may not, in certain matters, find difficulty in deciding. But rather it means not wobbling back and forth. Not vacillating. There may be an unwillingness to face up to the responsibility of making a decision, especially in something that affects one's life in a fundamental way. This consumes considerable energy, but it's not being used directly, it's not being channeled.

But if we do zazen when we get into these ego-driven states, and if we are determined to do zazen, then these states pass, sometimes quickly. It's as if they simply evaporate. Then again, they can take time to pass. Then we must be patient. If we are unable, because of where we are in our practice, to redirect or release such conditions immediately, then at least through zazen a certain calmness does come upon us, and in most cases this feeling will pass. And at least the body-mind, by virtue of being immobilized, is not floundering around, squandering its energies in habitual ways. One could have, of course, lots of thoughts. But if one continues to sit, then these thoughts will go, and one finds oneself, after this kind of a storm, much better able to get into practice.

On the other hand, if we give in to these negative states and just run off, doing all kinds of wild things, then we can be really thrown back, and it might take a long time to get back into one's practice again. In classical Buddhist terms, we can call this backsliding.

Why do fears and anxieties arise even when one is practicing single-mindedly? There can be many reasons, of course. Often people who are concerned about what they are going to do with their lives tell themselves that there is something that they have to do, some kind of goal that they have to realize, some kind of ambition that has to be achieved—ideas that are drilled into us by our parents and our schools. Or else people feel that they don't have a proper place in the world. They feel vulnerable, lacking protection, easily pushed into fearful mind-states. They long for wholeness, they long to get home, and often this is reflected in their dreams. This can become very painful.

First of all we must realize that the postulation of every goal is unreal in the sense that it involves living in the future. There's always a duality; we're always taking the present moment and dividing it, and as a consequence we're not living in the present moment, and of course the future hasn't come yet, so we're sort of in a no-man's-land. This in itself is a great source of anxiety. We must first learn to let go of our tendency to postulate goals and indulge our fantasies in long-range plans. This doesn't mean to stop planning activities that might require planning, such as taking care of children's needs or tasks at work or the requirements of a relationship. We're really talking about long-range ambitions, certain fixed ideals that we have in our mind that we feel *should* be fulfilled, that drive us. If we are able to live in the present moment, we begin to see that these things take care of themselves. One may reach a point, let's say, where one feels one needs more schooling. Then you go out and you do the things that are going to enable you to achieve that. If you're in love and want to get married, then you do what you need to bring that about.

Many times you've heard this quote from Lao-tzu: "To do nothing, yet to leave nothing undone." And this is really saying, "Be fully present. Let things emerge from your awareness and the activity that grows from it, *now*. Don't bet on long-range plans, they're all unrealistic." The Japanese have a saying, "The devil laughs at those who plan for the next year," or something to that effect. While this may sound extreme, at bottom it's all too true.

# Devotion
## (1978)

Let me say something about arousing the mind that yearns for Truth or, as it is called in Zen, "the mind that seeks the Way." Frequently, this comes up in dokusan: How can I arouse my own Bodhi-mind and strengthen my faith?

First of all, to arouse the mind that seeks the Way means to perceive or intuit, however dimly, the possibility, no, the inevitability, of our own enlightenment and Buddhahood. This is the moment when one becomes a genuine follower of the Buddha's Way and comes to long for one's True Home, and to take the first step on the Bodhisattvic path of self-sacrifice and heroic effort. When this takes place, the reciting of the Four Universal Bodhisattva Vows* takes on a fresh meaning, a deep and profound meaning. It's not just a formula repeated from the outside.

Of course, many steps lead to this, a good number of which are outlined in *The Awakening of Faith*, by Ashvaghosha. A good translation of this classic Mahayana text is by Prof. Yoshito S. Hakeda of Columbia University. First there is the all-important step of establishing a karmic connection with Buddhas and Bodhisattvas, those highly developed, enlightened beings—actually flesh-and-blood personages in the time of the Buddha—who were in fact the most developed disciples. The outstanding quality of both a Buddha and a Bodhisattva is an irrepressible desire to help others, especially in opening their

*Four Vows:
  All beings without number, I vow to liberate.
  Endless blind passions, I vow to uproot.
  Dharma gates beyond measure, I vow to penetrate.
  The Great Way of Buddha, I vow to attain.

eyes to the truth of their being, which in essence is no different from that of the universe. It is as natural for them to act in this way as it is for us to drink when thirsty. There is a mutual attraction between Buddhas and ourselves—otherwise the task might seem impossible. We need never despair, for we are assured an ultimate awakening once we put ourselves in their orbit. The problem then is how to evoke their aid.

There are many ways. Of course, reading the teachings of the Buddha and the Patriarchs, and developing a believing heart, is the first step. Also, we may make offerings. This is why we find on the altar flowers, incense, food—all offerings to Buddhas and Bodhisattvas. In this way we create an intimate relationship with them; they're not simply idols or statues, but living realities with the power to bring to consciousness, if we allow them, our Buddha-nature, of which they are the manifestation on a visible plane. In doing these things, and in bowing down out of respect, gratitude, and reverence to Buddhas and Bodhisattvas, we are gradually opening up to their power, to the long-frozen Buddhic forces within ourselves. We can rightly say that Buddhas and Bodhisattvas are our long-lost relatives, not unlike our blood relatives, and in performing rituals and rites we intrinsically and simultaneously create, deepen, and clarify our relationship with them.

So do devotions wholeheartedly, with a pure heart. By devotions, we mean chanting, making bows and prostrations, and presenting offerings. People often, particularly when they come to dokusan, prostrate mechanically. Some do it fast to get it over with so they can get on with the dokusan. They don't realize the true significance of these devotions. They aren't just formalities. They truly enrich and deepen our experience of the present moment. Such devotions have always played an important part in Zen training. In fact, during the great period of the T'ang-era masters we find these same devotions being performed. There's an excellent collection of the brilliant Dharma talks of Huang Po, translated, I believe, by John Blofeld, but interestingly there is hardly a word in the book that speaks about his devotional side. Yet go into any Zen monastery in Japan and complain that the ancient Zen masters *never* prostrated or engaged in devotions and you'll be told the story of how Obaku (Huang Po in Chinese) used to bow down before the Buddha with such zeal, burying his head in the carpet with such force, that he developed a permanent red mark there, which earned him the nickname Great Pearl, a name related to the mark on his forehead.

Too often Zen people fasten onto the iconoclastic aspects of Zen, the freedom to move about in ways people who don't practice Zen think are pretty zany. But remember, behind these and other free-flowing actions are always devotions based on a tremendous respect and reverence for the Buddha. The two go hand in hand. And this applies just as much after even a great enlightenment as before.

The position of gassho, with the hands placed palms together, is another gesture of respect and reverence, and it is also very ego-reducing. Another essential devotion is chanting portions of the sutras, as we do in ceremonies and at sesshin. These are all part of Zen training.

When these devotions are entered into with a pure heart, gradually the mind lets go of habitual obstructions, the disbelief and reservation growing out of ego. A new clarity and purity, a tender quality in the heart, all emerge. And we find that with all the masters, despite all of the vigorous and dramatic demonstrations of liberative technique that they're displaying, underneath there is always, in reality, a tender heart, one open to the sorrows of humanity and all living things. You'll remember that Dogen, when he came back from China after three years of hard work there, was asked what he had brought back to the people of Japan, what was his *omiage*—his gift to them. And he answered simply, "A tender, loving heart."

Dogen was one of the most profound, perhaps *the* most profound, minds of the Japanese Zen tradition. Yet, there it is, shining brightly in his answer: love and devotion.

## PART IV

ॐ

# ON ILLNESS,
# DYING,
# AND DEATH

# Illness, Dying, Caregiving, and Families: A Conversation in West Berlin

## (1985, 1996)

*How to deal with pain and with dying has always been part of Zen because it is so inescapably a part of life. Indeed the Buddha said he taught only one thing: a way beyond suffering. Zen Buddhism is, above all, a practical religion whose aim is simple—to help us live, and die, well. If Zen "works," indeed, if any religion can be said to "work," one test of its efficacy must surely be in the way it helps us face our inevitable dying and death.*

*To be able to look at death and suffering calmly is a step toward achieving a good, that is, conscious death. In facing our impermanence, we come into intimate contact with the Buddha's Four Noble Truths. These are, in essence: Life is suffering. It is so because we continually try to grasp and cling to what changes and cannot be grasped. There is a way beyond suffering. This is the eightfold Path of right view, right thoughts, right speech, right conduct, right livelihood, right effort, right concentration, and right wisdom. Through personal experience of these truths we begin to wake up to the spiritual nature of our existence. Facing our dying, we begin to live well.*

*The following was originally a conversation that I had during a 1985 visit to West Berlin with Sensei Bodhin Kjolhede, Dr. Peter Auhagen, and his wife, Dr. Christine Auhagen. It was transcribed and then revised in 1996 by Drs. Auhagen for this volume. Sensei Bodhin Kjolhede is Abbot of the Rochester Zen Center. Both Peter and Christine Auhagen studied medicine in*

*Germany, England, and Switzerland, where Christine Auhagen trained in internal medicine. She is also a trained psychotherapist and acupuncturist. Peter Auhagen was a surgeon for five years and is trained in traditional Chinese medicine and in Ericksonian therapy. Since 1991 the Auhagens have jointly maintained a private medical practice in Koln, Germany.*

DR. PETER AUHAGEN: Having worked now for about fifteen years both in hospitals and in private practice, taken care of people who are dying (or have died), and gone through the personal loss of my parents and dear friends, I would like to say something about the part played by doctors and nurses in the process of death and dying.

In my office (or private practice) where I see many cancer patients in all phases of their illness, I am confronted with all strata of the process, all the layers of human being: anatomical and physiological changes in the illness, psychological reactions, social aspects of illness, and the scope of individual spiritual achievement.

In the hospital it can be quite different. The first people to have the facts together about the person who is going to die are the nurses and doctors who are medically aware that a fatal illness exists but who might not know the person at all. We know that this person has a fatal illness and that he or she is going to die sooner rather than later. We have the task of answering the person's medical questions.

Patients who come to the hospital, especially the surgical department, are *all* afraid of dying. You can sense that many of them are afraid they will not wake up after their anesthesia. It's a very primal fear. They often ask as a joke, "Will I wake up?"

ROSHI PHILIP KAPLEAU: Regardless of the nature of their illness?

DR. PETER: Regardless of the nature of their illness. Even for an appendix operation anesthesia invokes quite a fear. And of course people who have all kinds of lumps and subconsciously fear it may be cancer, several days after the operation will get up their courage and ask, "Well, what was it?" This moment, if the person does have cancer, is the most difficult part of the work, this shows our relationship to a larger process.

DR. CHRISTINE AUHAGEN: I had a thought that comes from my work: that when some patients are afraid of dying they explicitly say, "I want to die." When you approach them they say, "Let me die. I want to die." I feel it often means "I have no strength."

ROSHI: And would this be true with a relatively minor illness?

DR. CHRISTINE: No, this would be with a fatal illness. Even if they don't intellectually know it, they feel that this is so.

ROSHI: Peter, let me come back to what you say about the "strata" or "layers" as you call them. You speak about "psychological" and "spiritual strata." How do you see them? What takes place there?

DR. PETER: The psychological identity is seen in the overall sum of both general and specific psychological patterns, traits, coping strategies, and the like. The spiritual "layer" (please note, I am not an expert) for me means how people see themselves in relation to the questions "Where do I come from?" "Where do I go after death?" "What belongs to me?" "What will remain after I die?" I do not mean philosophical speculations. I mean direct, tearful combat with the questions above, very often happening without any ideas of "spirituality" in mind.

ROSHI: Have you ever felt, based on what patients have said to either of you, that there's something that could be done to give them faith in living? Do you feel that at that point it is already too late to establish a philosophical or religious belief in the rebirth process that would enable them to die without fear and anxiety?

DR. PETER: Roshi, you are shooting three arrows at a time!

It is very possible to give faith in living; this is an inborn or subconscious knowledge. Here comfort is very important. I imagine this as mental hugging, stroking, humming a lullaby.

If a person is less than about fifty or fifty-five years old, and not yet physically very weak, it is possible to establish a better philosophical or stronger religious belief. Strangely enough, most people have an intuitive belief that death is not an end, but fear and anxiety can interfere with this. The relatives usually have fear and anxiety; somehow these are "contagious."

I have seen people like my father who seemed to have no fear or anxiety about death whatsoever (he had "died" several times during the tortures in the Gulag Archipelago), and others, like two of my close friends, who had difficult fear and anxiety that led them into painful technical treatment end up going through greater physical and psychological suffering in the end.

DR. CHRISTINE: My approach is to find out what the dying person thinks, to see if there's something in that consciousness of life and death that I can support. I try to both comfort and lead. I never hesitate to provide time for the dying person to accept his or her being a part of a greater reality than the mere body—being one with the family, participating in our shared beliefs and psychological insights. Finding out what the dying think is of primal importance.

ROSHI: What have you found?

DR. CHRISTINE: In the case of the death of my best friend just a month ago, I think I did a lot to try to enable her to die without fear and anxiety. We all sensed that she came to terms, in her own way, with departing from two small children, from a husband, and from life. In another person, a patient, I found, too, that there was something I could support. This patient was a young girl twenty years old and she knew she had a fatal illness. But she said, "I could die on the street as well. My situation is not different from my friends' situations, because anyone may face death at any time."

ROSHI: Did you have the feeling that these two people could face death without fear when it actually came?

DR. CHRISTINE: Yes, in the case of my friend I think she did, but I am not sure. In the case of the young girl in the hospital, she has not gone through the process of feeling fatally ill. She's now in the phase of pushing away fear.

DR. PETER: Working in a surgical department I have two types of patients. One type is pretty old—over seventy. I haven't met a single person from this group who would have the strength to establish a new belief. They are too thrown by the idea of a fatal illness at this point. The difficulty we doctors have is that these patients come to the hospital out of surroundings we don't know about. When you talk to them, you learn that they've led a normal life for sixty or seventy years, then all of a sudden they're facing death. Some of them say, "I want you to tell me about the likelihood because there are some things in my life I want to put in order." For such people that is their most prominent wish. Even a younger woman I knew who had a young daughter wanted to have all the necessary treatment so that she could put things in order for her daughter. In the case of younger patients—younger than fifteen—a fatal illness deals them a very severe blow.

Again we have the unfortunate situation of a doctor seeing fatally ill patients for only one month of a whole lifespan. You see them full of fear when they come into hospital, during the operation, and one week after the operation, during which they're not really normal. The operation is a heavy thing for the body. We try to pull them together for this physical assault on the body. A great problem for myself and my colleagues is that we do not know the patient over time. Then the families come, and they want to know the truth. We know that what we say is not all the truth; we give them some facts. You don't know the person, you meet him or her for the first time in a fatal situation, and you talk two or three times. What can you say?

ROSHI: You and I were talking recently about cancer and you said that sometimes when you have a patient who asks you, "Have I got cancer?" you don't give him a categorical answer. Why?

DR. PETER: First I want to find out what "cancer" means to the person. What do they know about it—what causes it, what cures it, how long is one ill with cancer? Breaking the word "cancer" into a whole lot of events, processes, treatment, and coping strategies is of vital importance for me. The word is a focus of fear, anxiety, the uncertainty of death, of operation, of chemotherapy, radiotherapy, biological therapy, physical pain. It is something so burdening that unless one is Hercules it is impossible to carry the burden.

DR. CHRISTINE: The point is that 30 percent of all cancers are cured. There are a lot of therapies, both innovative and traditional, that help a lot. But one needs a detailed knowledge of some of the lesser known fields of medicine as regional chemotherapy, oncological surgery, photo-chemic therapy, immunomodulators and, very important, a very up-to-date knowledge of how the mind works, knowledge of psychological processes and mechanisms.

ROSHI: How does the mind work?

DR. PETER: As to the psychological mind, I can by no means give a full picture, but many present-day psychotherapies, especially those associated with Milton Erickson, Carl Simonton, Jungian analysis, and depth psychology, point to a great versatility of the human psyche. And as for me, it is important to recognize the psycho-social pattern of the person so I can tune in at that level and take it from there. But listen, this sounds easy now when I talk about it here, but I'm afraid I get carried away into trying to lead or give advice much too often.

DR. CHRISTINE: Cancer is curable in 30 percent of all cases. But the name of the demon has remained: cancer is a killer. People are now living longer than they were even twenty years ago; techniques for discovering cancer have grown. In medicine now the idea that cancer is a disease resulting in death is not prominent. There is no longer the feeling that when an illness continues over a long time, it must be cancer.

SENSEI BODHIN KJOLHEDE: So you're saying that if someone asks you, "Do I have cancer?" and you say "Yes," that can be very misleading?

DR. PETER: It can be misleading before one understands whom one is talking to.

ROSHI: So what do you usually say to a person in the hospital who asks you, "Do I have cancer?"

DR. PETER: I try to describe to them their condition. I say, "You have no pain at the present; you had this lump, which is a growth; we've taken this lump out, but we've not cured you of the disease which caused the lump." If some of the cancer remains in the body, as it does in some abdominal operations, I say, "Some of this tissue remains in the body and will, at a slow rate, still be growing. So we haven't cured the disease, but the most imminent dangers have been removed." Then very often they ask, "What's going to happen?" I say, "I don't know what's going to happen, but we haven't cured your disease." Very few people will ask, "How is this going to end?"

I remember one woman who was pressing us to tell her whether she had cancer. She said, "Tell me! Do I have cancer: yes or no?" A friend and I kept telling her, "You have certain cells which have a malignant character, but we cannot say for sure these are malignant cells." We definitely don't like to use the word "cancer" because, even in her case, the pathologist wasn't sure. She went to another doctor and showed him what the pathologist had written. This guy told her, "You have cancer." She came back raging at us, "Why didn't you tell me I had cancer? This other doctor told me the truth!" The pathologist had written, "These cells are atypical and look like malignant cells." You can take this "look like" to be "they are" or you can take it to mean "they are not" or "they can become." You cannot be sure.

DR. CHRISTINE: Each person has a concept of what cancer is as a disease. I would try to find out what a person thinks. Maybe you could use the word then?

DR. PETER: Yes, you are right. Because there is nothing wrong with the word cancer once there is understanding, rapport. But we felt we were being pushed heavily and all that we knew was that there were cells that appeared malignant.

ROSHI: Was there no way to determine whether they were all malignant or not?

DR. PETER: No, because this was an early stage of development, and luckily for her it was taken out at this early stage when the cells were just beginning to change.

DR. CHRISTINE: I really feel that when a patient is so fixed on this word "cancer" the best approach is to ask what cancer means to her.

DR. PETER: Yes, you are right. But she wouldn't talk about it.

SENSEI: To people who are so emotionally charged, definitions are secondary.

ROSHI: Let me ask you this, Peter: From your experience with patients, do you feel that, in a situation such as you have just described, it is the fear of pain or the fear of death itself—extinction, or however one conceives of that—which arouses the most anxiety or terror in these patients?

DR. PETER: I think it is the sudden realization that *they're* going to die. It strikes them with great force. Up until then death has been an abstraction. You're going to die sometime, of course. But suddenly you're faced with the fact that you're going to be dead in a very short time. It is the fear of extinction. This is why cancer is such a focus: because cancer can develop very quickly. Death itself becomes real; the extinction may come sooner than next Christmas!

ROSHI: But is it the fear of pain or death that causes the greater anxiety?

DR. CHRISTINE: Generally, there are two kinds of people: the first is the person who has experienced the death of a friend or relative from cancer and has seen agonies associated with it. This person is afraid of the process of dying. Such people have witnessed the experience of losing through this process and that loss is a fact. This may include, for example, leaving children alone, not being able to be in accordance with the ethical vows of caring for a family or bringing the money home, relinquishing the guidance of your children through life. This is *painful*. And speaking from my own experience, it forces you as a friend or a relative to think in *practical* terms about your own death. These practical issues can become a huge obstacle to going through the process of dying if they are not adequately attended to.

The second type is the person who has not had a personal experience of the process, or has suppressed the experience. Such a person is more afraid of extinction. This is what Hamlet meant when he said that death is an "undiscover'd country from whose bourn no traveler returns" and that this "puzzles the will, and makes us rather bear those ills we have." I'm quoting from Shakespeare, from my memory of Hamlet's soliloquy.

DR. PETER: And I would like to add yet another side, another practical one. I believe that it's often not the fear of pain that makes one pull back. When physical death is stretched out over time, it is a very difficult and even humiliating process. When people who have cancer cannot hold their stool, cannot hold their urine, are weak, fall down, become confused mentally, not recognizing others or shouting at them—this is very difficult to witness. This whole process of the disintegration of the body-mind is what has spooked many people who have taken care of relatives at home. The constant presence day and night of the sick person, going to work and coming back at five o'clock to feed and wash the sick person, is like caring for a small child. And yet it is different too because an old person may not give back the joys of a child and besides, you know that the process will end in death.

ROSHI: Do you feel that the person with life-threatening illness experiences the disintegration too, and that this causes fear and anxiety?

DR. PETER: I'm always amazed at how many of these people, though they know they're seriously ill, cling to life, and repeatedly say, "I'm going to get better; I'm going to go home." But everyone knows that they are coming to die in the hospital.

DR. CHRISTINE: Yes, this was so difficult for me to understand. How even very experienced physicians *simply do not see* this resistance clearly and so they don't take action by clarifying the truth. It is as if the seriously ill and those surrounding them try to "conserve" a state of resistance that cannot be stopped.

SENSEI: Here's an interesting question: When you're faced with death, or a life-threatening illness, how much do you fight and how much do you let go? That is, when do you stop fighting? When is it a positive fighting-spirit and when is it clinging?

ROSHI: That's a difficult thing to determine, either for oneself or for others. There's such a fine line. I remember asking my teacher, Yasutani Roshi, one time, "If you were faced with death now, would you mind dying?" This was his answer: "I don't mind dying, but because I feel I've got things to do yet I would like to live longer." We didn't discuss pain. Do you feel that pain enters into this?

DR. PETER: I haven't myself experienced pain, so I can't talk from my personal experience. I have seen people in pain, however, who were not fatally ill, just solidly in pain, body and mind. They would tell me, "You know, I could never understand before why people could jump out of a window because of pain, but now I can understand it." Pain seems to take over their whole existence. I've seen several patients whose pain was so intense that we felt very guilty because we couldn't do very much about it.

ROSHI: Isn't it true that for people in great pain the ability to withstand it depends a great deal on attitude? For example, someone who has a strong belief in God, or survival after death, could take a lot more pain than somebody else without such a strong and supportive philosophy of life.

DR. PETER: Yes, Roshi. My father, for instance, was able, during unbelievable tortures during the Stalin era, to switch off pain. Milton Erickson, the famous physician and psychotherapist, was able to endure his own pain *while* treating patients, and was a very successful teacher who had an immense sense of humor and a unique attitude to life. I am sorry to say that what academic medicine teaches doctors about pain reveals only part of the picture. And yet there is enough material in print to help professionals get the bigger picture if they make an effort to find it.

ROSHI: I remember reading a study that was made of some twenty or twenty-five people and the manner in which they were enduring pain. Those who were sustained by some kind of philosophy—some kind of ideal—endured it much better than others without a sustaining belief. I suppose you could say, though, that some people's nerves are so constituted that they can tolerate pain better. What do you think about that?

DR. PETER: Yes, I agree with you. The belief system, the social background, the history of pain in your own family, in the family of your parents, your philosophical or spiritual experience can all help—and they can produce changes in the chemical transmission of the pain sensation or in the production of pain-soothing hormonelike substances. Response to pain is different in Swedes, Germans, Italians, Turks, and Arabs. Response to pain is a language, part of the character, part even of a belief system, as far as we can tell.

ROSHI: For certain North American Indians it was a sign of weakness to show a response to pain or to complain about it. When the Iroquois, for example, took prisoners they might have them "run the gauntlet." Those who showed fear or gave way to the pain might be treated more harshly than those who did not.

SENSEI: From what I understand that could be true of the Japanese, too.

ROSHI: During the American occupation of Japan people who were not servicemen or families of servicemen would have to go to a Japanese hospital or a Japanese clinic if they needed treatment. They complained very strongly that the Japanese doctors were sadists. Unlike American doctors, who try to relieve even a small pain, the Japanese doctors made no attempt to do that. I had a talk with a Japanese doctor about that very subject one time, and his answer went something like this: "In our culture we believe that pain is a condition of life, and that one has to learn how to endure pain. To prescribe drugs, as you do in your American culture, for every ache and pain does not strengthen people but weakens them." It was interesting to see the reaction of those Americans who were not accustomed to that sort of thing.

DR. PETER: Coming back to pain. I would like to ask you, Christine, as I know you have had a lot of back pain, what do you think of pain without a fatal illness and pain during a fatal illness?

DR. CHRISTINE: In both conditions it is vital to first relieve the immediate pain so the person can start to think normally. When one is in pain there is only one wish—to stop the pain. So drugs *are* vital. But then one has, as a psychologically working physician, to find out which course is to be taken for this *particular* person. But this is a very, very long story.

DR. PETER: Just a picture that could make our point more vivid. The surgeon cuts and takes out; the internist gives pain medication; the physiotherapist works with exercise; the naturopathic doctor treats with acupuncture and similar things; the psychotherapist uses psychotherapy; the spiritual teacher soothes the mind. So everyone is a musician in this pain-treating orchestra. But who will be the conductor?

DR. CHRISTINE: The ideal physician! If you find him or her, please give me a call (*laughs*). But seriously, the more professional knowledge a physician has, and I will put psychotherapy, hypnotherapy, physiotherapy on the *must* side, the more she or he can help. And as for spiritual teachers, we have you, a roshi and a sensei (*laughs*). Why do *we* have to care!

ROSHI: Peter, on the basis of your experience with patients, what do you feel is the single most important thing that one can do, before one has a fatal illness, to prepare oneself for eventual death, as we call it? And what do you feel a patient who already has a fatal illness can do to deal with the fears and anxieties and terrors of death?

DR. PETER: The single most important thing is to establish a firm belief or, even better, *experiential* knowledge about rebirth and the impermanence of the self. I have had the extremely favorable karma to experience the rebirth of our two children. So for me, death will be a transition, a big transition, but a transition all the same. So I can hope that when my time comes to move into the next cycle, I will have enough strength to remember it. And another thing—in situations of the death of my parents, deaths of friends, or life-threatening situations, I find that the Prajna Paramita sutra emerges spontaneously in my mind and I recite portions of it.

As for patients who have a fatal illness, it is important that they find something or someone in their own personal history: a teaching, a book, a spiritual friend or a teacher, a physician, someone with a great heart, from which they can get words of comfort that can be transferred into their own being. Soothing and gently embracing these words while opening the door to what comes next—the heavenly kingdom, paradise, next lifetime. Also we must create a conducive, comforting environment. A depressed spouse in a lonely hospital room is not so soothing, is it?

ROSHI: Is it fair, then, to infer that people who have a strong religious background—however one may interpret the word "religious" here—people who are sustained by some belief in an afterlife, or a future life, face the physical death at the end of a lifetime or life cut short by illness better than people who don't have such a philosophy or belief?

DR. PETER: I would positively affirm that the person who has some kind of belief system is better equipped to face life and death than one who hasn't. I have known many people who say, "I believe in God, and I know . . ." with an air of tranquillity about them. It makes us doctors feel that we don't have to take the whole burden on ourselves. When you see a person who is standing on his or her own two feet, you can discuss with them spending that time at home.

ROSHI: That brings up the next question: Do you feel that, as a doctor, in many cases patients with life-threatening illness would be better off in their own home rather than in the hospital?

DR. PETER: This brings about an aspect we haven't spoken about yet: the family. Here you have a koan. You have to ask, as a doctor, "What is this family like? What is the family bond?" These members, who haven't personally experienced the fatality of the illness, haven't yet understood, the way the patient has. For them, the dragon of fear may be bigger than the illness. For the patient, who is fatally ill, his life hasn't changed: he eats the same food, he wears the same socks. This is something I try to point out to the patient: "Do you feel any different now that you've had the operation?" And he says "No." The patient has this experience of "I'm fatally ill, but I'm still functioning well."

But the relatives have the image of the Grim Reaper. It's very difficult to assess in a short time how the family is going to react to a person who is going to die. People are afraid to take their relatives home because they are afraid they cannot provide the proper medical care and often they are right. They say, "My wife and I both work and we can't take care of our relative." It is true that if the patient is old, she or he can consume all their energy. The question is, do these relatives have some kind of a social and spiritual support system?

I remember one woman—a very interesting case—who had a fatal illness with no possibility of operation. It turned out that she had very strong Christian beliefs. I talked to her and said, "I don't know how long you're going to live, but your condition is not going to get better; it might stay the same." She said, "I want to go home." She had been about four weeks in the hospital. She had between two weeks and eight months to live, but I never gave her any exact time. Her son and daughter came home from their vacations and were told by the nurse that their mother was going home. My colleague didn't explain to them exactly what had happened and they became furious at the hospital, saying "Why are you releasing our mother who is fatally ill? What kind of people are you?" My colleague couldn't get through to them, so they came to me. I talked with the son and daughter for about an hour, explaining to them that I'd talked with their mother and that, for us, it was most important to respect her wishes. In the end the relatives understood that if they couldn't cope with their mother at home—if she got a high fever, for example—they could take her back to the hospital. We were not dumping the patient on them, but were trying to let this woman, who still had a sharp mind, live in natural surroundings. I asked the daughter what she would like to do if she were fatally ill but in possession of her mind, and she said, "Well, I would like to go home, too." But it took an incredible amount of energy for me to talk to this woman like this for one hour, because it touches the most basic issues of one's own life, and it is not easy. Another woman, a physician without a family, went through every possible chemotherapy, operation, radiation therapy—and died lonely, disillusioned, and feeling rejected. And she was a very nice, intuitive person, a former journalist, then physician. You never know. . . . I want to listen to what the dying person has to say, to try to understand and not talk so much about the facts. I always try to get away from the "How long am I going to live?" or "How long is she going to live?" "What is the name of the disease?" There's a deeper need in all of us to come to terms with something.

SENSEI: On the other hand, when I put myself in the place of a patient with a life-threatening illness, I can very well understand that I'd want to know—as exactly as possible—how much time I have left and what it is I have.

ROSHI: Why do you suppose most people want to know these things?

SENSEI: Probably to know how best to face this thing.

ROSHI: Do you think it is what was mentioned earlier, namely, making a will and that sort of thing?

SENSEI: I think that is definitely part of it. But just not knowing—the unknown—they want to get a handle on it.

DR. PETER: But how much time do you have now?

SENSEI: I'd say I have fifty years, the way we normally think . . .

ROSHI: I think what Peter's trying to say is that the time is not so important; to get people in touch with something that transcends time and is basic to life and death is the important thing. And when the patient says, "I want to know!" this is a great spiritual opportunity to bring home, if you can do it, the truths that all one's life one is trying to teach. When people are not sick they think they will live forever, and it's very hard to get them to think about death, but when they're faced with a life-threatening illness, suddenly they become open. That is the time to talk to the patient about spiritual matters.

SENSEI: But wouldn't you be more open to it if you heard you had two weeks to live than you would be if you heard that you had two years to live?

DR. PETER: You are right for you. I too would like to know as exactly as possible for myself too. But it is my experience that most people ask the question *wanting* to hear "many months" or "years." I think most people know in themselves how long they could live. So now I am turning the question around. "How much time do you think you have to live?"

The object here is to conceive of the final process in terms of many activities, emotional expressions, sunsets, movies, rituals, maybe letters, saying good-bye. When a doctor says, "You have another six months" or "I give this person four weeks," this is misleading and the wrong orientation.

ROSHI: It almost sounds omniscient.

DR. PETER: Yes. And you find out by trial and error that you don't really know, so you tell them, "I don't think there's anyone in the world who can tell you how long you will live." Then I try to discuss with them the quality of their life.

DR. CHRISTINE: When you say there is something that transcends the question of "how long" and "how will it end," how do patients without spiritual supports face this?

ROSHI: Let me try to rephrase your question. Following up on what Sensei Bodhin said, that if a patient were told, for example, "You have six months to live," it might create in the patient a sense of urgency about wanting to know the meaning of life and death, and therefore the patient might be receptive to teaching—if it's from the right person. Or has it been your experience that it doesn't make any difference, even if you give him an exact time, in terms of receptivity to spiritual matters?

DR. PETER: My experience has been that whenever you start talking about numbers, length of time, you get away from the underlying matter. People then think, "How will I spend this time?" The relatives look upon this as a sword of Damocles which is going to fall after six months because the doctor said "Six months." Even with people who are not religious in any sense, when one talks with them, trying to get away from the names and times, they very well understand their present situation and they often get in touch with the tranquility lying beneath the fear. They understand that the quality of their lives is most important. About the meaning of life and death—I have met maybe four or five patients who developed the want-to-know-it state of mind. Most of the others who have died—about a hundred and fifty or two hundred people—were just busy coping, basically doing what they did before. I am not speaking about the last days, when most people calm down by themselves.

ROSHI: Doesn't it come down to this? Before a patient will attempt to get in touch with his or her essential nature, which transcends all names and times, a good life or a bad one, there has to be strong motivation. That motivation has to be a belief in rebirth. If there is no belief in rebirth, if the person thinks death of the physical body is the end, then one of two things may emerge. One is to live whatever life they have left according to the philosophy of "Make the most of the time ye yet may spend before ye too into dust descend," which could be a very wild kind of thing—wine, women, and song—or if the person longs to travel, he or she may go to all the places the person has been wanting to go to. The other kind of thing is just the enormous sense of loss and despair, a sinking into depression and fear.

But if you have the feeling that this is not the end, or that this is just the beginning and what will follow will be a new kind of life, then you will try to prepare for that life. Unfortunately, when people have no true knowledge of rebirth, they may take it to be a very unrealistic thing: living up in the clouds or wanting to go to heaven. So they say, "Well, you're missing life here." This is not, of course, the Buddhist idea of rebirth at all. Obviously it's a complex situation and you have to take a patient's own assumption into consideration.

SENSEI: You say it would make a difference that they believed in rebirth. Would you say the same if they believed in an afterlife?

ROSHI: Yes.

SENSEI: It might not be rebirth; it might be heaven.

ROSHI: An afterlife, from a Buddhist point of view, is very unrealistic. It suggests a heavenly kind of thing, not rebirth into this mundane world of pain and struggle but into some nebulous, abstract heaven where things will be beautiful forever. Permanency.

And of course all of you know the difference between reincarnation, which implies a migrating soul, and rebirth, which is not the transference of a substance but the continuation of a process.

But getting back to the doctor's point of view, it seems to me that the doctor has to become not a preacher, but a person of pure spirituality to be able to counsel the dying. Everything's against it, if you work in a hospital, with the stresses and strains a doctor undergoes. Even ministers or priests or rabbis labor under certain difficulties when they go into hospitals trying to help—except perhaps in the case of last rites. You sit down and try to talk with a patient, but the TV is on. You face certain social problems that are almost insuperable.

DR. CHRISTINE: There are inner problems, too, for a doctor working in a hospital. To be peaceful and calm when you sit with a patient is quite difficult. When I was a young doctor in 1986 it was impossible. I did not have the necessary peace working in the hospital because I knew I had twenty things to do that were urgent and difficult for me to do. It takes a lot of energy to be calm. But now in 1996 somehow things are different. I can stay mentally with an ill person as I stayed with my best friend and her family for half a year. It did cost a lot of effort and energy and I fell ill *afterward*, but I think I contributed some to her peaceful exit.

DR. PETER: It is not just being calm; in talking with a patient for five or ten minutes you should be able to draw upon your whole energy potential. You have to be able, for five or ten minutes, to be *absolutely* present, and that taps a lot of your primal energies. If you have no strong energy root it may be impossible. If I sit in zazen it will give me a lot of energy when I go into the hospital. Now going to my private office I tap into some energies of my continuous practice of Zen. Particularly if I have chanted the Prajna Paramita to myself once or twice on the way there.

ROSHI: It's vital to be able to draw energy from the Prajna Paramita or from some other source. For me it's looking at a powerful Buddha figure. Of course the basic thing is zazen. When I was in London in the museum I was so energized by looking at those powerful Buddha figures there! If one were faced, as you two are, with the kinds of situations you face in the hospital every day, then zazen would be a tremendous source of strength which one could communicate to the patient, provided one had a reasonable opportunity to be alone with the patient. One needs to have some kind of source to draw upon, especially these days when we're living under such hectic circumstances. For Peter, the Prajna Paramita is a very strong source; other people use chanting or music. You need something that turns you inward so that you can draw upon these inner resources. We all have this tremendous amount of energy, you know, but ordinarily we just can't evoke it.

DR. PETER: There is something that comes to mind when we talk about the stresses we work under in the hospital or in our office. One has to be with so many people in different stages of life experience—patients with *all* kinds of diseases, symptoms, troubles, colleagues, our staff, relatives of friends, and stay in touch with yourself and earn money. What has proven to be very helpful to me is to experience or to think about the Oneness of Mind and of the uniqueness of every patient.

Sometimes I even understand what people do not say. And believe me or not, the most astonishing thing is that the Zen koans I have worked on just bubble up in all different situations with my patients, as well as what I have learned from you, Roshi and you, Sensei. These things benefit (as I hope) a lot of patients.

So, if I can sum it up for myself: The teaching of Zen Buddhism with zazen, koans, and chants is a basic guiding factor for me in my highly complicated profession. And I hope for me that Zen Buddhism will guide me home on a moonless night.

# Dying: A Conversation with Jon Sheldon, M.D.

## (1985)

*Jon Sheldon is now a family physician practicing in Denver,
Colorado. He is an old friend with many years of Zen training.*

ROSHI PHILIP KAPLEAU: You are a resident in family medicine.
How long have you been working in hospitals?

JON SHELDON: Three years.

ROSHI: How would you describe the way in which patients in
the hospital generally die? In other words, what are the different dying states you have observed?

JON: In my experience almost all patients in the hospital die
poorly.

ROSHI: What exactly do you mean by "poorly"?

JON: When people are born in the hospital they are attended to
with great care, but when they die, they often die alone. That
is, they are separated from the people who have loved them
all their lives. In some cases they are separated from a decent
amount of medical and nursing care.

ROSHI: Is this situation inherent in the way hospitals are obliged
to operate or is it one that can be improved?

JON: I think the situation is inherent in the doctors and nurses,
not in the hospital, which is, after all, a building. Because
medical caretakers have so little experience with dying, we
have this situation in hospitals. Of course on one level, caretakers have had a great deal of experience. They have been
involved with a great many people who have died. But in
terms of human feeling, of insight and understanding, of the
ability to put themselves in the position of someone dying,

there is a great lack. It doesn't take a lot of insight to recognize that a person going through this major transformation, of passing from one side of life to another, has need for a great deal of sympathy. Unfortunately, in the hospital that sort of thing is often totally lacking.

ROSHI: Would you say this is true because family members are excluded from the hospital at the time that someone is dying, or is it because the main caretakers, the doctors and nurses, lack the caring attitude so essential when one is dying?

JON: Both. The intensive care unit—if we take that as an example—can be an intimidating place for the family. Unless there is an active effort to involve the family, most families, in my experience, tend to stand back and let the hospital people, who seem so at ease in what is to the family a strange and foreign environment, take over. As for the second part of your question, whether what is missing is a lack of sympathy on the part of the doctors and nurses, I don't think they lack sympathy; they lack training. Or perhaps it is better to say that it does not occur to them that the dying state has considerable significance for the patient.

ROSHI: Would you say that these lacks on the part of doctors and nurses spring essentially from an absence of spiritual or religious training, or otherwise?

JON: *Inclination* would be a better term. This is not to say that doctors and nurses are irreligious in terms of whatever religious beliefs they hold. Many of them are religious in the ordinary sense. The difficulty is that religions do not deal with this issue in my experience. These people may be devout and even attend religious services, but those qualities do not prepare doctors and nurses for the experience of dealing with dying patients. It is a totally unknown realm to them. It is a terrible thing to say, but that is exactly the way they act.

ROSHI: Can you describe in some detail how patients die as you've observed them? That is, do they die fearfully or bitterly, or do many of them at the moment before death seem to have accepted or become reconciled to the fact of their imminent death?

JON: That is a question I can't really address myself to, because the deaths I have been involved with in the hospital concern people who have either died suddenly or who have slipped into a coma or who have been allowed to die—that is, for whom a decision was made to turn off the machines. I haven't been fortunate enough to experience the dying process with these patients. When I get to them, they are usually on their way out. They are not conscious.

ROSHI: Have most of the patients you have observed or been involved with been heavily sedated before dying?

JON: No, they have not. When I see them, they are usually semi-comatose or comatose, or they have died suddenly. When patients have metabolic problems they are auto-sedated. They lose consciousness, which is not the result of the medication we are giving them.

ROSHI: Can you mention some situation in which you have been involved in which you felt the doctors demonstrated a lack of insight or understanding? I am talking about hospital situations.

JON: I had a patient, a thirty-eight-year-old woman, who had a long-standing illness that had reached the terminal stage, and the family made the decision, with her approval, to have her life support system disconnected. After that was done the patient's heart began to fail, and this was obvious from the cardiac monitor at her bedside. As this began to happen, one of the doctors in the room said, "The patient is beginning to slip away. We should ask the family to leave the room." My response was, "Now is the time for *us* to leave the room." He looked at me in surprise, but not having any better idea of what to do, went along with my suggestion.

ROSHI: Why did he say, "Now is the time for the family to leave the room"?

JON: I think he didn't know what else to do. He felt that as a doctor he should do something, but he didn't know what, so he fell back on an old familiar routine, taking charge and doing things, which was listening to the heart and looking at the numbers on the dials of the cardiac monitor.

ROSHI: What was the purpose of looking at the numbers of the cardiac monitor?

JON: We Americans seem to have a morbid fascination with, a pathological addiction to, the television screen in any form. When babies are born, it is common to see parents as well as doctors and nurses staring intently at the fetal monitor even while the woman is in active labor. Likewise, the death scene often includes family members and health care professionals—doctors and nurses—gazing intently at the display on the cardiac monitor as the patient is dying—in other words, is undergoing the most significant transition.

ROSHI: Are you saying that a truly caring doctor or nurse wouldn't be distracted by the cardiac monitor but would be more directly involved with the patient?

JON: I am not saying that attention to the monitor screen means that good medical care has not been delivered, but that once all medical steps have been taken and the patient's death is imminent, many human things that could be done for the patient are not done, such as, for example, holding the patient's hand or speaking calmly or giving words of encouragement, or even placing a cold towel on the forehead.

ROSHI: Do you feel, then, that if doctors and nurses were better educated in how to deal with the dying, the latter would die with greater serenity and dignity?

JON: Absolutely. It does not take ten or more years of meditation or spiritual insight for them to act compassionately; it takes psychological awareness.

May I tell you about another case? A woman was dying from an overwhelming infection, and after a long and very difficult illness she fell into an irreversible coma. After keeping a long bedside vigil, her family made the difficult decision to discontinue her life supports and let her die. This was agreed upon by all concerned, and a time was set for this to happen. When the appointed time came and the family were in the room, the hospital administration suddenly decided that it needed an opinion from the hospital lawyer whether that decision by the family was in the best interest of the hospital. Just imagine the situation: Here is a family that has made a terribly difficult decision, yet they are made to wait for several hours in the hallway, of all places, while the hospital administrators check the matter out with their lawyer. The anguish of the family must have been terribly great. In any other situation the family would likely have taken charge. But since all this took place in a hospital—actually in the intensive care unit—the family was totally disenfranchised.

All our medical technology is clearly a two-edged sword. It accomplishes what can rightly be called miracles of modern medicine, but once the usefulness of this technology is over, it becomes an obstacle to seeing the patient as a human being. Even for a novice doctor to enter one of these intensive care units for the first time is a frightening and even a terrifying experience. Imagine how much more so this must be for the family, who in most cases lack any medical sophistication.

ROSHI: Do you feel that the hospice programs help mitigate the worst aspects of what you have just described?

JON: Absolutely.

ROSHI: Is there anything else you would like to add?

JON: Yes. The scene in the hospital is not entirely grim. There are times when patients and families are accorded the dignity they deserve. I recall the case of a patient, an elderly woman, who had a massive stroke and whose family immediately gathered around the bedside. As it became clear that the patient would not regain consciousness, the family made the decision that if her heart stopped beating, no attempts would be made to resuscitate her. It so happened that that evening the patient had a heart attack and died with her family in attendance. Had they not made that decision, a medical team would have arrived when the patient had the heart attack and would have kicked—yes, that is just the word—the family out of the room and begun vigorous resuscitation efforts despite the fact that this woman had massive and irreversible brain damage.

I recall the case of another woman who went into respiratory failure and was the object of intensive efforts at resuscitation. Halfway through the attempt the patient's private physician decided that resuscitation shouldn't continue. At that point a most unusual and disturbing thing happened. Everyone left the room, and this patient, who moments before had been the object of intensive efforts, no longer was of medical interest. It was as if she had ceased to exist as a human being despite the fact that she was still alive. No one thought to provide medicine for her comfort, much less spend any time with her.

ROSHI: Why did her physician want the resuscitation stopped?

JON: She had an irreversible illness and the only thing we could do was prolong her life artificially on a ventilator. Her doctor knew she didn't want this. In fact, we called her physician as we usually do and asked him, "What do you want us to do?" He replied, "I would like you to stop your efforts and let her go peacefully." When this announcement was made, all of the nurses and doctors quickly left the room.

ROSHI: Why did they do that?

JON: They felt that because their instructions were to allow her to die, there was nothing else that could be done, and so they took their medicines and machines and left her alone to die.

ROSHI: What period of time would you say elapsed from that point until she was declared clinically dead?

JON: About thirty hours.

ROSHI: During that thirty hours, did any doctor or nurse remain with her and try to make her comfortable in a physical way? Did any nurses or clergy remain with her until she actually died? In other words, could they have remained with her without breaking the rules of the hospital?

JON: Yes, it was a simple matter to provide her with a few medications to make her breathing easier.

ROSHI: This may sound personal, but did you remain with her?

JON: Yes, but I don't want to make myself out to be a hero. The point is that once it was pointed out what was happening, in essence we abandoned our patient. It would have been easy to enlist the help of the nursing staff to assure this woman's being comfortable during her last hours. I might also point out that when we left the room initially, we didn't know how long she might live. In fact she lived, as I said, for thirty hours. My central concern here is to clarify the importance of continuing to help a hospitalized dying patient *after* it has been decided to discontinue artificial life supports.

# Death and Dying:
## A Conversation with
## Penny Townsend, R.N.

### (1985)

*Penny Townsend-Quill, R.N., has been a nurse since 1978. Her focus has been on community health and hospice work.*

PENNY TOWNSEND-QUILL: I work for the Monroe County Health Department [in New York State] in a hospice program that is a community effort. We go into people's homes, and the Visiting Nurses Service of the Monroe County Health Department supplies the nurses for the program.

ROSHI PHILIP KAPLEAU: You say that dying persons rarely talk about their death. Why do you suppose that is?

PENNY: I have directly asked them about death, but it is something that people don't usually talk about. They can't find the words, or else they don't know what kind of questions to ask. Many families would like to know from the dying patient what it feels like to die.

ROSHI: Have the terminally ill who have a relationship with a clergyperson ever told you what was said to them about death?

PENNY: Usually the clergyman is a Catholic priest. The time spent with the dying person is usually structured: prayer or last rites. I know that the patient usually wants reassurance that everything is going to be all right after death.

ROSHI: Have you ever asked such a person, "What do you mean by 'all right'?"

PENNY: Yes.

ROSHI: What does the person say?

215

PENNY: "Because of the life I have led"—and there could be assorted sins or problems mentioned—"I will have no after-life" or "I will not be received by God" or "I am going to hell" or "my soul will not be everlasting." Also, "Can I atone for my sins?" or "Will I be forgiven for such and such that happened earlier in my life?" But this is a rare conversation, you must understand.

ROSHI: Do you feel that if the dying person could somehow establish belief in the rebirth process, it would tend to relieve anxieties he or she may be experiencing?

PENNY: Yes, I think it would. But another anxiety is about separation from loved ones and those left behind. There are also fears about what is going to happen during the dying process: the pain, physical distress, loss of breath, and the like.

Mainly I work with cancer patients, people who have been told they are going to die, so they probably have a better-defined life span than the rest of us.

ROSHI: Going back to the question of a future life, has any patient said to you, "I don't want to be born again if the nature of my future life depends on what I did and said in this life, because I would have to suffer a great deal for the terrible things I have done to myself and others"?

PENNY: No, although in a way there is a parallel to that in the Catholic belief. Maybe you ought to talk to Catholics about how the priest steps in, and through confession sins are forgiven, and everything is okay—supposedly. I don't think the average person could face the question you're posing.

ROSHI: Based on your wide experience with dying people, what do you feel can be done for them that usually is not done? I mean spiritually or religiously, not medically.

PENNY: Anybody at all?

ROSHI: Yes.

PENNY: She or he needs someone who is going to be completely there. I feel this more than I can say it—someone who can really forget herself, put herself away and just be there. One of the greatest fears of the dying person is the fear of being abandoned while still alive. It is really a very complex matter, because everyone is so different and you have to throw the rules away, so to speak—that is what I mean when I say you have to forget yourself—leave your shoes outside the door.

ROSHI: Can only a professional do that, or do you think that any caring family member can perform that task?

PENNY: Either could do it. But some professional people come in with the Kübler-Ross philosophy, that is, that this person needs to share her feelings and needs with others. These professionals or others may come with a set of rules or conceptions: the dying person is in the denial stage or is not accepting "and we need to help him learn to accept"—when, as a matter of fact, that person doesn't need that kind of help at all.

ROSHI: Could you say a little more about what you call the Kübler-Ross philosophy?

PENNY: As you know, Dr. Kübler-Ross was a great pioneer, the first person who brought to public attention the needs of the dying person. She formulated the theory that each person goes through five stages: denial and isolation, anger, bargaining, depression, and acceptance.

This theory was postulated some ten or fifteen years ago, and these stages were thought to be the accepted mode of the dying person. Then it began to be realized that not everyone went through those sequential steps. Some people stay in one stage and never go through any of the others.

Most professionals, I think, have a high regard for Dr. Kübler-Ross, but many no longer accept these expectations as laid out by her. According to Kübler-Ross, the dying person eventually accepts her death, but that may not be so. Some die angry or determined to get well again and perhaps live another six months or more.

ROSHI: Are there people who die with great fear and anxiety?

PENNY: Yes. You never know what will happen. One man, for instance, never spoke a word the last six months of his life.

ROSHI: On the basis of your eight years' experience with dying patients, can you tell me in what way you feel the subject of rebirth can be made to have a positive impact on the dying?

PENNY: The problem I have with that is introducing it as a new idea. Those who have been most spiritually aware or leaned most heavily on some religious persuasion, or spent most of their adult life practicing a religion, find that as their death comes closer their spirituality becomes stronger. With such people rebirth or some idea of life continuing beyond death would, I think, work well. But someone who has had no religious orientation—I don't know how such a person would respond to the idea of rebirth. Almost always it is women, and not men, who are more receptive to these ideas.

ROSHI: Why is that?

PENNY: I don't know. Perhaps it is because it is easier for women to talk about their fears and anxieties.

Caretakers coming forth with an idea such as rebirth would have to be very careful, especially if they don't know the family's position on such a matter. The caretaker might feel that this is a new idea that will fall on fertile ground, but that is a dangerous assumption. People who are involved with another religion might misinterpret or resent having the dying person hear about rebirth. This should be left to the family priest or minister, if there is one.

ROSHI: Can you think of anything else?

PENNY: Yes. In your book *The Wheel of Life and Death* you say that family members and friends should leave the room when death is imminent and that only the clergy should remain. However, for most dying people it would be very hard to have family and friends leave at the moment of death. It is a very important time for them and this is when family needs to be present.

We have been talking about people who die at home from a terminal illness. But what about people who die in an intensive care unit or nursing home? Actually they constitute the bulk of dying people. A person who would naturally die of a stroke is now kept alive by respirators and other instruments. And what about the newborn infants kept alive in incubators? Or take the case of the septuplets born in California, aided by all kinds of medical technology? What I have dealt with here is only the simplest of situations.

ROSHI: I suppose you have heard of cases where persons are declared clinically dead by a doctor and it turns out later that they aren't. Have you dealt with such people?

PENNY: Yes. Usually it is after a cardiac arrest. The patient is having an out-of-body experience and is looking down on the team of doctors and nurses frantically working to save her life. But this person has such a feeling of peace that she doesn't want to come back at all. "Just let me go on," she says. Only reluctantly do such people come back to life.

ROSHI: Can you say more about that?

PENNY: There are cases of people who have been declared clinically dead and who have observed themselves being resuscitated. I think you are going to have more sophisticated ways of saving people's lives in the future, and therefore very possibly you will have more of this type of case.

ROSHI: Is there anything else you want to add?

PENNY: Just this: People usually die the way they have lived their lives. Their strengths become stronger. During the dying process everything seems to be exaggerated, both the positive and negative qualities. Dualistic notions emerge strongly, such as, "Have I been good? Have I been bad?"

ROSHI: Can you suggest what the caring family can do to reduce that sort of thing or to help the dying patient deal with it more positively?

PENNY: Yes, to emphasize that these things really don't matter—in fact, they never have mattered. But that may not be realistic. Anyway, they don't matter now and they are not going to matter.

ROSHI: If a person is overwhelmed by feelings of guilt because of the way she has lived and this feeling is now being exaggerated during the time of dying, what do you feel can be done to help the person through this period of great stress?

PENNY: I don't think there are any right words. I don't think you can say anything to anyone to make things better, to sprinkle fairy dust on the situation. Those things are real. That person needs to talk and relive incidents over and over again. That sort of thing needs to be allowed, but you do need to try to make that person understand that everything is going to be all right.

ROSHI: But if one believes in karma, that is, that you get your just desserts upon rebirth, what can you do to help such a person?

PENNY: What would you do, Roshi?

ROSHI: I would tell him to try to empty his mind of all thoughts and try to pass from this side of life to the next no-mindedly— that is, simply to become one with the dying process and not to separate himself or herself from the dying by such thoughts, whether they be unpleasant or pleasant.

PENNY: That is really hard for the average person to do, and without training probably impossibly hard.

ROSHI: Don't you agree that that is a good reason why people who still have their health and physical and mental faculties intact should develop a spiritual practice now, because, as you said, people die the way they have lived?

PENNY: That is true.

ROSHI: Another thing: Do you believe that if one had something like a mantra that could be recited in all kinds of distressful situations, then at the time of physical death it would come to one naturally and easily and would be of great help?

PENNY: Yes, absolutely.

# On Confronting a Chronic Illness

## (1991)

Usually when people talk about what they've learned about their illness, you feel that the illness has been going on for a long time. My illness, to put it in its narrowest terms, is only about two months old, although the doctor tells me that probably the beginnings of it took place much earlier. My condition was diagnosed as what is now becoming a common disease, Parkinson's disease. Half a million people got Parkinson's disease in the past year, according to some statistics that I saw. And the interesting—if that's the right word—fact is that there is no known cause of it and no known cure for it.

The best thing that can be said about it is that it can be controlled. Many new drugs have been devised to keep this disease in check. And these drugs are pretty powerful—at least to somebody like myself, for whom taking any kind of drug, even an aspirin, was seen to be an affront to the Buddha. Of course, that isn't true. But for me, for a long time, given my karma, it seemed so. Well, after not having taken any drugs at all it was a new experience to suddenly find myself with four or five different ones. Among other things, it made me feel that drugs certainly have a place—allopathic medicine has a place—in the scheme of things.

Usually the first six weeks of treatment for Parkinson's are the worst, because it's a time of experimentation, of trying to find how much of a particular drug the body can take, when, and just what effect it has on your condition. There are many degrees of Parkinson's. I don't know what degree I am in at all. But, I can certainly still do a lot of things that I previously did.

You may think, especially if you're doing Zen, that you have

221

good protection against shock from a sudden announcement that you have to take drugs for the rest of your life—that there's no cure and the best you can hope for is that if you take care of yourself, you'll be able to do many things that you did before: carry on a normal life with some limitations. I remember that when I was first told this by the doctor, it made absolutely no impression on me.

But then, suddenly one day it hit me: "Do you realize what the doctor said? For the rest of your life you're going to be taking heavy drugs, and there's no cure, and that's it!" And that's when a lot of negative, dark thoughts began entering my mind. Parkinson's is a terribly debilitating disease; I had absolutely no energy. It was a strange experience, to have all these dark thoughts that I hadn't had for *years*, thoughts about death—not thinking of life and death in a philosophical kind of way, but of how it impacts the things that you want to do, have to do, need to do, before you die.

One of the clearest insights that came to me during this period was that there's no such thing as death. Now, we've all heard that, of course, and read about it, and I've even written about it. It struck me that this whole duality of life-and-death/life-against-death was 100 percent wrong. It's not that you're either alive or dead, and if you're alive, you're in one condition, and if you're dead, you're in another condition, and there's absolutely no connection between the two of them. That sort of thinking begins very early. We see death around us, but we never stop to think that death might be an aspect of life, that there's nothing but life. This is what struck me with great force: that this is an alive universe, this is not an inert universe. We can never compare life with death because there's only life—death is just a term we use because we don't have another. We don't think about it as taking a turn, that death is life in another form. Thus we continue to use the word *death* and it takes on a life of its own. So we go wrong right from the very start, by dualistically thinking about life and death.

And then another insight came to me: the disease is now yours, it's inseparable from you. The only way, it seemed to me,

222

to deal with a chronic disease (and I may not be entitled to speak about it yet because I've hardly begun having it) is to accept it as part of you, as part of your life, not something isolated that you just have a marginal relationship with.

When something serious happens to people—something like cancer—people often ask, "Why should this have happened to me? What have I done to deserve this?" What had Ramana Maharishi, one of modern India's most spiritually developed individuals, done to deserve to die from cancer? What sort of karmic retribution caused the death of India's Ramakrishna by cancer? Coming to our own times, did Shunryu Suzuki Roshi, Katagiri Roshi, and Maureen Stuart Roshi, all of whom were felled by cancer, ask themselves, "Why should this have happened to me?" No, they did not. They understood the deep complexities of karma. And they were present in their lives every minute. Actually I can't imagine any Zen person asking these questions. I certainly didn't. And I didn't because as Zen students we know that we have earned everything that happens to us, good and bad. Reflecting on this, I feel that this deep awareness made it easier to accept Parkinson's disease.

I'm sure that I will learn a great deal as I get further into this Parkinson's. One doctor, in a statement I read, said that every person before death will have one degree or another of Parkinson's. So many things are happening throughout the brain, so many changes are taking place. Some of these events resemble Parkinson's. For those of you who may not be familiar with this disease, Parkinson's patients have trembling of one or both hands, they have difficulty walking, a great deal of muscular rigidity, the face becomes masklike, they walk slowly, their voice becomes soft, and they experience a great tiredness. What it really centers around is dopamine, which is a neurotransmitter that causes the muscles to move. The cells that supply dopamine suddenly dry up and there isn't enough supply getting to the body. So what these modern, remarkable drugs have done is to mimic the dopamine. They cause the muscles to move, and the more exercise you do, the better off you are.

Since I've been taking these drugs, I'm told my condition has changed considerably for the better. If nothing else, my valuation of drugs has gone up tremendously. Of course it means living a regulated life; you have to take these pills every four hours, and you can't take them without food—at least I can't, so you have to change your whole style of eating: small meals. For me, one of the positive features of Parkinson's is the extreme importance of physical exercise. I began swimming in the pool more, playing at different games, throwing the ball around, doing hatha yoga, and walking on the beach at night. All this makes a tremendous difference. So, it hasn't altered my life outwardly in many ways, but of course inwardly is another matter.

So, where does Zen come into this, specifically? You think that when you're doing zazen fairly regularly, you're learning a great deal about yourself—and of course you are. But I don't think you really come to grips with your problems unless you're in an extreme position, where you think you may die.

Never before that I can remember in my mature years had I been in a condition where I thought each breath was going to be my last. There was no pain, or at least no physical pain, and yet I felt worse than if I had physical pain. And so my mind turned in certain directions: it takes strong zazen to overcome that pull. I was getting up in the middle of the night. I could hardly breathe. I couldn't sleep. I found that there was nothing else to do but zazen. So I began doing zazen when I woke up in the night and found that it established a kind of equilibrium.

Now, I'm talking about myself: I certainly don't presume to speak for other Zen people; everybody's different. But one of the things that I did find helpful was that I always had zazen to sustain me. I think it was enormously valuable to have that kind of a sustaining practice.

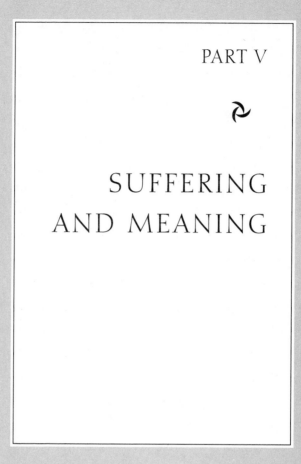

PART V

SUFFERING
AND MEANING

# An Age of Destruction
and Spiritual Resurgence:
A Conversation
with Vondell Petry

(1991)

*Vondell Petry, a longtime Zen student and friend, conducted this interview at my home in Florida. It first appeared in* Quality Living *magazine in 1991. Some of her questions were unique, giving me an opportunity to explore issues of Zen and our society—and its future—that I've rarely had the chance to discuss elsewhere.*

VONDELL PETRY: We're confronted by so much negativity in the world and yet there are signs of a spiritual resurgence in many places. What do you make of this?

ROSHI PHILIP KAPLEAU: Obviously—or maybe not so obviously—what is driving people to Zen Buddhism and other spiritual traditions is the lamentable state of the world: pollution and destruction of the environment, population pressures, the pain of war, increasing poverty, the decline of the economy, the scarcity of vital resources, and a general fear and anxiety stemming from one or another of these causes and conditions. Clearly we're in a period of great instability.

VONDELL: Do you feel, as some do, that we are approaching the end of a world cycle?

ROSHI: I have felt for some time that the negative karma of the peoples of this world cycle has ripened and is beginning to

227

confront us. The debt is coming due and has to be paid. Additionally, many negative cosmic forces unleashed into our world are both the cause and effect of so many disastrous conditions in our midst today.

VONDELL: What can we do in the face of such overwhelming obstacles?

ROSHI: For one thing, on a spiritual level, those who feel empowered through meditation and other means can work to counter or neutralize the negative forces suffusing the consciousness of people everywhere. Particularly, with a massive war of violence such as we had in the Persian Gulf, the negative vibrations reverberating from such conflicts have an adverse effect on all of us, provoking fear, anxiety, anger, depression, and other unhealthy emotions. It's obvious that in a physical and social sense, we need to work together to save our imperiled planet.

VONDELL: So the work must continue on the material and spiritual levels?

ROSHI: Yes, inwardly and outwardly.

VONDELL: But that order is a large one, since it seems we are so busily creating our own disasters.

ROSHI: There are those of us who believe that certain destructive thoughts and actions of human beings can and do help create earthquakes, floods, and similar disasters. On a massive scale we are altering the environment in ways that are making it more prone to disasters.

VONDELL: Would you say this is one of the most difficult times human beings have faced since the dawn of history?

ROSHI: The way I read and intuit history, we're in one of the worst periods of human existence. Probably no period in history equals the fury of mankind in the twentieth century, given the amount of blood that has been shed and the sufferings inflicted.

VONDELL: It is obvious that to counter such immense negative energy requires immeasurable courage.

ROSHI: Courage, imagination, and the will to survive.

VONDELL: Can we, as human beings with our great defects and

limitations, survive the horrors and catastrophes we ourselves have created and continue to create?

ROSHI: Only if we transcend those limitations in a superhuman leap of faith and will. Don't forget, the same force, or energy, that is destroying the world can also save it, for essentially they are no different.

VONDELL: The ability to transcend our limitations, to rouse a superhuman leap of faith and will, is a very big order.

ROSHI: It is probably the biggest challenge we humans have faced in our long sojourn on this earth.

VONDELL: And the hope that we can do this, where is that?

ROSHI: The hope is that there is a way if there is a will. Still there comes a time when the karma of the peoples of this world cycle will have exhausted itself and our civilization will disappear, like others in the past.

VONDELL: How will we know that the karma of our era is exhausted?

ROSHI: There will be an intensification of all the negative aspects of our society and culture that we are experiencing now. It's as with an individual. Death could come to him suddenly, as in a violent car or plane crash or from an obliterating nuclear blast. Or it could be a slow dying, as from a worsening fatal illness.

VONDELL: Do you see the growth of suicide among the young and elderly as connected with the enormous violence in every aspect of our society?

ROSHI: I'm not a sociologist or an expert in these matters, but it is obvious that the sanctity of human life in our violence-ridden society has become devalued and demeaned. When that happens, everyone's life is endangered, including, of course, one's own. Violence breeds more violence, and as the Buddha said, "One who kills another digs two graves." Killing and physical abuse on our streets and in our homes is today almost the rule rather than the exception. Whereas in earlier times a slap or a push or a beating sufficed to allay the anger of two quarreling people, these days a bullet or a knife blade settles the argument permanently.

And then there is the violence of the "killing fields," of the numerous "small wars" around the globe euphemistically described as wars of liberation. The recent war in the Persian Gulf, though only of six weeks' duration, resulted in an estimated fifty thousand Iraqis dead, civilians and soldiers, with total casualties close to two hundred thousand, according to media reports. American and coalition warplanes, we are told, flew eighty thousand "sorties" [bombing missions]. What blood and tears, what carnage, lies behind that innocuous-sounding word *sortie!* To my knowledge, not one of our political leaders condemned these ruthless bombing attacks. On the contrary, after the cease-fire, the American mood was one of jubilation, and even gloating, over our triumph. Instead of gloating, we ought to heed the wise and compassionate counsel of Lao-tzu, the legendary sage of China:

> *The death of a multitude is cause for mourning.*
> *Conduct your triumph as a funeral.*

VONDELL: Is what we are currently experiencing in the way of violence vastly different from what has gone on since the beginning of time?

ROSHI: Of course there have been similar periods in history of unrestrained killing and maiming, but because technology has increased our power to act destructively, our capacity for evil has multiplied threefold.

VONDELL: It sounds as though the very life force is imperiled.

ROSHI: I'm not saying that the life force will disappear with the physical destruction of the world. It won't, because what is behind the creation of the universe is deathless, and it's deathless because it has no finite self. But . . . that may be small comfort for many.

VONDELL: What about the legacy of pain and suffering an apocalypse will bring? What about the survival of billions of years of evolution of life on earth?

ROSHI: Remember, for something unique and wonderful to be born, there must first be death, which is inseparable from life.

VONDELL: Are you saying that after this Dharma-ending age passes, a more humane age will follow?

ROSHI: A higher and more humane consciousness, yes. If I may use traditional Buddhist terminology, the age of Buddhas [beings who have ascended to the highest rung of the ladder of human consciousness], of Buddhahood, will be ushered in, and it will be the wisest, the most compassionate and humane we have yet known on earth. The Buddha himself predicted that. Like Christianity, Buddhism is also imbued with apocalypticism, but it has, I think, a slightly different flavor.

VONDELL: Would you say, then, that what we witness as both spiritual and physical events is energy stumbling toward this eventuality?

ROSHI: Yes, but with many downs and ups, many detours on the way. It may also be relevant to point out that the evolutions of technology, useful as they have been, in many respects have been a stumbling block to the full spiritual development of human beings. That's why it's been said that "technology makes major contributions to minor needs of human beings."

VONDELL: What else do you think will characterize this new age?

ROSHI: If, as it now seems, we are going through a period of alienation and disintegration, the new age of Buddhas will be characterized by a more pervasive realization of the unity and solidarity that defines our True Nature.

VONDELL: You are talking about fully mature human beings.

ROSHI: Yes, fully mature human beings who still have, among other unique attributes, a childlike spontaneity and innocence, along with a completely mature wisdom and compassion.

The following is a prayer I delivered on June 30, 1989, at the International Ecumenical Conference for Peace held at the Cathedral of Mexico City and sponsored by the cardinal of Mexico. All major world religions were represented, including the Dalai Lama and myself, among others, representing Buddhism. The prayer expresses my heartfelt longings for our difficult era. I think it sums up a lot of what we've been talking about.

In the Lotus sutra, a Buddhist scripture, it is written that when the planet is threatened by great disasters, Bodhisattvas will spring up everywhere to neutralize the forces of evil seeking to engulf the world. Bodhisattvas are personifications of the transcendent wisdom and love lying at the core of the human heart. My prayer therefore was this:

May we all exert ourselves to the utmost to mobilize our innate wisdom, compassion, and courage at this crucial time in our world history to rescue our ailing planet with its suffering inhabitants, both human and nonhuman, from the catastrophes awaiting it. In short, I pray that by our actions we choose nonviolent Life and not extinction.

# Man's Justice and
# God's Justice

## (1994)

I'd like to talk about an unusual Turkish story or dialogue that
has many qualities of a Zen koan—and a fascinating koan at
that. Although these days the word koan has become a buzz-
word describing or referring to any insoluble problem, strictly
speaking, a Zen koan revolves around the sayings and doings of
the Zen masters. Etymologically, the word means "a place
where there is truth," not unlike a case at law which serves as a
precedent for resolving future cases. But I call this Turkish story
a koan most because it has a "bite" to it, a contradictory element
that cannot be logically resolved. The purpose of every koan, of
course, is to help the student refine spiritual understanding.
Moreover, like every koan, this one points directly to ultimate
truth. Here is the story:

Once the Hodja (literally, "venerable teacher"), sitting in one of
his accustomed places, namely under the branches of a walnut
tree, was approached by a delegation of children who had fallen
into dispute.

"Hodja," their spokesman said, "we have a case which needs
your judgment. We have gathered all the walnuts under this tree
and wish to divide them equally among ourselves. There are
four of us, and we have shared equally in the labor of gathering,
but after dividing them all there are still three walnuts remain-
ing. We have searched all around the tree for another, but have
found none. It seems that one of us must be deprived of a walnut,
but we cannot decide which. Your wisdom in such matters is
well-known to all of us—for have you not settled disputes in our

village these many years when matters could not be taken before the cadi? Please now advise us how we should decide."

The Hodja listened carefully to this impassioned plea and thoughtfully stroked his beard. After some time he asked, "Would you wish God's justice in this matter, or man's justice?"

The child who had spoken turned to his companions in puzzlement. Evidently there were two kinds of justice possible in such affairs, and now they must choose between them. The children talked the matter over.

"Listen," said one of them, "we know man's justice only too well. Have we not seen how bribes must be paid to the cadi in order to receive a favorable judgment? In this case, too, a bribe will be expected, and whoever pays the least will be deprived of a walnut. I therefore vote for God's justice."

"I, too, would vote for God's justice," said another. "For does not God provide for all? And do not our holy men—among whom we must surely count the Hodja—endeavor to administer God's ways among men? It is my belief that the Hodja will shake down a fourth walnut so that we may all have an equal share in order that God's justice be fulfilled."

Said the third, "As each of us has many times observed, man's justice is a phantom, and largely because those who administer it are thieves who steal for themselves the very property under judgment. Quite apart from any bribes we might have to pay, we can fully expect the Hodja to take more than any of us, and we must be content with what remains. I join my vote with yours."

"The matter is decided then," said the fourth child. "For why would anyone choose the wisdom of man in preference to that of God, almighty and compassionate? Regardless of how things go among men, one should always call upon God alone for help in such matters, even if the matter is as small as a single walnut."

"Hodja," said the spokesman when the children had reached their decision, "with one voice we choose God's justice over man's. Knowing that you will execute that justice in precise accordance with divine wisdom, we ask for your judgment in the matter of the walnuts."

"You have chosen well," said the Hodja with a smile. And to

the first child he gave fifty walnuts, to the second thirty, to the third three, and to the fourth none at all.

The obvious question we must ask ourselves is, "Why does Hodja distribute the nuts in the manner he does?" Is it perhaps because Hodja knows that the last boy had not really done his share of the work of gathering the walnuts but had "goofed off" unbeknownst to his companions? Or that Hodja, through his psychic powers, had perceived that the boy who got the most walnuts deserved them for other good and sufficient reasons? Or is God, through Hodja, testing the boys' characters to see how they will respond to His distribution, i.e., to see whether the boy who received nothing will complain bitterly and the one who received the most preen himself on being the most deserving? We don't know how the boys responded, of course, for the dialogue does not tell us. Most importantly, is Hodja trying to teach the boys through his seemingly unfair distribution that God's world is beyond the ethical considerations that govern man's world—that justice in God's world cannot be equated with justice in man's world? Or to put it another way, can it be that the fourth boy got no nuts because God, having the holographic vision that man lacks, sees into the boy's past lifetimes and knows that at one time he created negative karma for himself by reason of evil or unjust actions? Man's justice, we know, issues from a moral vision that looks from one side at that which has infinite dimensions. God's justice embraces all those infinite dimensions.

But is God's justice just if it relates actions committed by the fourth boy in a past lifetime to this lifetime? Is it fair, in other words, to punish the boy now for what he did in a previous lifetime and probably doesn't remember anymore?

A contemporary Zen master, Shibayama Roshi (in his book *Zen Comments on the Mumonkan*), commenting on a certain koan, observed that "it is the mysterious work of God to create the new and true world. There everybody, everything, lives in God, and all the provisional names and defilements of this world are never found in the least." Is he implying that in God's kingdom such concepts as justice and injustice, of holy men and

235

worldly ones, of names such as *walnuts* and *walnut tree* are nonexistent? Man's justice, we know, is rooted in morality, in notions of right and wrong. God's justice, on the other hand, transcends right and wrong, but does not leave them behind. Although God's justice is found in part in man's justice, God's justice goes beyond man's. In short, God's justice is above man's, but man's justice is not below God's.

What precisely do we mean by *justice?* Webster's defines the word as "the quality of being righteous; impartiality, fairness; a deserved penalty, just desserts." It also refers to "the use of authority and power; upholding what is right, just, or lawful." Asked, "Who are the just?" Meister Eckehart replied, "They are just who give to God what is His, to the angels what is theirs, and to their fellow men what is theirs." The children, obviously wise beyond their years, have already learned how man's justice, when divorced from God's, is easily corrupted by displays of power, dishonesty, and other unlovely qualities. Understandably, then, they opt for God's justice, which they believe to be untainted by the selfish scheming of humans, and which is therefore fair and impartial.

Ask believers about God's ways and His justice, and very likely you will be told that His ways are not ours, that God moves in mysterious fashion His wonders to perform (or as a Portuguese proverb has it, "God writes straight with crooked lines"), and that humans, with their limited and clouded intellect, cannot hope to fathom God's "zigzags" even as He pursues a steady course straight ahead.

Yet, though we speak of wonders and justice, where is there justice and wonder in the floods and droughts and earthquakes that have claimed the lives of untold millions? Where is there wonder in the creation of such diseases as malaria, tuberculosis, influenza, and the numerous microorganisms that have caused so much suffering and death to billions of innocent victims, most of whom have been children? What defector from belief in God's supposed wisdom and love in the face of the violence and suffering of this calamitous twentieth century hasn't cried out, "How can an all-knowing, omnipotent, and benevolent God allow countless millions of people to suffer and die in two horrendous world wars? If He has the power to intervene in human history, why did He allow Hitler to come into power and do nothing to prevent him from snuffing out the lives of six million innocent Jews in the Nazi gas chambers, or permit millions more to be slaughtered in the Crusades and the Wars of Religion, all in His name? Where was His mercy when one million Cambodians were ruthlessly destroyed during the Khmer Rouge's four-year reign of terror? For what mysterious reason has God not intervened in the enormous oppression and cruelties inflicted on countless blacks by whites—all supposedly God's children—throughout the world and throughout time? If God is all-powerful, why doesn't He prevent such calamities? Is He unaware or indifferent to them? If so, why? And what about the loss and anguish and pain that come into people's lives through no fault of their own: the sudden, meaningless death of a loved child; the wanton spraying of bullets into an innocent crowd killing people indiscriminately. Why does God permit such tragedies? If God can stop them and doesn't, He must be cruel and unfeeling.

We cannot exonerate God from responsibility for such disasters by arguing that they are the outcome of man's defection from God's divine law. After all, didn't God create man in His own image, which is to say he is a creature of God? Moreover, there is even less reason to exempt God from culpability for His "natural acts" in which the earth quakes, rivers overflow, and humans and animals in a frenzy of fear and pain vanish from the earth. Are these creatures the victims of the wrath of a vengeful God? Or is there some hidden meaning? To put it baldly, what could have motivated a benevolent God to create a world in which there is so much pain and sorrow?

The Buddhist patriarch Ashvaghosha pinpointed the perplexing problem posed by the notion of a benevolent God the Creator who is the source of everything: "If God is the cause of all that happens, what is the use of striving?" That is, what is the use of striving to realize one's highest spiritual potential through meditation and other means? If everything is foreordained by God, who is said to predestine certain souls to salvation and others to damnation, where is there room for self-effort, for free will, for the operation of the karmic law of cause and effect, which decrees that we are personally responsible for what we are and what we will become; that no act done intentionally is free of consequences, whether painful or pleasurable; that just as the thoughts and actions of past lives fashioned this life, so how we live in this life will determine the nature and quality of our next life.

At all events, we must now confront another vital question. If God, without sin Himself, created a sinless, perfect world ("God created the world and said, "Yes, it is true, it is good"), how did sin or evil—that is, murder, torture, cruelty, and suffering—enter the world of humanity? The Old Testament tells us that evil originated with Adam and Eve, whom God cast out of the paradise of the Garden of Eden (with the loss of their primal innocence), after they disobeyed Him and succumbed to the temptation to eat the fruit of the tree of the knowledge of good and evil. With this disobedient act, their and our unitary nature became fractured; thus arose the dualistic notions of self and other, good and evil, life and death, et cetera, and concomitantly the myopic view of a fractured world of opposites.

What do the "God-intoxicated" ones, the mystics, have to say about their relation to God and about the problem of evil and man's sufferings? Meister Eckehart wrote, "If I am changed into God and He makes me one with Himself, then there is no distinction between us." He also declared, "The eye with which I see God is the eye with which God sees me." And Angelus Silesius, another mystic, boldly proclaimed:

> I know that without me God cannot live at all.
> Were I to go, He he also to his death must fall.
> I am as great as He
> And He as small as me.
> He cannot be above, nor I below Him be.

The poet Rainer Maria Rilke wrote in his *Book of Hours:*

*What will you do, God, when I die?*
*When I, your pitcher, broken, lie?*
*When I, your drink, go stale or dry?*
*I am your garb, the trade you ply,*
*you lose your meaning, losing me.*

*Homeless without me, you will be*
*robbed of your welcome, warm and sweet.*
*I am your sandals: your tired feet*
*will wander bare for want of me.*

*Your mighty cloak will fall away.*
*Your glance that on my cheek was laid*
*and pillowed warm, will sink, dismayed,*
*the comfort that I offered once—*
*to lie, as sunset colors fade*
*in the cold lap of alien stones.*

*What will you do, God? I am afraid.*

Eckehart seems to be implying that if God makes him one with Himself and he lives in God's goodness, he can do no evil. He also appears to be saying that for those who, like himself, are privy to God's mysterious ways and who live in His goodness, sin and suffering are transcended and are therefore no longer a problem. Silesius and Rilke, for their part, affirm that God's existence is inextricably bound up with theirs. In effect, these exemplars of God's wisdom and justice seem to be saying, "God and I are not two." Are they also acknowledging thereby their coresponsibility with God for the existence of so much suffering in the world?

Those liberated souls whose spiritual eye is clearly opened, and who therefore know the true nature of life and death (without having invoked the aid of God), say that though there are earthquakes and floods, fires and drought, pain and anguish, struggle and death, yet inseparable from this turmoil and destruction an unmovable calm and nirvanic joy prevails. For these enlightened beings, to live is a form of our True Self at one time and one place, and to die also a form of True Self at one time and one place. Life and death, then, are essentially no different. Moreover, these Buddha-like beings affirm that the world is a phantasmagoria, a passing show, like the blowing of bubbles, which burst and reappear no matter how often they are broken. So long as we view the world through the distorting veil of our discriminating, dualistic, ego-dominated intellect, we humans will remain ignorant of the true nature of life and death, and therefore the illusion of a discrete self opposed by an alien "other" will arise: thus suffering is inevitable. Because suffering is the lot of those who confuse the apparent with the real, suffering won't cease until ignorance, and the misguided actions that flow from it, segues into Knowledge.

What about the contention that God is callous or indifferent toward suffering and therefore cannot be called an all-loving God? Those who seem to be marching to God's drumbeat insist He is not callous or indifferent; it is merely that He is not powerful enough to prevent the disasters that lead to pain and suffering. In the beginning His power was complete, but when out of His love for His creatures He decided to endow humans and angels with free will, God had to surrender His unlimited sovereignty over those creatures; otherwise they would not be truly free to choose what *they* wanted and not what God wanted. Nevertheless, they insist, God remains powerful enough to bring about His ultimate plan of salvation for all His creatures even though His omnipotence is no longer absolute but limited by His creatures' freedom.

Notwithstanding, how does a true spiritual seeker penetrate God's kingdom? Certain religionists answer, "By prayer, by reading, by reflecting on the teachings of the sacred books of the great religions, which books Emerson called 'the sanctuary of the intuitions,' one can come to know God's unsurpassing justice, goodness, and wisdom." But what are we to make of this baffling passage in the Old Testament: "You cannot see God and live"? For many, it makes as much sense, or nonsense, as the question "How many angels can fit on the head of a pin?" Are, then, the biblical statement and the question about angels both without spiritual significance? Let us see.

In Letter Five of the Bassui letters (in *The Three Pillars of Zen*) you will find Zen Master Bassui proclaiming, "Your Buddha-nature is like the jewel sword of the Vajra king. Whoever touches it is killed." Doesn't Bassui's pronouncement hew closely to the biblical one? So how does one live in the realm of God? To live in God's world ("where all names are provisional") means to die to the old world dominated by our discriminating intellect. Clinging to our name-calling, ego-centered mind, therefore, and making it the touchstone of ultimate truth, bifurcates the world into the specious categories of good and evil, man's justice and God's justice, wise men and fools, and so on. The more we assert man's world of dualistic thinking, the further God's unitary world of Oneness recedes. Although God's world transcends man's (the latter being merely an imprint of the pure world of God), they are not fundamentally apart; it is our ignorance that makes it seem so. The truth is, man is God and God is man. As it is said, "God became man that man could become God." Yet man is man and God is God. Still, God's existence depends as much on us as ours does upon Him; in *substance* we are not different.

Returning to the theological problem of "How many angels can fit on the head of a pin?"—if you were asked that question, how would you respond? I once asked a Zen adept that same question and this is what he told me: "Isn't it so that Zen deals with the concrete, the real, and not the abstract or theoretical? We know that koans, although paradoxical and baffling in their formulation, do point to ultimate truth—in their own terms they do make sense; they are valid spiritual problems. But the question 'How many angels can fit on the head of a pin?' is for me a conundrum, not a koan. It's nonsense that challenges one to take it seriously."

In the monotheistic religions, angels are said to be bodiless immortal spirits, limited in knowledge and power, of higher and lower ranks, who take on human form when they need to communicate with human beings. Many of you undoubtedly are familiar with the story of the archangel Lucifer, who, we are told, was an angel of light so long as he remained content with his place in the celestial hierarchy. He became the prince of darkness when he sought to usurp the position higher than the one that had been allotted him and then, unbelievably, led a revolt of the angels against God. As a result he was cast into the hell of eternal damnation where God turned him into Satan, the incarnation of evil. Imagine—rebelling against God! This must be the ultimate madness.

For a clue to the significance of the "angel koan," let us compare it with similar statements in the Buddhist scriptures. Those of you familiar with the marvelous Vimalakirti sutra (as translated into English by Robert Thurman) will see a connection at once. Here is the background of the sutra: The great Buddhist layman Vimalakirti is ill, so the Buddha calls upon his ten great Bodhisattvas to visit Vimalakirti and convey his condolences. Astonishingly, they beg off, one by one, citing Vimalakirti's overwhelming spiritual powers in Dharma combat—combat in which he again and again demolishes them. Like an Asiatic Socrates, Vimalakirti has roamed the countryside searching out these accomplished Bodhisattvas and engaging them in debate on the subtle teachings of the Buddha's Way—debate that in the end leaves them speechless and humiliated. After all the others have begged off, the Buddha turns to Manjusri, who, as the head of the Bodhisattvas, cannot refuse his request. Manjusri therefore says he will go and convey the Buddha's condolences to Vimalakirti.

When word spreads that the great Bodhisattva Manjusri, will be confronting the great layman, Vimalakirti, in Dharma combat and that the ensuing dialogue will "scorch the heavens," tens of thousands of shakras, brahmas, lokapalas, Bodhisattvas, disciples, gods, and goddesses from all the ten quarters, we are told, gathered in Vimalakirti's simple ten-foot-square room. All fit in comfortably! Manjusri begins by conveying the Buddha's well-wishes and then asking Vimalakirti why he is sick. Vimalakirti responds in his now famous words: "I am sick because the whole world is sick." Then, after all the other Bodhisattvas have responded to the same question, he asks Manjusri, "What is the state of mind of a Bodhisattva who has entered the gate of nonduality?" Manjusri replies, "This is what I think: In respect to all things, there is nothing to say, nothing to teach, nothing to point to, nothing to know, and no questions and answers to be concerned with. This is entering the gate of nonduality." Then Manjusri, addressing Vimalakirti, adds, "We have all given our explanations. Now, good man, give us yours." The audience is then awestruck by the "thunderous silence" of Vimalakirti, who sits silently, in profound Awareness, and says nothing. It's a great moment in a great and inspiring sutra.

If you do not perceive the truth of the sutra and of the question of how many angels can fit on the head of a pin, or can't yet see their connection with the koan man's justice and God's justice, consider this pronouncement of Hua-yen Master Fa-tsang: "Ten thousand Buddhas preached the Dharma on the tip of a hair"; and that of Zen Master Hakuin, who wrote, "Apart from Mind there is no Buddha. . . . In reality, Buddhas have no form. They have been given form out of our necessity." Aren't these two masters saying that ultimate truth is beyond the senses and yet not apart from them; that the tip of a hair is ultimate truth; that the poisoning venom of a snake is ultimate truth; and that the head of a pin is no less than ultimate truth?

In genuine Zen training, of course, you can't resolve a koan by simply conceptualizing about it as I am doing now. You must present a live, convincing demonstration of your understanding. Now, how would you demonstrate this koan of man's justice and God's justice if you were facing your teacher in the privacy of his teaching chamber? Be careful! If you say something like, "I would take all the nuts, crack them, and then divide the meat equally," you have missed the point of the koan.

Let me conclude this commentary by telling you of a tragic event that occurred while I was living in Japan and that bears on the problems we have been discussing. It was a Saturday night, and a crowded train was speeding from Tokyo toward Yokohama. From the opposite direction another speeding train on the same track was also heading toward Yokohama. They crashed head-on in Yokohama. Many people were instantly killed and a number of others injured, some seriously, some slightly. A few survived unhurt. Among the last were three students of Yasutani Roshi. The next day they attended our *zazenkai* (all-day sitting) in Kamakura, where I was living at the time and where Yasutani Roshi held a one-day sitting each week. After a brief lunch, a heated discussion ensued about the train wreck. A person who had been on one of the wrecked trains asked Yasutani Roshi, "Does karma come into this problem, and if so, in what way?" From a legal standpoint, of course, there was no question that the engineers of both trains were guilty of negligence inasmuch as they mistook or ignored certain signals; in a criminal or civil court of law they would undoubtedly be held accountable for their negligent behavior. That was clear. But what about the *karmic* consequences? The roshi's response left everyone gaping in disbelief:

"Karmically speaking, all those who boarded either train freely, of their own volition, are at least fifty percent responsible for their injuries or death."

"What!" exclaimed those who had survived the head-on crash unhurt. "They did nothing to cause that crash, so how can they be held karmically responsible for their injuries or death?"

The roshi, Hodja-like, held his ground: "Since nobody forced them to get on those trains and they freely chose to do so, I can only repeat, they are at least fifty percent karmically responsible for what happened to them."

Now let me ask all of you: From what standpoint does the roshi make that statement? Is he speaking from the perspective of man's justice or God's justice? If you equate karma only with God's justice, your understanding of karma is still imperfect. Yet if you say that karma has nothing to do with God's justice, you have not yet caught even a glimpse of God's justice. So what will you say? Speak now with no hesitation. Man's justice? God's justice? What is the truth of your life? That is what Zen is really all about.

# Epilogue: Practical Zen—
# a Conversation with Kenneth Kraft

## (1991)

*This article first appeared in* Yoga Journal, *July–August 1991. It has been adapted somewhat here. Ken Kraft is an associate professor of Japanese religions at Lehigh University, Bethlehem, Pennsylvania. He is the editor of* Zen: Tradition and Transition; Inner Peace, World Peace: Essays on Buddhism and Non-Violence; *and the author of* Eloquent Zen: Daito and Early Japanese Zen. *He is also a longtime Zen student and a good friend. I found that his questions touched important areas, and they help clarify vital aspects of Zen training and Zen experience.*

KENNETH KRAFT: May I ask you about your own religious background before you encountered Zen? Were you exposed to deep faith as a child?

ROSHI PHILIP KAPLEAU: I come from mixed Jewish and Christian parents, neither of whom was very religious. As I got older, I tried Catholic, Protestant, and Jewish places of worship, but could find no fulfillment in any of them. Then I became an ardent atheist, a step that shows how strong my religious aspiration really was.

KENNETH: In what sense?

ROSHI: Paul Tillich, the distinguished Protestant theologian, used to say that a fervent atheist is much closer to God than a person who routinely goes to church once a week and feels he has thereby surrendered himself to God. The atheist who vehemently claims, "There is no God!" is actually affirming God, for he can only deny God in the name of God. So atheism can often be a vital stage on the way to true religiosity.

KENNETH: How do you assess the notion of God as it has developed in the West? Sometimes it seems to be a matter of religious vocabularies—that is, there might be Buddhist concepts or experiences that one could call God if that label didn't have so many charged associations for a Westerner.

ROSHI: Buddhism certainly upholds a transcendent experience, but it is more than a semantic problem. The absence of a God in Buddhism invariably prompts people to say, "How can you have a religion without God? Buddhism can't be a religion in the same sense that Christianity and Judaism are religions." And they are right. If by religion one means a belief in an all-powerful Supreme Being who created and rules the universe, and who is to be obeyed and worshiped, then Buddhism is not a religion.

For others, however, religion is an all-encompassing truth that provides answers to the perennial questions: To what end was I born? What is the purpose of my life? Why must I die? What is my relation to my fellow creatures? Judged by that standard, Buddhism is certainly a religion.

When a student from a devout Christian or Jewish background comes to me and says, "I like what Buddhism has to offer, but frankly I'm bothered by the absence of a God in its teachings," I usually assign him or her the koan "What is God?" As most people now know, a koan is a spiritual puzzle that cannot be solved by the intellect alone. A practitioner uses a koan in meditation to attain a state of deep concentration and self-forgetfulness. If one truly experiences the reality behind the word *God*, one realizes that "if I speak of God, it is not God of whom I speak."

KENNETH: Generally Buddhism prefers not to personify the transcendent.

ROSHI: Ultimate truth cannot be named or described—it is beyond all categories. Personifying the transcendent can have great value, but there are drawbacks, too. In my new book, *The Wheel of Life and Death* (now retitled as *The Zen Art of Living and Dying*), I discuss the plight of a woman who was a pious Catholic. She had been married just a short time and was very much in love with her husband, when he was sent to fight in the Vietnam War. He was killed within three months. A shady character from the same neighborhood, however, came through the whole war without a scratch. And so she turned from loving God to hating Him. "Why would a loving and just God do this to me?" she bitterly asked herself over and over. That is the problem of personifying God. Most people cannot accept, "Ours is not to reason why . . ."

KENNETH: It's a classic problem in Christian theology: If God is truly all-powerful and all-merciful, why is there evil and suffering?

ROSHI: It is easier for Buddhists to deal with that kind of problem because of the doctrine of karma. Simply defined, karma is the law of cause and effect that embraces the moral implications of action. Viewed more broadly, karma is the creator, the maintainer, and the destroyer of the universe. And in other contexts, Buddhism does not even posit a beginning of the universe, much less a creator God. Perhaps this is why you don't find in Asian art the despairing, agonizing quality that has been so prominent in Western art.

KENNETH: There are many fine people who have no religious background; and there are others who have had long years of religious training but do not seem to manifest its benefits. How would you compare the effects of a deep spiritual experience—such as kensho in Zen—with the effects of character, whatever you might include in that? Are there people who have had an awakening experience but who are unable to develop spiritual maturity due to certain weaknesses of character?

ROSHI: This is a vital question. To begin with, there is considerable misunderstanding about the word *kensho*. As you know, *ken* means "to see," and *sho* is "True-nature," so the term has the literal meaning of "seeing into your True-nature." But a penetration into truth can be shallow or deep. In Japan the word *kensho* is generally used to describe a relatively shallow awakening, and we use it the same way.

Now a shallow penetration—even two or three such experiences—will have little effect on character. It takes long training to establish firm character. Long training not only includes correct immobile and mobile meditation, but also such things as chanting, repentance, and the various devotional activities that are very much a part of Zen. Most important, until one has integrated an awakening into one's daily life so that one is able to *live* by what one knows to be true, one is not really enlightened.

KENNETH: How does training affect character? Usually we think of character as something more or less innate—we come into the world with a certain character, and it doesn't change very much in the course of our lives.

ROSHI: Again, the doctrine of karma is helpful here. We all have different karmas. That is, we come into this world with different backgrounds, dispositions, and the like. The way we respond to people and events establishes certain patterns, and that is also karma. We can, though, change our karma—the direction and quality of our life. If we couldn't, there would be no point to spiritual training. Training enables one to change one's karma, through understanding and compassion, and thereby to develop a strong character and a warm personality. The importance of faith should also be noted: if one has faith in oneself and faith in the Buddhist teachings, training moves along much faster.

But it is a mistake to think that simply by sitting, simply by passing koans, you are going to develop a strong character. Unfortunately, there are people who have been exposed to Zen for many years but whose training, it can honestly be said, is defective.

KENNETH: One of the images that some people have of Zen enlightenment is that once you get it, whatever it is, then life is joyous and peaceful from then on. It's more subtle than that, isn't it? Don't people of considerable Zen attainment still have to confront painful situations in their lives?

ROSHI: They do, yes. So much of the violence and turmoil in the world today is painful to spiritually sensitive persons because it is vicariously felt. As for personal pain, once it is seen as karmic retribution, it becomes more bearable.

KENNETH: Does one experience the painful aspects of life differently after enlightenment?

ROSHI: Yes. Before real insight, pain usually brings up a kind of resentment: "Why should this happen to me? What have I done to deserve this?" But somebody who has seen into the oneness of life and gained a practiced understanding of karma would never respond in that way.

KENNETH: In one of your books you suggest that instead of asking "Why me?" at such times, we could more profitably ask ourselves, "Why *not* me?"

ROSHI: That's right. "Have I lived in such a way that I have a perfect karmic slate? Have my thoughts and actions in this life—not to mention previous lives—been free of greed, anger, and delusion?" As one begins to experience the indivisibility of life, one can, as I said, accept a painful situation as one's own karma, without bitterness.

KENNETH: Your best-known book, *The Three Pillars of Zen,* includes a section entitled "Contemporary Enlightenment Experiences." In one case a husband and wife are attending their very first Zen retreat, in Hawaii, and both of them have an experience that is sanctioned by the master as enlightenment. Might not that account create a misleading impression of Zen training?

ROSHI: Yes, it might, if understood as "enlightenment." But I seriously doubt that the word *enlightenment* was used by Yasutani Roshi, the master in question. Rarely does a roshi say, "You are enlightened," or words to that effect, for such a pat on the back could reinvigorate an ego that has been merely dislodged but not wholly banished. I feel certain that the tenuous nature of their penetration was pointed out to them by Yasutani Roshi, who would have urged them to continue their training, to expand and deepen what they had barely tasted.

KENNETH: Do Zen teachers sometimes have difficulty evaluating people who are certain that they've had an awakening experience?

ROSHI: Not really. A teacher can very quickly deal with people who feel they have some kind of Zen realization. You simply ask them, "Do you want me to test you?" If you put it that way, it's hard for them to say no.

KENNETH: After such testing, if your response is negative, do most people accept it?

ROSHI: Yes, most do.

KENNETH: They don't go away saying, "Well, you may think I'm not, but I'm sure that I am"?

ROSHI: I remember one older woman who challenged me in an interesting way. I had tested her with questions such as, "Are you in the universe, or is the universe in you?" Then I extended my hand and said, "Don't call this a hand, but tell me, what is it?" Protesting, she replied, "I don't understand Zen terminology. I've only been exposed to Zen recently, so I can't answer the Zen way. But I know I've had a genuine insight." However, I hadn't used any Zen terminology.

KENNETH: I see her point, though. Even if there are no Zen technical terms in those particular questions, there is a Zen context, even a Zen culture, from which questions like that arise. And there are ways to respond appropriately according to that Zen culture.

ROSHI: Perhaps, but there are also people who know very little about Zen, and yet because they have seen into the truth in some measure, they have no trouble handling a master's testing questions.

KENNETH: I've heard some Zen insiders say that once you learn how to negotiate the koan system, it's possible to fool a teacher.

ROSHI: Not if the teacher—assuming he or she is competent—doesn't want to be "fooled." In certain cases a teacher will allow a student to pass through one or more koans even if the student's understanding is not deep. To some people it may seem as if the teacher has been fooled, but actually the teacher is consciously trying to encourage the student. It's more important, I believe, to help a sincere student than to uphold a system.

KENNETH: Sometimes it is necessary for a student to continue his or her training with another teacher. What happens then? In Japanese Zen at least, it's not uncommon for the second teacher to make the student start all over again with one of the initial koans, no matter how much training the student has had.

ROSHI: A second teacher who does that is not necessarily acting in an arbitrary manner, because the standards of roshis differ. To give an analogy, suppose you fracture an arm and your doctor has it x-rayed. Then you move to another city, taking the x rays with you, and you consult a different doctor. Invariably, the second doctor will have his own x rays taken regardless of the quality of the first set. The same koan may have several acceptable answers, according to the various lineages. It's an indication of the richness of koans.

KENNETH: Zen masters have likened their task to "selling water by a river." What is the role of a teacher in Zen?

ROSHI: In Zen it is said that the role of the teacher is to preserve the student from his, the teacher's, influence. Personally, I see myself as someone who shares with others what he does seriously for himself. In Zen there is no need to think of a teacher as someone who has a special wisdom or compassion that few other people possess. At a critical point in Zen training the teacher is like a midwife, who can help deliver a child when it is ready to be born. In the same way, the teacher can help a student only when the student has helped himself to such an extent that his or her mind is ripe for a breakthrough. The teacher is not, as someone put it, a big daddy.

KENNETH: As you know, Zen teachers are sometimes criticized for being too authoritarian.

ROSHI: Some Zen teachers are indeed authoritarian, and some are quite the opposite. One finds the same mix in Hinduism and many other traditions. Every teacher who is going to be effective must sometimes lay down the law, and at other times he has to relax and let up a bit. In other words, a wise teacher doesn't let the stick overshadow the carrot, and vice versa.

KENNETH: Authority has been a troublesome issue in many

American Buddhist centers. Westerners commonly want the teacher-student relationship to be less hierarchical. And there have been clear-cut abuses of authority. Let's assume that the teacher is qualified—might there be cases where students' demands for a more egalitarian setup actually hamper a teacher's effectiveness?

ROSHI: Yes, that can happen. Usually those demands are made by beginners, people who have not gone very far into the teaching. An insistence on more "democracy" often reflects certain frustrations that students encounter in their Zen training. In our culture, we expect to be given answers much more quickly than they are given in Zen. But it is important to develop the capacity to work things out for ourselves. That is what koans compel us to do and is one of the reasons why koans are so valuable to work on. Those who resent this approach perceive the teacher as cold or unfair or authoritarian. "Why don't you explain what you mean?" they demand. "How do you expect us to understand?"

KENNETH: You have trained five or six disciples who have become teachers in their own right; they are now running centers in the United States and Canada. What does it mean to sanction a person to teach?

ROSHI: Zen has many branches and lineages, and the criteria vary among them. A future teacher must complete a prescribed course of training, but even in a given temple or center, that training may not be the same for every student. In our Sangha, one must first pass about forty preliminary koans and then go on to the classic koan collections, the *Gateless Barrier* and the *Blue Rock Record*. Including certain verses, that's another two hundred koans, and we go through all of them twice. Finally, there are about fifty koans dealing with the Ten Cardinal Precepts of Buddhism. Even for students who are working continuously with the teacher, this kind of intensive training can take ten years or longer.

KENNETH: Are there further requirements as well?

ROSHI: At the Rochester Center, a person tracked to be a teacher is encouraged to undertake a pilgrimage to the Asian Buddhist countries, to interact with teachers and students in monasteries and other training centers. Someone who is about to take on Zen students must also have a steadfast character and a warm, flowing personality. Ideally, one's understanding should have matured to the point where it equals or surpasses the insight of one's own teacher.

KENNETH: Many Westerners interested in Zen may not initially have access to a teacher. They do the best they can on their own—reading books, attending talks, perhaps meditating with a small group of like-minded people. Can one practice Zen authentically without a teacher?

ROSHI: Yes, up to a point. Books can certainly help one get started, but there comes a point when just reading books is not enough. You can't ask a book questions. The value of a teacher is that he or she has been through the whole process that the new student has yet to experience, so the teacher can perform important functions as a guide.

KENNETH: What does a Buddhist community offer a beginner?

ROSHI: A great deal if it is a harmonious community with a trained teacher. Crucial support and encouragement will come from all sides. To be able to meditate with people who are much more experienced than you are, people who perhaps have had some kind of awakening, can be enormously stimulating to a beginner. In most centers, the place where the group meditates is reserved for that activity only. So it acquires a certain atmosphere that enables you to unify and focus the mind much more easily than if you are trying to meditate in your own bedroom or living room.

KENNETH: What does commitment mean in Zen?

ROSHI: It's a pledge or promise to yourself to give all that you can to your Zen training and your life, which are not really two. Once you have established a rapport with a qualified teacher, then a commitment to that teacher is essential. If we state it in terms of a Zen community or Buddhist Sangha, you must be willing to make certain sacrifices, sensible ones, for the sake of the group. In short, it means to scruff off one's self-centeredness and see oneself in relation to the whole.

KENNETH: When you reflect upon the past thirty years, were there significant developments that you did not foresee? What has surprised you the most?

ROSHI: The biggest surprise was the quick decline and virtual extinction of the spirit of the sixties and early seventies, the so-called counterculture. I never anticipated that after the marvelous—and that's the right word—responses of the young people who were so interested in spiritual training, there would be such a 100 percent turnaround. In that era there was a real appreciation of simplicity, an indifference to money, finery, and material things. It's hard to believe that it passed so quickly.

KENNETH: Many of the people who were strongly influenced by the counterculture continue to feel a sense of loss about the passing of the sixties.

ROSHI: Still, I see some signs that the best features of the counterculture—the unselfishness, the desire to work for others, the spiritual aspiration—are starting to surface again, often in new ways. It may now have a stronger, sounder base. For the past five years or so, we Zen teachers have been deploring how few young people were coming into Zen. But now they are beginning to attend workshops and training programs in greater numbers.

KENNETH: As you look a few years ahead, do you have any personal goals or any goals for the Zen Center? Maybe you are goal-less at last!

ROSHI: I hope so. It seems that my karma at this stage is to live knocking around, traveling here and there . . .

KENNETH: Wandering like "clouds and water"?

ROSHI: Like clouds and water, exactly.

KENNETH: If you would permit me to ask, how would you like to be remembered?

ROSHI: I'd be happy if my students said of me what a Zen adept of old observed about his teacher: "My teacher was great in what he said, but he was even greater in what he didn't say."

# About the Author

In 1953, recognizing the urgency of spiritual questions in his life, Philip Kapleau quit his successful career in court reporting at the age of forty-two, sold his belongings, and bought a one-way ticket from Connecticut to Japan. He intended to pursue Zen practice at a Buddhist monastery, and attain enlightenment. A few years earlier he had been sent to Tokyo as a court reporter for the War Crimes Tribunal of Japan, and there had met the eminent Buddhist scholar D. T. Suzuki. Kapleau's participation in the Tokyo Tribunal, and his earlier post as chief court reporter at the International Military Tribunal in Nuremberg, Germany, had left him with penetrating questions about cruelty and suffering.

For thirteen years Kapleau remained in Japan while he trained under two distinguished masters of Zen Buddhism, the late Harada Roshi and his successor, the late Yasutani Roshi.

Kapleau returned from Japan to the United States in 1965 and the following year founded the Zen Center of Rochester, New York. Since its founding in 1966, the Zen Center has attracted students from all parts of the world. The teachings and influence of Roshi Kapleau have now expanded into many other affiliated centers and groups in the United States, Canada, Mexico, Costa Rica, and other countries in Europe.

*The Three Pillars of Zen,* Kapleau's first book, has been the bible of several generations of American Zen practitioners. A classic now, it has been translated into twelve other languages, including Polish and Chinese. Three additional books followed: *To Cherish All Life: A Buddhist Case for Becoming Vegetarian; Zen: Merging of East and West;* and *The Zen Art of Living and Dying.*

Now in his eighties, Roshi Kapleau resides in south Florida.

# About the Editors

Rafe Martin is a noted storyteller and author of many books, including *The Hungry Tigress: Buddhist Myths, Tales, and Legends* and *One Hand Clapping: Zen Stories for All Ages*. He has been a student of Zen, training with Roshi Kapleau, since 1970, and lives in Rochester, New York.

Polly Young-Eisendrath, Ph.D., is a psychologist and a Jungian psychoanalyst practicing in Burlington, Vermont. She is a clinical associate professor of psychiatry at the University of Vermont, and the author and editor of many books, the most recent of which is *The Resilient Spirit*. She became a student of Roshi Kapleau's in 1971.